The Cubans of Union City

Yolanda Prieto

The Cubans of Union City

Immigrants and Exiles in a New Jersey Community

TEMPLE UNIVERSITY PRESS
Philadelphia

Temple University Press
Philadelphia PA 19122
www.temple.edu/tempress

Published 2009
Printed in the United States of America

Library of Congress Cataloging-in-Publication Data

Prieto, Yolanda.
The Cubans of Union City : immigrants and exiles in a New Jersey community / Yolanda Prieto.
p. cm.
Includes bibliographical references and index.
ISBN 978-1-59213-299-7 (cloth : alk. paper) — ISBN 978-1-59213-300-0 (pbk. : alk. paper)
1. Cuban Americans—New Jersey—Union City—Social conditions. 2. Immigrants—New Jersey—Union City—Social conditions. 3. Exiles—New Jersey—Union City—Social conditions. 4. Social change—New Jersey—Union City. 5. Community life—New Jersey—Union City. 6. Political culture—New Jersey—Union City. 7. Sex roles—New Jersey—Union City. 8. Union City (N.J.)—Ethnic relations. 9. Union City (N.J.)—Social conditions. 10. Union City (N.J.)—Religious life and customs. I. Title.
F144.U58P754 2009
305.868'7291074926—dc22 2008043768

010813P

To the memory of my parents Juana E. and Porfirio Prieto,
Cuban immigrants to Union City

Contents

Preface ix

Acknowledgments xv

1 Introduction 1

2 Cuban Union City: Origins, Development, and Change 17

3 Building Community: Economic Growth and the Rise of Local Organizations 39

4 Women Leave Home for the Factory: Gender, Work, and Family 63

5 Saint Augustine Parish and Cuban Adaptation: Religion and Reconciliation 85

6 Exile, Ethnic Identity, and Political Culture 113

7 Union City Cubans and Community Change: Some Theoretical Considerations 141

Abbreviations 165

Notes 167

Bibliography 183

Index 195

Preface

This book is an ethnographic study of Cubans in Union City, New Jersey. It captures the journey of this community from the late 1940s, when the first Cubans moved there. It continues with the growth of this settlement when the 1960s exiles arrived, and finally it explores changes in Union City as many older Cubans moved away and new Cuban immigrants have come into the area. This work proposes that a welcoming reception of Cubans by the U.S. government, especially after the revolution of 1959, and the entrepreneurial characteristics of the group, helped Union City Cubans integrate into their new society.

The Book

As the story of this book is also my story, it is at once an insider's tale and a sociological treatise. This study documents the facets of Cuban life in Union City that I see as most important. It also points out unique aspects of this Cuban settlement. Chapter 1 provides an introduction to the Union City Cuban community and a background discussion on the Cuban migration to the United States, especially after the 1959 revolution. Chapter 2 looks at the formation and characteristics of the Cuban community in Union City, including the pre-revolutionary immigrants, the post-1959 exiles, and those arriving since the 1980s and 1990s. Chapter 3 explores especially the late 1960s and 1970s, the period of heavy exile migration into the community and its economic boom. It discusses the changes that have occurred since then, especially the Cuban business flight in recent years as other groups have moved into the area. Chapter 3 also looks into the development and decline of civic and other associations. In Chapter 4, I address the pivotal role of women in the migration, especially in relation to family and work. Chapter 5 examines the role of a Catholic church, Saint Augustine Parish, which aided many Cubans, especially post-1959 exiles, when they arrived in Union City. This chapter also recounts the relationship between Cubans and their church of origin. Cubans in the United States have had tense relations with the Church in Cuba because they believe that the Church there is not sufficiently critical of the Castro government. Pope John Paul II's visit to Cuba in 1998 helped dissipate some of these tensions, as the exiles learned about the good work that the Church was doing for the poor and others in Cuba. In Chapter 6, I concentrate on the role that ethnicity and Cuban political culture have played in the Union City Cuban community. This chapter compares and contrasts the political activities of older exiles with those of younger Cuban Americans. In general, younger Cubans are not so interested in anti-Castro politics and concentrate more on local and national politics. Chapter 7 deals with the theoretical underpinnings of this work. The main theoretical claim is that a positive, welcoming immigration policy toward Cubans helped them integrate socially and economically. As Alejandro Portes and Rubén G. Rumbaut assert in *Immigrant America: A Portrait,* "For immigrants, the most relevant contexts of reception are defined by the policies of the receiving government, the conditions of the host labor market, and the characteristics of their own ethnic communities. The combination of positive and negative features encountered at each of these levels determines the distinct mode of newcomers' incorporation."[1] Integration, however, does not mean that most Cubans have rejected their culture. Even those who have left Union City, including younger Cubans, generally know and maintain the use of Spanish, observe their holidays, and eat Cuban food. In this chapter I address the importance of themes such as assimilation, race, ethnicity, social class, gender, religion, identity, and immigration in the light of the changes that have transpired in Union City. Questions regarding the reasons for the dispersal of Cubans to other areas are explored. Who leaves? Who stays? Why? This chapter studies contemporary changes more extensively. In particular, I want to examine how the above-mentioned variables influence Cubans' relationships among themselves and with other groups in the area.

Some Comments on Methodology

Conceived as an ethnographic community study of Cuban Union City, this work combines participant observation, available statistics, and in-depth interviews. My goal is to write this story through the voices of the protagonists, including my own.

A new interest in the study of communities is reemerging in sociology. For years, community studies were mainly identified with the classical works of Chicago sociologists. Suggestive titles like *The Hobo: The Sociology of the Homeless Man* by Niels Anderson (1923), *The Gold Coast and the Slum* by Harvey Zorbaugh (1929), and *The Ghetto* by Louis Wirth (1929) are only a few among the impressive production of the Chicago school of community sociology in less than a decade. In addition to the classical studies of Chicago sociologists, there were other perspectives in community studies; for example, the holistic studies, best exemplified by Robert and Helen Lynd's research in the Midwest. Their volumes *Middletown* and *Middletown in Transition* (1929 and 1937) studied the everyday life of the typical small city in the American heartland. What all these studies had in common was the use of a variety of methods: detailed ethnographies, participant observation, the collection of life histories, and the use of official statistics.[2] Yet community studies in the first half of the twentieth century were concerned with local phenomena. Many of the titles cited above are about Chicago, a city that has received more attention than any other. Perhaps the "localism" with which American community studies were charged contributed to their decline.[3] From descriptive analyses of communities, American sociology moved to "national studies of groups based not on community of residence, but rather on [variables] such as age, race, sex, and social class."[4] More recently, some sociologists have produced community studies that look at the impact of global economic and political forces on local communities. Examples of these are *Canarsie: The Jews and Italians of Brooklyn Against Liberalism* by Jonathan Rieder (1985), *Black*

Picket Fences: Privilege and Peril Among the Black Middle Class by Mary Patillo-McCoy (1999), *Working Class Heroes: Protecting Home, Community, and Nation in a Chicago Neighborhood* by Maria Kefalas (2003), and *There Goes the Neighborhood: Racial, Ethnic, and Class Tensions in Four Chicago Neighborhoods and their Meaning for America* by William Julius Wilson and Richard P. Taub (2006).

The recurring importance of ethnicity and immigration in the American social landscape is reinforcing the need to study local communities. The spatial concentration of immigrants poses questions about their integration (or lack of it) into American society.[5] Immigrants' economic and social conditions, relationships with other immigrant groups, and their relations with the general population and with their societies of origin have been studied not only by sociologists and anthropologists, but also by historians.[6] What is new about contemporary community studies is the focus on a dynamic that is both local and global. In an internationalized world, it is impossible to look at a group of neighborhood residents and ignore how their lives are affected by processes that go beyond local economic and political decisions. In the case of immigrants, it is imperative to explore the transnational ties that they maintain with their original countries. For instance, among some groups, immigrants' remittances to relatives in their home countries become major sources of revenue for those countries. Contemporary community studies present new challenges and new opportunities, especially for those studying immigrant communities.

In this book, I blend the local perspective and methods of classical community studies with contemporary global approaches. As most recent studies do, I ask questions that link local and global layers of community experiences. The politicized nature of the post-1959 Cuban migration to the United States makes most Cuban immigrants and exiles very responsive to what goes on in their country of origin. Thus, I cannot study Cubans in Union City separated from their history and their present relationship to Cuba. Neither can I study them outside the context of the rapid demographic changes going on in that community.

This work has a large subjective component. A significant part of it is based on the experiences, the memories, and the meanings that the participants have shared with me. As such, it is a collective narrative mediated by my interpretation as a researcher and as a Cuban. This kind of reflection implies that something might get lost in the translation from the participant's experience as it is lived to the researcher's articulation of it. Philosophy and the social sciences have become more aware of the importance of the subjective and of the relationship between experience itself and its articulation.[7] Interviewees may select what they prefer to present to the researcher as "true" and suppress those issues that may be traumatic. In the case of Cubans, questions related to Cuba and politics are a good example. Accounts of the same events or facts by different participants may not coincide. The researcher has to be conscious of the importance of the subjective element, and, at the same time, optimize her/his position by establishing the best possible rapport with the participants. Yet, in this study, I was a Cuban researcher, something that could be seen as an asset or a liability, depending on how much distance is desired from the topic of investigation. I personally believe that being Cuban gave me a great advantage in studying this community. I have tried to be as balanced and fair in my descriptions and analyses as possible, always mindful that my own experiences may have colored my explanations.

For this project, I used ethnographic techniques. Although I back assertions with statistics, most of the methods I used to describe and explain the everyday life of Cubans in Union City are qualitative. My own lived experience in Union City was added to the hours of participant observation I did with families and organizations, in churches, and in the streets. I interviewed 102 Cubans and Cuban Americans.[8] Of those, sixty-two lived in Union City and forty had moved from Union City to other towns or cities in New Jersey. I also interviewed nine non-Cubans: six white Americans and three Latin Americans from other countries. The interviews mainly took place from 1999 to 2008. A few interviews took place before 1999.[9] The length of time between the beginning of the interviewing period and the end gave me a good sense of the social, economic, and cultural changes that this community has undergone. The great majority of the interviews were conducted in Spanish, with the exception of some interviews with Cuban Americans and with the few white Americans who participated. The interviewees included community, religious, business, and political leaders as well as ordinary folk. For each chapter, I interviewed individuals relevant to the chapter's topic. For example, for Chapter 4 on women, I interviewed women from different generations as well as the leadership of the major Cuban women's organization. Participants signed agreements to be interviewed. Many of them wanted to remain anonymous, and in those cases I use pseudonyms. The interviews ranged from two to three hours, and they were not structured. I only asked leading questions and probed later on, if necessary. I was more interested in what the participants wanted to say. All spoke very freely and enthusiastically. It is primarily because of them that this book was possible.

Acknowledgments

Writing this book has encompassed a long personal and intellectual journey. Because I came to Union City with my parents and my sister in the late 1960s, I felt the need to understand the settlement of the Cuban community there, long before I became a sociologist. I had experienced some years of the Cuban Revolution, and later migration to the United States—with all the human cost that such major upheavals imply. I had also witnessed the changing roles of my parents; my father from retired worker in the railroad industry to a presser in a New Jersey factory; my mother from seamstress working at home to a factory worker in the garment industry. My sister, the youngest of us, also experienced difficult changes. From a familiar school in Cuba to a completely different one in Union City, in a language she did not understand. Perhaps it was my need to understand the Cuban Revolution and its impact on my life that led me to study those aspects of it of which I was part: the migration to the United States, and in particular to Union City, New Jersey.

I want to thank many individuals who have helped me in the process of researching and writing this book. Above all, I thank the 102 Cuban and Cuban American men and women whom I interviewed. I'd also like to thank the nine non-Cubans who participated. Although not all are quoted directly, their collective stories constitute the backbone of this work, and

I hope that their voices come through. Any errors in interpretation are, of course, solely mine.

Lourdes Casal was a special source of inspiration. I worked with her on various projects about the Cuban migration to the United States. She died in Cuba in February, 1981, but her memory lives throughout the pages of this book. Marifeli Pérez-Stable read the chapter on politics. As a good friend does, she lent her support as well as a critical eye. A special note of thanks goes to my friend Jill Hamberg. From reading parts of the manuscript, to forwarding relevant information, to helping me with computer troubles, she was very instrumental in the completion of this project. As a long-time West New York resident, Roland Alum served as an anthropologist *in situ*. He gave me innumerable suggestions, procured me interviews with leaders of the community, and read parts of the manuscript. Other friends and colleagues read individual chapters: Patricia Keeton, Sydney Weinberg, Sherry Gorelick, Barbara Schroder and Joyce Polistena. To all of you—my sincere appreciation. Erin Augis and Liliana Cotto provided invaluable suggestions and made parts of the manuscript much better.

Several friends contributed information, artwork, photographic talent, and enthusiastic support. I want to thank them all: Ana Meseguer, José Hernández, Hilda Díaz, María Cristina Herrera, María de los Angeles García, William Duque and Hildalina Oropesa. Judith Staley and Gordon Bear helped me make sense of confusing statistics.

There are many friends and colleagues whose scholarly work or lived experiences provided inspiration. Some helped me raise questions about the material. Others were part, in one way or another, of this work's trajectory: Helen Safa, Henry Bischoff, Kathie Friedman-Kasaba, Iraida López, Albor Ruiz, Mariana Gastón, Reverend Raymond Rafferty, Reverend Eduardo De Zayas, Nesecan Balkan, Gail Lerner, S. Priyadarsini, Clayton Hartjen, Patricia Connors and Daniel Schulgasser. In Cuba, I want to deeply thank Juan Valdés Paz, Martha Nuñez Sarmiento and the late Jorge Ramírez Calzadilla for their encouragement.

Many institutions assisted in the completion of this project. Hudson County Economic Department of Planning and Economic Development provided maps and relevant information. Librarians at the Union City Public Library, Ramapo College Library, personnel at the Hudson County Department of Human Services, and personnel at the Regional Census Office were most gracious in guiding me to needed information. I especially want to thank Shirley Knight at Ramapo College Library for helping me navigate through U.S. government documents. The Separately Budgeted Research Program of Ramapo College granted me release time on more than one occasion to work on my research. Also at Ramapo, I appreciate the support of friends, colleagues, and kindred spirits who either expressed enthusiasm for my work or made the often heavy teaching and governance load not only bearable, but pleasant: Henry Frundt, Martha Ecker, Susan Scher, David Greene, Donna Crawley, Mary Starke, Robert Becklen, Trent Schroyer, Charles Carreras, Ellen Ross, Mitchell Kahn, Carole Campana, Fredric L. Weiss, Patricia Hunt-Perry, Phillip McLewin, Beate Riesterer, Carol Duncan, Peter Scheckner, Michael Riff, Diana Alspach, Zewde Petros and Samuel Rosenberg.

Financial assistance was provided in part by the Cushwa Center for the Study of Catholicism at Notre Dame University in the form of an award to study Saint Augustine Roman Catholic Church in Union City. The ethnography that I conducted at the church informs much of Chapter 5 of this book.

I am immensely grateful to Christina Johnson, the initial copyeditor of this work and to the final copyeditors for their expertise and editing skills. At Temple University Press I wish to thank Janet Francendese, Editor-In-Chief, who always showed respect for my work. Also, I am grateful for the work of Emily Taber, David Wilson, and Gary Kramer. My appreciation to two anonymous readers of the manuscript. Their comments and suggestions proved to be invaluable.

The constant support of my family sustained me during light and tough times. My love and thanks go to Zoila, David, Christina, Michael, Jenell, and Matthew.

Finally, I owe a special debt of gratitude to James D. Meltzer, who believed in my ability to complete this project. And, as usual, he was right.

1

Introduction

On March 19, 1968, a few days after leaving Cuba, I arrived with my family at Newark Airport in New Jersey. Like many other Cubans, my family had decided to leave their country after the radical changes brought about by the Revolution of 1959. My uncle was waiting for us at the airport, and after a short ride on the New Jersey Turnpike, we reached Union City, our final destination. My uncle and his family had lived there since the early 1960s and they had seen this city change from a community mostly of European extraction into the second largest concentration of Cubans in the United States after Miami, Florida.

Although our relatives helped immensely in our transition to a new country, my adjustment was not easy. I had not wanted to leave Cuba. At twenty-one, it was difficult to leave behind not only my familiar environment, other relatives, and friends, but also the youthful dream, based on my religious beliefs, that I could contribute to a harmonious dialogue among believers, revolutionaries, and all those professing disparate ideologies but committed to creating a more equitable society. Instead, I found myself in another land, honoring my family's decision to leave a political system under which they did not want my sister and me to live. I could not remain in Cuba by myself. As my father said many times, "We either leave together, or we all stay here." His undisputed authority as the man of the house in a traditional, small Cuban town was stronger than my desire to stay, even though I was an adult. And, independently of how I feel today about our departure, my father's good intentions did not make the pain of leaving any easier for me at the time. I still shudder when I remember waking up on Saturday mornings in Union City forty-one years ago. The slow pace of the weekend magnified the unfamiliar sounds coming from the street, giving me a sense of unreality, a dreamlike feeling that was not eased by the fact that I knew some English. I can also relive the grief, fear, anticipation, and all the other emotions involved in the experience of migration.

Some Cubans had been in Union City since before the 1959 revolution, but the bulk of the community was formed in the 1960s and 1970s by those escaping the revolutionary government. Cubans who migrated after 1959 initially went to Florida, but the magnitude of the migration became too much for the state to handle, and many were resettled in other states. Union City, known as "the embroidery capital of the world" for the number of needlework factories located there, was a logical destination because of the number of jobs available to the newcomers. Within a short time, the adjacent towns of Union City and West New York in northern Hudson County, which overlook the Manhattan skyline along the New Jersey side of the Hudson River, practically became "Cuban towns," and Union City began to be referred to by many as "the second Cuban capital in exile."[1] This book traces the history of this migration, of which I am a part.

Union City Cubans were predominantly of working-class background. Those who had come before 1959 had been in search of economic opportunities, and the exiles left Cuba when economic conditions worsened after the Revolution in the late 1960s. Small entrepreneurs fled when they lost their businesses due to the Ofensiva Revolucionaria or Revolutionary Offensive, which nationalized what was left of private property. A good number of professionals also came to Union City as political refugees. Most medical doctors were able to validate their credentials. Other professionals, such as lawyers, found it more difficult to do so, and they became teachers or social workers. Although many Cubans were from Havana, the majority came from smaller cities and towns, especially in Las Villas, now Villa Clara, a province in central Cuba. This had been true since the 1950s, when people from Fomento and Placetas in Villa Clara constituted the great majority of

Cubans in Union City. Being from Camagüey in eastern Cuba, we were in a minority. But my family fit the typical profile of Union City Cubans. My father had worked in the railroad industry, and my mother, like many Cuban women, had been a seamstress who worked at home. Although generally of lower socioeconomic status than those who came in the early 1960s, Cuban refugees of the late 1960s and 1970s also shared strong anticommunist feelings. The waves of Cuban migrants up to the 1970s were considered the true political exiles.

Union City has experienced changes. Since the mid-1980s, a significant number of immigrants from elsewhere, mainly from other Latin American countries, have settled there. Additionally, many Cuban refugees from the Mariel exodus in 1980, and *balseros* who left Cuba in the 1990s by boat or homemade rafts, have come to Union City. As the new groups moved in, many of the early exiles began to leave. Some moved to neighboring cities in affluent Bergen County, and others left for Florida, but some remained. At the same time, legal Cuban immigrants have been arriving since a 1994 migratory accord signed by Cuba and the United States, and they are replenishing, if in some minimal way, the diluted Cuban presence in these towns. These new Cubans are encountering a very diverse community, made up of a myriad of nationalities: Dominicans, Puerto Ricans, Colombians, Salvadorans, Ecuadorians, Mexicans, and many more. Despite the diversity of the community, Cubans still hold some economic and political power, and Union City is still considered, at least symbolically, "the northernmost Cuban province."

That many of the early exiles moved out of Union City after two decades is hardly a surprise. We could say that history repeats itself. Traditionally in the United States, we have seen immigrants move away from the area of original concentration after they attain some economic security. Better schools for their children, the peace and quiet of the suburbs, the feeling that their old neighborhoods deteriorate as new immigrants arrive, and the attempt to assimilate into the mainstream of American society and culture have generally explained why immigrants move. In industrial Hudson County, the flight to the suburbs has been the experience for the Germans, Irish, Poles, Italians, Armenians, eastern European Jews, and others who were there before the Cubans came. Sociologists have conceptualized this phenomenon as "queuing" theory, and, especially in urban settings, it has been the predominant model of immigrant settlement.[2] What is different about the Cubans and other Latinos at present is that the immigrants are moving away from the original concentration, as opposed to their European predecessors, who usually became suburbanites in the second generation. Even more striking, as reported by the 2000 census, is that a greater proportion of newcomers are going directly to the suburbs.[3]

Not only in New Jersey, but also throughout the United States, the dynamics of current immigration are different from those that played out at the turn of the century. Contemporary migrants come predominantly from Asia and Latin America, not from Europe, and while the diversity within these populations in the United States is astounding, the immigrants of today are more visible because most are considered nonwhite.

The study of immigration and of the integration of immigrants into their new society is also changing. Traditional assimilation theories have been challenged by new perspectives. For example, some contemporary sociologists claim that immigrant concentration in certain locations may continue to be part of the nation's ethnic map, even for new generations. From a different point of view, many anthropologists and sociologists talk about transnational migrations, in which an immigrant experience is divided between the country of origin and the country of residence.[4] Instead of wanting to become part of their new home completely, new immigrants maintain regular contact with their home nations through visits, remittances, telephone calls, and, more recently for some, electronic communication. For many immigrants, the hope of returning permanently to their countries after they make some money becomes a goal. There is evidence that in the past, too, many longed for their homeland, and some wanted to return. However, going back was far more difficult than it is for today's immigrants.[5] Transportation was not advanced, and trips were very slow, costly, and time consuming. This is not to say that many of those who plan to return at present do so. Despite the benefits of modern technology and travel, most contemporary immigrants stay, raising their children here, just as earlier groups did. But there is an accelerated motion of people and resources around the world today that makes the migration phenomenon far more complex, and the analytical model of transnationalism increasingly accurate.

At the root of this movement are the profound changes brought about by the growing globalization of the economy. One of the negative consequences of this trend is that the polarization between rich and poor nations becomes more acute and the need for poor people in less developed countries to migrate to more developed ones more critical. Moreover, this economic dislocation is not restricted to one class. Although poor, uneducated labor migrants still represent the bulk of immigration in the United States, middle-class professionals and their families have also been joining the flow since the 1970s. In fact, an increasing proportion of recent immigrants are professionals and entrepreneurs.[6] Besides economic factors, people also leave their countries for political, religious, and ideological reasons. In many cases, some or all of these motivations converge. Thus, the traditional categorical distinctions between economic and political migrants may not be as useful in analyzing the very complex, multifaceted, contemporary population movements.

The Cuban Case

Although there were Cubans in the United States before 1959 who came primarily as economic migrants, the majority of those who entered this country after 1959 were afforded the status of *political exile* when they arrived. The long-term conflict between Cuba and the United States since the Revolution of 1959 explains why this group is treated differently. But even when strong economic reasons motivated Cubans to leave the island after 1959, Cubans' self-perceptions and the perceptions of non-Cubans characterize this group as different from other migrants. Politics, specifically anticommunist politics, is the motor that drives the Cuban community in the United States. Many scholars have written about the Cuban migration, particularly the post-1959 exodus.[7] Hence, I will only offer an overview as a necessary context for the subject of this book.

Cubans have emigrated to many parts of the world in different historical periods. However, the greatest share of the diaspora has settled in the United States. Ever since the days of the Spanish exploration and conquest of the New World, there has been a close link between Cuba and the United States, most notably with the Florida peninsula, but also with New York. Cuban immigration began in the nineteenth century. Perhaps the most notable immigrant of this period was Father Félix Varela, a priest who was involved in the movement for Cuban independence from Spain. Father Varela came to New York in 1823 after being expelled from Spain for advocating for greater Cuban autonomy. He died in Saint Augustine, Florida and never went back to Cuba. In 1869, immediately at the beginning of the Ten Years' War of Independence in Cuba, some cigar manufacturers moved their businesses to Key West, after which a flow of Cuban immigrants came to work in the cigar trade. The United States also served as a refuge for Cuban political exiles. The best known of these exiles is Cuban formost patriot José Martí, who lived in New York for fourteen years writing prolifically and striving for the island's independence.

During the first half of the twentieth century, U.S. investments in sugar production strengthened a sector that was already central in the late nineteenth century, but reinforced Cuba's economic dependence on the United States, its principal customer.[8] The volatile nature of the sugar market generated periods of growth and decline, creating opportunities for some, but dislocating many other citizens. During phases of economic depression, the country experienced high levels of unemployment, decreased wages, and heightened political instability. These hardships resulted in increased Cuban emigration to Florida and New York.

By 1950 there were 33,700 Cubans in the United States. However, the massive inflow of Cubans into this country started after the Revolution of 1959. In 1970, the first time the U.S. census separated the Hispanic population into nationalities, the number of Cubans had escalated to 439,000,[9] and it continued to climb in 1980 and 1990. The 2000 census reported 1,240,685 Cubans in the United States, including individuals of Cuban parentage.[10]

This massive Cuban migration was the result of radical changes brought about by the Revolution of 1959. Because of this, the social composition of this group, especially the early post-1959 refugees, was different from that of other Latin American communities in the United States. Post-1959 Cuban refugees were also different from the earlier Cuban immigrants. People leaving Cuba at the time were precisely those who in other poor countries do not need to migrate. The first wave of Cubans who came in the early 1960s represented the sectors of society that were most negatively affected by revolutionary changes: officers and personnel of the former Batista government, the mainly white, upper middle-classes, and professionals.[11] They left during the first couple of stormy years after the Revolution thinking that their return to the island was imminent because Fidel Castro's government would not last long.

Since the early 1960s, the U.S. government has played a major role in the Cuban immigration to this country and in the status of Cubans when they arrive here. In practice, U.S. immigration policy toward Cuban émigrés has been consistent with the country's refugee policy since the end of the Second World War. Refugee status was granted primarily to those immigrants coming from formerly communist countries. Special treatment of Cuban migrants thus began very soon after 1959. Between 1959 and 1962, Cubans who wanted to leave their country could obtain American visas in the American embassy in Havana or the American consulate in Santiago de Cuba. After the break of diplomatic relations between the two countries in 1961 and the missile crisis in October, 1962, it was more difficult to emigrate. With the escalation of tensions, the Cuban government suspended commercial flights to the United States in 1962. In the meantime, a "visa waiver" program was implemented by the U.S. State Department with the agreement of the Justice Department that authorized Cubans to enter the United States. These waivers were issued by the Swiss embassy, which agreed to represent U.S. interests in Havana. Once Cubans received the visa waiver from the United States, they had to obtain an exit permit from the Cuban Ministry of The Interior. Then, in the United States, the Cubans were granted "indefinite voluntary departure" or "parole" status.[12] After 1962 it was hard to leave even after obtaining a visa waiver since there were no commercial flights between the two countries and the only way out was through a third country, namely Mexico or Spain.

One of the most disputed chapters of the early migration was Operación Pedro Pan or Operation Peter Pan. This program, which began in December, 1960, brought over 14,000 unaccompanied children to the United States. Designed and managed by the Catholic archdiocese of Miami, the exodus of children from Cuba responded to the great fears of many parents about the fate of their offspring under communism. The nationalization of private schools by the government, coupled with rumors that the authorities were going to remove the *patria potestas,* or parental rights, and send children to the Soviet Union, created panic among many Cuban parents, especially those from urban, middle-class backgrounds.[13] The removal of parental rights never took place, and Cuban authorities have always claimed that these rumors and actions were mere propaganda aimed at discrediting the Revolution.[14] Once in the United States, these children went to camps, orphanages, and foster homes. Most of their parents joined them later, but the trauma of being sent away at a very early age was not easily forgotten. After all these years, most "Peter Pan children" deeply appreciate what they see as their parents' sacrifice to send them to freedom, but others, even when they prefer to live here, profoundly resent a separation that they feel caused them irreparable damage.

During the first months of the Cuban exodus in the early 1960s, help to the refugees was provided by the state of Florida, but the extent of the migration overtaxed state resources and exacerbated frustrations among local residents about this massive human flood in their community. President Eisenhower authorized the funding of the Cuban Refugee Emergency Center to coordinate relief efforts and to administer a program of resettlement to other states. Resettlement of refugees had previously occurred in the United States with Hungarians fleeing the 1956 revolution in their country. But the Cuban Refugee Program (CRP), as it was called when President Kennedy became involved after 1961, became the largest, most expensive, and most ambitious program for handling refugees in U.S. history. Resettlement was handled through four voluntary agencies: The United States Catholic Conference, the Church World Service (Protestant), the United HIAS (Hebrew Immigrant Aid), and the International Rescue Committee (nonsectarian). Whether resettled refugees were going to relatives in other state's, to sponsors, or were simply taking jobs at a distance, they were given money for their transportation expenses and received a transitional grant by the CRP to help in their adjustment. In addition, Cubans received food, clothing, medical care, job training, college tuition loans, and other benefits. Perhaps the most important advantage offered to the exiles was the passage and implementation of the 1966 Cuban Adjustment Act, which facilitated permanent residency status to Cubans a year and a day after entry into the United States. These benefits, coupled with the group's middle-class work ethic, have been instrumental in the integration of most Cubans into American society. There were obvious humanitarian reasons for accepting the exiles, but the political reason for bolstering the migration was pivotal. The small island of Cuba was key in the geopolitical battles of the cold war. The exodus from Cuba undermined a revolution that sided with the communist enemies.

As years passed, and their expectations of a prompt return to the island seemed less realistic, Cubans began to embrace their new country. They were successful in creating a prosperous economic enclave in Miami, which they consider the Cuban Mecca, but also in other places where they settled. Most wanted to bring relatives from the island to join them, but after the breakdown of diplomatic relations between the two countries, that was difficult if not impossible. As mentioned before, Cubans leaving the island between 1962 and 1965 had to do so through a third country, generally Spain or Mexico. Then, on September 28, 1965, Fidel Castro unexpectedly announced that the port of Camarioca in Matanzas province would be opened for all those who wanted to leave the country. Cubans in Miami rushed down to pick up relatives. To normalize the flow of immigrants, Cuba and the United States signed a memorandum of understanding starting the "Freedom Flights" as they were known here. These flights lasted between 1965 and 1973, and they brought the second vast wave of Cubans to the United States. This group included a higher proportion of blue-collar workers and small business owners than the previous one. Many of the typical Union City refugees came during this period. The second group was not very well received initially by the earlier exiles, mainly due to social-class differences, but gradually they were accepted. Overall, until the early 1980s, these two waves of Cubans were overwhelmingly white, had relatively high levels of education, and were ardently anticommunist. Their mainly middle-class positions or aspirations in Cuban society shaped their values, which brought them closer to mainstream America than to the majority of their Latino counterparts. Despite internal differentiations, these groups set the tone for both Cubans' self-perceptions, and the perceptions of others about Cubans in the United States. Cubans did not feel that they were a "minority," and they often became the example for Hispanic and other immigrants because of their hard-work ethic and their adherence to American ideals.

The third wave of Cuban migrants came when Fidel Castro opened the port of Mariel in Cuba in 1980 and permitted families in the United States to come and pick up their relatives. The Mariel exodus was preceded by a series of events that resulted in a major international crisis. These included a number of embassy invasions in Havana (mainly Latin American embassies), hijackings of Cuban planes and vessels, the continuing decline of the Cuban economy, and pressures from disaffected Cubans who wanted to emigrate.[15] The most dramatic event occurred on March 28, 1980, when a bus full of people who wanted to leave the country crashed into the Peruvian embassy in Havana and the occupants requested political asylum. A Cuban guard was killed during the incident. On April 4th, the Cuban government withdrew the guards from the embassy and announced that those seeking asylum would be allowed to leave the country. Within forty-eight hours, more than 10,000 Cubans had taken refuge on the grounds of the Peruvian embassy. After a series of flights from Cuba to Costa Rica, Spain, and Peru, which allowed the evacuation of the Peruvian Embassy, the Cuban government announced that the port of Mariel would be open for all Cubans wanting to leave. Cubans in Florida immediately organized a flotilla, which began ferrying the Cubans from Mariel across the Straits of Florida to Key West. About 125,000 Cubans came through the Mariel boatlift.[16] They were not from upper- or middle-class backgrounds. They were not even similar to the latest wave of the late 1960s and 1970s that brought a large number of working-class people. The refugees of the 1980s were generally younger and predominantly male, and the number of black Cubans in this group was significantly higher than that of previous exile waves: approximately 20 percent, compared with 3 percent.[17] There were also some law breakers and mentally ill people who were placed on refugee boats by government officials. Cuba's unofficial argument was that if the United States had for years encouraged the migration of well-educated, professional sectors of Cuban society, they should receive some poor, sick, and delinquent Cubans too. However, although the media inaccurately and undeservedly focused the attention on the criminals, many of the Mariel refugees were families. Research and personal testimonials demonstrate that many immigrants from this group have been as successful as their predecessors.[18] But for the first time in the Cuban migration, a high percentage of poor, dark-skinned, and less educated people, more representative of the Cuban population on the island, was added to the earlier waves of exiles. At first, Mariel Cubans were seen as heroes escaping to attain freedom, but when the differences between these and the early exiles became more evident, the Mariel migrants were discriminated against, even by their own people.

After Mariel, the U.S. government agreed to authorize 20,000 yearly visas for Cubans who wanted to emigrate. In reality, however, between 1980 and 1993 there was limited immigration from Cuba. The fourth wave of immigrants came in the summer of 1994 when masses of people left the country by boats or homemade rafts. The Cuban government openly allowed those who wanted to leave to do so. This decision came at a time when the country was experiencing the most severe economic crisis in its history. The 1989 collapse of the Soviet Union compounded the effects of the U.S.-imposed embargo. Large Soviet subsidies to the Cuban economy were no longer available. The response of the government to this emergency was to implement a *período especial,* or special period, a government program that enacted severe laws to combat the crisis in the long run, but which imposed further limits on consumption and restricted access to already scarce resources. One of these measures, implemented in 1993, was to legalize the use of the dollar as currency. Since then, life has become easier for those Cubans working in sectors such as tourism, where they are partly paid in dollars, or more importantly, for those who receive remittances from relatives in the United States. Others, who depend only on the devalued Cuban peso, face extreme difficulties. The discontent created by the special period has had social and political repercussions. A street riot, as well as the chaotic departure of thousands of Cubans, marked the summer of 1994. The dramatic events of that year included the death of dozens of people when a tugboat carrying adults and children trying to leave the country was intercepted and sunk by the Cuban coast guard. The United States accepted all boat migrants at first, but a change in U.S. policy directed the balseros, or rafters, to Guantanamo, the U.S. base in Cuba. Cubans in Guantanamo lived in very crowded and harsh conditions for months, but eventually they were allowed to come to the United States. When the balseros were brought from Guantanamo, another agreement resolved that the United States would return to Cuba all escapees found at sea.[19] While refugees picked up at sea were returned to Cuba, those who reached U.S. shores could stay and benefit from the 1966 Cuban Adjustment Act. This policy is known as the wet foot–dry foot policy. As expected, these migrants came mostly from the poorest sectors of Cuban society and were those hurt the most by the economic crisis.

The 1994 migration chaos led to lengthy conversations between the United States and Cuba and the migration agreement mentioned above got under way, in which the United States agreed to grant 20,000 visas a year for Cubans who wanted to emigrate. Through a lottery system, Cubans who have presented proper documentation are randomly selected. They are interviewed by the U.S. Interests Section in Havana for approval. After this, they need to get their exit papers from the Cuban Ministry of The Interior. Those who are authorized to leave have to pay their airfare in dollars, which is usually done by their families in the United States.

Current migration from Cuba is different from earlier periods. Even when most migrants are opposed to the government, the majority of those leaving Cuba now cite economics as their primary reason for leaving. They come from all segments of society. They include the poor, but also a high proportion of professionals who were raised and educated in contemporary Cuba, which constitutes another "brain drain" for the island.

For Cuba, the emigration of its citizens to the United States has often provided economic, political, and ideological escape valves for internal pressures, albeit the departure of disaffected individuals has been portrayed as a betrayal of the Revolution. For the United States, the Cuban immigration has always been part of its foreign policy toward Cuba, although it has represented different things at different times. For example, the upper- and middle-classes and professionals left Cuba in the early 1960s because they strongly opposed the new government. That was also true of the migrants of the 1970s. These people were welcomed here as political refugees. Their presence helped the U.S. economy without creating great social upheaval. This selective immigration policy benefited the United States. Conversely, as discontent mounted on the island, the full boats of Cubans coming from Mariel in 1980 became a dilemma for the United States, not only because the migrants were different from the earlier exiles economically, socially, and racially, but also because a simultaneous flow of Haitian and other boat people was reaching Florida, making entry by Cubans more complicated. Shortly after Mariel migrants came, the exclusively Cuban relief system was replaced by the federally funded Refugee Resettlement Program (RRP) and the Cuban/Haitian Entrant Program. Cubans who had entered the United States before October 1, 1978, and had registered with the Cuban Refugee Center in Miami continued to be eligible for assistance under the CRP, but effective December 1, 1980, the program was phased out. The *marielitos*, as the Mariel refugees are sometimes known, received help through both the RRP and the Cuban/Haitian Entrant Program under the category of "entrants."[20]

The Mariel exodus was a factor in the change of refugee policy. The Refugee Act of 1980, signed into law by President Jimmy Carter, was intended to aid all refugees, irrespective of national origin. An obvious reason for this policy change was the strong criticism faced by the U.S. government in the wake of the simultaneous and chaotic influx of boat people from Cuba and Haiti. While Cubans were automatically being granted political asylum because they came from a communist country, Haitians were being denied that status even though they were fleeing very dangerous political conditions in their country.

Neither the marielitos nor the balseros encompassed the same social and political gains for the United States as the earlier exiles. With mounting anti-immigrant feeling in this country, the fact that many dark, poor people from Cuba were trying to illegally enter the country became a problem.[21] These migrants were not welcomed, not even by their own compatriots, who considered them rough, uneducated, and often lazy, attitudes that are changing as many of the recent arrivals become integrated into the new society. Nevertheless, although recent accords between the two countries have diminished the deluge of Cubans coming to the United States, many people continue to reach the Miami shores and some perish at sea. The famous case of Elián González, the six-year-old Cuban boy who survived a shipwreck in November, 1999, is one example.[22]

Though recent Cuban immigrants are no longer viewed as special, as the earlier exiles had been, all still enjoy preferences over other immigrants. Political refugees from other countries—Vietnam, Haiti, eastern Europe before the collapse of communism, El Salvador—have been granted entry into the United States, but Cubans enjoy additional benefits. The most important difference is the Cuban Adjustment Act of 1966, referred to earlier, which is designed to facilitate the adjustment of Cubans' legal status after they arrive. Cubans who come legally as visitors, tourists, or in an official capacity and stay when their visas expire are allowed to apply for permanent residence after one year and one day of uninterrupted stay. These benefits are unique to Cubans, to individuals married to Cubans, or to children of Cubans. Critics of these policies claim that some of the forces that generate the Cuban migration are actually a Caribbean, even global, phenomenon. In the western hemisphere, Haitians and Dominicans escape dire conditions in their countries and do not receive the same treatment as Cubans do when they arrive here.[23]

The main reason for Cubans to leave their country now may be economic rather than political, but many recent immigrants have tended to claim political motives upon arriving in the United States. One reason is the pressure that they receive from the dominant, conservative voices of the exile community. A related reason may be that, by adopting the exile status, they obtain social and political advantages in their new country. On the other hand, some recently arrived Cubans have become disappointed with the conditions in the United States because they had an idealized notion of life in this country. Their value systems were shaped in a very different economic, social, and political context. Also, many are critical about exile politics, which they see as undemocratic. They believe that many Cuban-American political leaders engage in the same repressive and intimidating practices as the ones they criticize in Cuba.

As a result of the various moments in the history of Cuba, of the Cuban diaspora, and U.S.-Cuba policy described above, Cubans in the United States today have become a much more diverse population than they were in the 1960s and 1970s. Most exiles establish a difference between themselves and the "new Cubans."[24] They see themselves as socially superior and politically purer in their anti-Castro convictions than more recent refugees. The new Cuban immigrants, however, are more representative of Cuban society. They are professionals, artists, workers, black, and white. They also differ from the exiles in their relationship with Cuba. While the early wave generally shuns any openness to the island, most recent migrants hope for an end to hostilities between the two countries. Above all, they want their counterparts in Cuba to improve their living conditions. Many members of the first wave oppose visiting the island based on an ideological opposition to Fidel Castro's government, now headed by his brother Raúl. They believe that these visits help the communist government survive by bringing dollars into the country. Also, in many cases, they no longer have relatives there. On the other hand, the new Cuban immigrants return to the island very frequently to help their relatives with necessary dollars and goods. In part, their more frequent contact with the island responds to a relaxation in migration policy by the Cuban government. The early refugees were not allowed to return to Cuba until 1979, almost twenty years after the beginning of the mass postrevolutionary migration. Since the summer of 2004, however, it is the U.S. government that has imposed severe restrictions on visits back to Cuba.

The diversity of the Cuban community in the United States today raises a number of questions. How are Cubans from the different waves influencing each other? Will they continue to live in separate worlds? Given its present heterogeneity, will the Cuban community in the United States move to more moderate stands toward Cuba, and more realistic expectations of the United States? How do Cubans compare themselves with other Hispanics? Are Cubans different depending on the region of the country where they have settled? The answers to these questions require study. In some cases only time will tell. With this book, I want to make a contribution toward a greater understanding of these issues, which are both professionally and personally important to me.

2

Cuban Union City

Origins, Development, and Change

When the first Cuban families arrived in Union City in the late 1940s, they were following in the footsteps of many other immigrant groups. As in other parts of the Northeast, waves of immigrants contributed to the urbanization of today's Hudson County, a 46.4 square mile area located within minutes of New York City. The county consists of twelve municipalities: Bayonne, East Newark, Gutenberg, Harrison, Hoboken, Jersey City, Kearney, North Bergen, Secaucus, Union City, Weehawken, and West New York. It has the highest population density level in New Jersey, with 13,000 persons per square mile in 2000.[1]

The first true settlers of Union City were eighteenth-century Dutch and English merchants who divided a dense forest into large land parcels. Prior to them, there had been some isolated, small Dutch outposts and transient fur trappers, traders, hunters, fishermen, and woodcutters. In the middle of the nineteenth century, after the revolutionary wars that erupted in 1848 Europe, there was a large influx of refugees into Manhattan. A number of German immigrants living in New York City decided to move to a less crowded and more residential area. These first families came to West Hoboken, the lower section near the Jersey City boundary, and the uptown section, or Union Hill, north of 32nd Street. West Hoboken and Union Hill were consolidated into a single town, Union

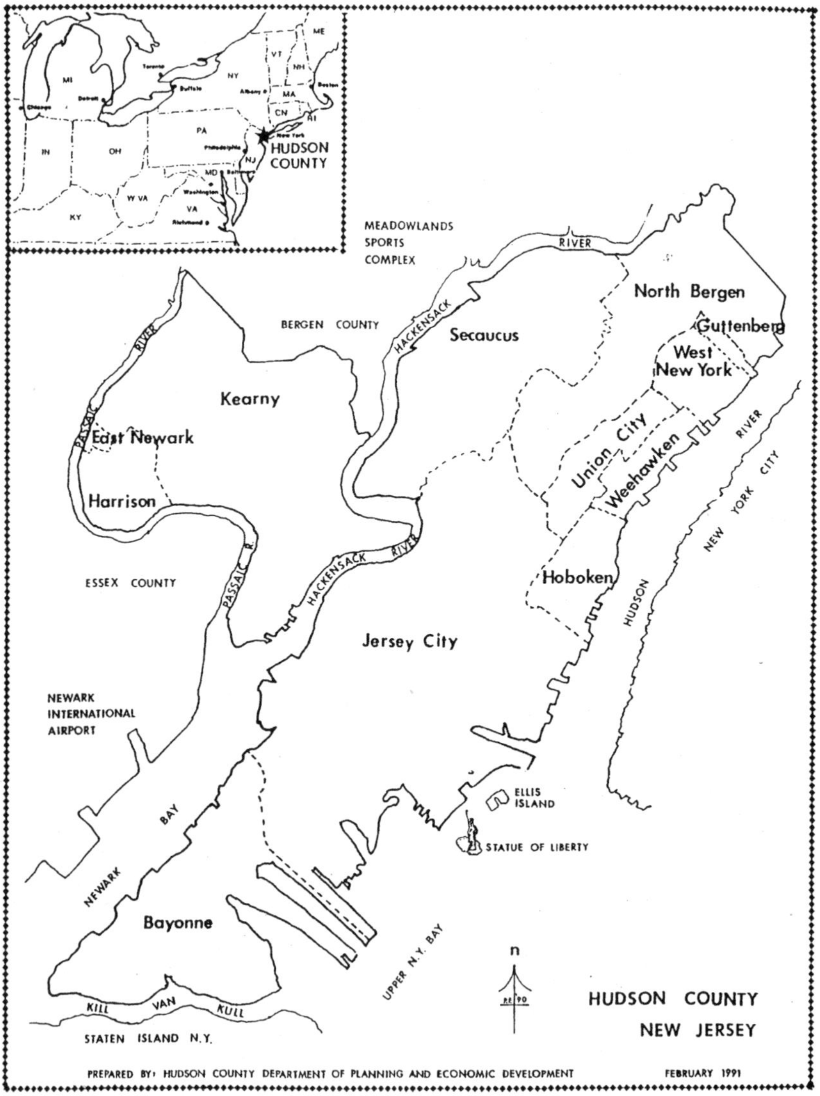

FIGURE 2.1 *Map of Hudson County.* (Hudson County Economic Department of Planning and Economic Development)

FIGURE 2.2 *Bergenline Avenue at 32nd Street ca. 1890.* (Collection of William Duque)

City, in 1925.[2] Union City was practically a German-speaking enclave in northern New Jersey at first. Eventually, it also became the home of Irish, Poles, Armenians, Syrians, eastern European Jews, and Italians, who mostly came in search of economic opportunities.

During the early twentieth century, Union City became established as the home of the American embroidery industry, following the introduction of the first embroidery machine in the United States. Immigrants produced a range of products, from luxury laces to military emblems and insignias during World War II. There were also many silk mills and several beer breweries located throughout the city. In time, Union City thrived on commercial activity, and Bergenline Avenue, a central thoroughfare, was bustling with stores, banks, and other businesses.

By the 1960s, upwardly mobile Union City residents had started to disperse. The Germans had largely assimilated into American culture. Many other European Americans had left the area too. The city showed signs of economic deterioration. Many stores closed and buildings became unkempt. Beginning in the middle of the 1960s, a stream of Cuban exiles began to join the group of Cuban families that had been living there since the 1940s. Cubans represented the first massive Hispanic presence in the city, and as their population grew many of the remaining ethnic Americans still living in Union City left. Others, of course, stayed and accepted the newcomers. They felt that Union City was their home. Some members of ethnic groups even welcomed Cuban émigrés. Susan, a working-class German American woman who was living in Union City in the 1960s, told me:

> My husband made a Cuban friend named Manny. His father owned a little grocery store. The business grew and from that he went into real estate. Cubans were very enterprising. Besides Manny, we made very good Cuban friends. They were good families, very gregarious. Some Americans were very negative toward Cubans, but many were not. Some people feared they were taking their jobs away. My whole family liked them. As Europeans, they were used to accents. (Interviewed on February 28, 2000)

Margaret, a working-class Italian American woman reiterated the rejection of some and the good feelings of others about the newcomers:

> When the Cubans came some people felt resentful, in particular those families who had been in Union City for generations. I really didn't experience much of that. My family felt it was wonderful. Though at times . . . there were mixed feelings expressed at the dinner table, but most of us felt very positive. After all, Italians were immigrants too! (Interviewed on November 8, 2002)

As will be discussed in Chapter 3, Union City experienced an economic boom with the arrival of great numbers of Cubans. But Union City, like other northern industrial cities, felt the impact of the economic decline of the late 1970s and 1980s, when it lost industrial jobs to less developed areas of the country and the world. Since the 1980s, a new wave of immigrants from Central and South America began arriving in Union City, as well as Cuban refugees from the Mariel exodus. More immigrants have come in the 1990s and 2000s. These recent arrivals do not fare as well due to the precipitous decline of manufacturing. Yet this economic change does not seem to deter them from coming to Union City, which, with 42,000

FIGURE 2.3 *Bergenline Aveune at 32nd St., 2008.* (José Hernández)

residents per square mile, is the most densely populated area of the United States today.[3] The newcomers take jobs in the service sector, and work for the many small factories, often sweatshop-like operations, which are eager to find cheap labor.

The Establishment of a Cuban Community

Most Cubans who arrived in Union City in the 1940s and 1950s had migrated from New York City. They wanted a quiet place to live, work, and raise their families. Small in number and not very visible, their presence still drew their Cuban relatives and other compatriots to the area when they arrived en masse in the 1960s.

Some of my interviewees recall those early years. A retired woman in her early 70s told me how difficult it was for the first Cubans:

> When we got here there were no Hispanics. Only a handful of Puerto Rican families and they helped us a lot. Many of our Cuban friends who had overstayed their visas lived with us for a while.

> There was a lot of fear that they would be caught by immigration. Before the exiles came, Cubans were treated pretty badly. Some Cubans who came early on worked hard and were successful. But many were not. It was very hard to find apartments because of discrimination. We were seen as "problematic." The majority of apartments that we could afford were poorly furnished and had shared bathrooms. The city was so ugly and depressing. But it was better than staying in Cuba, where it wasn't easy to find good employment. No matter how difficult it's been, I still think this is a wonderful country! There are so many opportunities. And some immigrants don't appreciate it. They only complain. (Interviewed on June 27, 2001)

The majority of Union City prerevolutionary migrants came from small towns and rural areas, such as Fomento in central Villa Clara province in Cuba. They came to the United States primarily in search of economic opportunities. They were mostly white, since the nonwhite population in Cuba was concentrated in urban areas. The same woman quoted above, added: "In Cuba, you couldn't get a good job. It was not easy to *desenvolverse,* or get ahead. That's why my husband and I left Fomento for the United States in 1955."

Julio Bello, a Cuban American, expressed similar feelings about his parents, who came to Union City in 1956:

> My father is from Fomento and my mother from Buena Vista, also in Villa Clara province. My mother had completed the eighth grade, but my father only finished second grade. You can imagine that my father's hopes for a good job in Cuba were minimal, so they decided to leave the country. My father became disillusioned in the United States after he came. He had a different idea of this country. He didn't like it that, here, women had to work. Also, the family did not spend a lot of time together. (Interviewed on July 22, 2001)

Not all Union City Cuban pioneers came from New York. In 1949, while on their honeymoon in Miami, Manuel and Lyda Rodríguez took advantage of an invitation from a New Jersey woman, Florence Colarusso, to come up north with her. Manuel and Lyda, who were in their early 20s and wanted a better life than they had in their native Cuba, decided to start anew. They traveled by car, along with Colarusso and a friend. They were among the first Cubans who came to Union City as immigrants. As Juan Forero remarked:

> Colarusso's good deed . . . didn't just help one young couple start a new life. The Rodriguezes, from the small town of Fomento in central Cuba, would become remarkably successful business people and help dozens of relatives and fellow townspeople emigrate to New Jersey . . . In the process, the newcomers from Fomento would create a small but vibrant Cuban American community where there had been none before. So when Fidel Castro took power in 1959, setting off an exodus of U.S.-bound Cubans, it was natural that tens of thousands would arrive in Hudson County.[4]

Politics was a reason for many of the early immigrants to leave Cuba. In the late 1950s, the political scenario on the island was marked by increasing conflict between the Batista government and opposition forces. The fighting rebels, led by Fidel Castro, were gaining ground politically and militarily. Cuban nationalism, historically very strong, was manifested in support of the rebel cause both inside and outside of the country. As will be discussed in Chapter 6, many Cuban immigrants were involved in revolutionary activities. A good number of them collaborated with U.S. cells of the 26th of July Movement, the leading revolutionary organization in the struggle against the Batista government. These political units had a great deal of support among Cuban immigrants in New Jersey and New York. Silverio Rodríguez told me that he became involved with the Movement after he arrived in Union City with his parents in 1954. Silverio added, "I met Fidel Castro. He used to visit the revolutionary groups around here from time to time. I met him when he came to Union City to talk to us in the late 1950s. I remember that I met him at the *bodega* that's on 26th Street and Bergenline Avenue." A former farmer from Fomento, Silverio's father participated in anti-Batista activities in Cuba and in the United States. After the triumph of Castro's revolution, Silverio's parents went back to Cuba, where they started to face political problems. Now a fierce

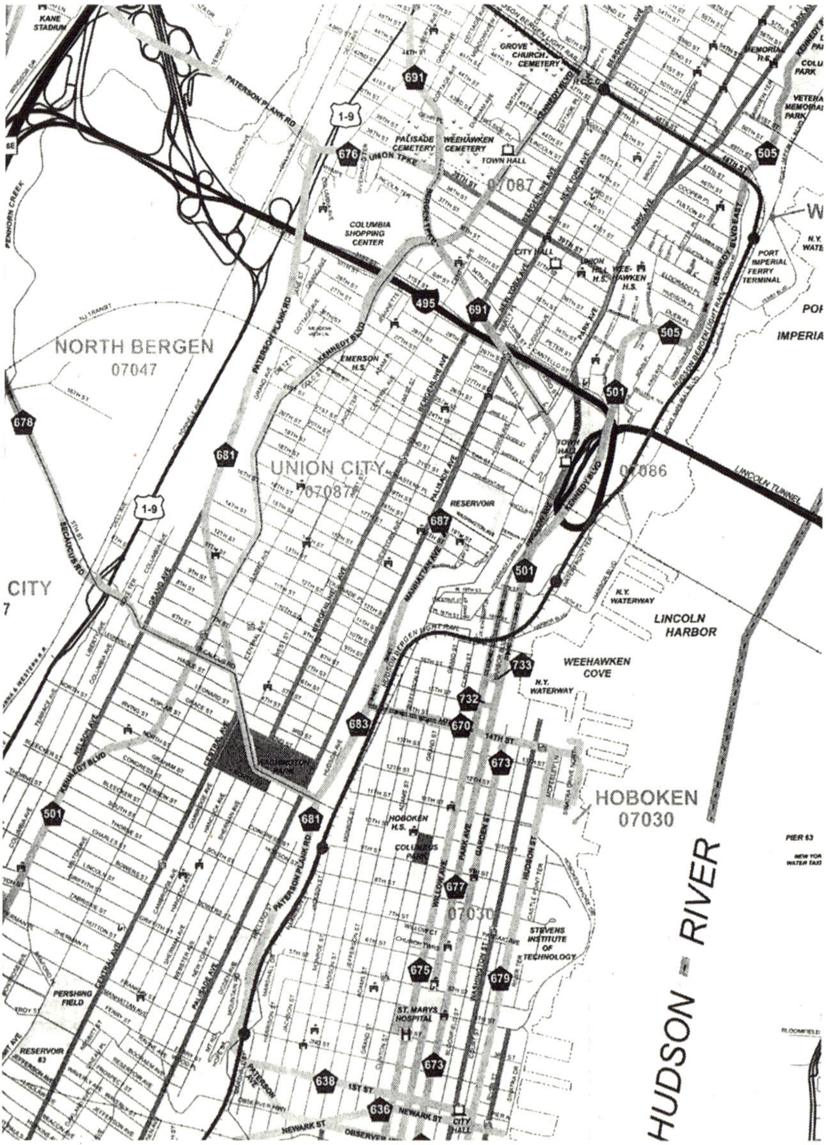

Figure 2.4 *Map of Union City.* (Hudson County Department of Planning and Economic Development)

anti-Castro activist, Silverio confided: "My father saw many injustices. He went to jail for a while. Since I had stayed here, I sent for them. I got them out of the country two years later through Spain" (interviewed on November 14, 1999). Dionisio Villanueva lived in Sagua de Tánamo, in Oriente province. He remembers that his mother insisted on sending him and his brother to the United States after "the town was burnt by the rebels," at the peak of the anti-Batista struggle. He came on a student visa in 1958. After the Castro government took over they went back to Cuba, only to return to New Jersey permanently a year later (interviewed on August 7, 2001).

A small group of tightly knit families, the pre-1959 Cuban immigrants set the stage for what was going to become the second largest concentration of Cubans in the United States, after Miami, Florida. They provided Union City with necessary labor; they took jobs in the embroidery, textile, and other manufacturing industries. Before the exiles of the 1960s arrived, the immigrant Cubans of Union City were beginning to succeed in business and starting to build social organizations. I will discuss this topic further in Chapter 3.

The Exiles

The large number of exiles who came in the late 1960s were, decidedly, the ones who gave Union City its Cuban character. The sheer magnitude of the migration changed the social composition of the city, which is a mere 1.4-square-mile area (forty-nine blocks long, and, at its widest point, seven blocks wide). In 1970, over 39,000 persons of Cuban birth or parentage lived in Hudson County. Only Dade County, Florida, the location of Miami, held a higher concentration of Cubans living inside the boundaries of a single county. Union City and the neighboring town of West New York absorbed the majority of the exiles. While the Hudson county population as a whole had been steadily declining since 1960, Union City counted 57,305 residents in 1970, a 10 percent growth in population since 1960.[5] In West New York, Cubans represented 51.1 percent of the population in 1970, compared to 0.1 percent in 1960.[6] As the exile flow into the county continued unabated during the early 1970s, the Cuban-origin population continued to increase. According to the 1980 census, there were 45,719

FIGURE 2.5 *The Pérez family being greeted by their Union City relatives at John F. Kennedy Airport when they arrived from Cuba in 1962.* (Collection of Hildalina Oropesa)

Cubans in Hudson County, of whom 72 percent lived in those two municipalities. Before the 1980 Mariel refugees came into the area, there were almost 18,000 Cubans in Union City and over 15,000 in West New York. Many thousands more lived in the adjacent county towns of Hoboken, North Bergen, Weehawken, and Gutenberg.[7]

When Cubans arrived in Miami, they registered with the Cuban Refugee Center. One of the top priorities of the program since its inception in 1961 (as described in Chapter 1)was to resettle refugees away from the Miami area. As of December 1972, 51 percent of all resettled refugees had come to the New York/New Jersey metropolitan area. Other popular states were California and Illinois. In New Jersey, Hudson County received most of the exiles.[8] The Cuban Refugee Program was not officially established in New Jersey until 1965, when the second wave of immigrants started to arrive. Lourdes Gil recalls:

> Before 1965, a few Cuban exiles of the early 1960s who were licensed as social workers offered courses to arriving Cubans. Many of these were professionals and needed guidance as to how to proceed with the accreditation of Cuban degrees. I remember that my mother and other social workers used the Newark office that had previously housed the Hungarian Refugee Relief effort in the 1950s for that purpose. (Interviewed on July 9, 2001)

This initial aid system was called the Cuban Welfare Program, and it received funds from the Division of Public Welfare of the State of New Jersey. After 1965, the Cuban Refugee Program was established. Mr. James Orrico became its director, later succeeded by Conchita Valdés Muñoz.[9] Hudson County Division of Social Services provided modest cash assistance, medical expenses, food stamps, at least a month's rent payment until the recipient found a job, and financial help for education and training. I personally received help for education. Like many other Cuban exile students, I was granted the "Cuban loan," financial help for higher education that was given exclusively to Cubans. Other refugees recount their experiences with educational training opportunities. Luisa, a former Cuban Refugee Program worker commented:

> I was a science professor at the University of Villa Clara in Cuba. When I came to the United States, I went back to school and benefited from the training programs they had for Cubans. Many Cubans went to Montclair State College to study. I got a Master in Education from Montclair because I wanted to work in education. But I had some personal problems and went to work at the Cuban Refugee Program until very recently, when I retired. (Interviewed on August 22, 2001)

When help for older refugees ran out in the Cuban program, they were transferred to Social Security, Supplemental Security Income (SSI), and programs for the disabled. Federal Cuban Relief Program monies were channeled through state and county governments to the municipalities where Cubans were relocating. Communities outside Miami seemed to experience more difficulty in getting funds from the federal government. Ms. Angelica Harrison, Director of Hudson County Division of Social Services, complained, "New Jersey didn't get as much money for the Cuba program. We were cheated, as secondary ports of entry usually are. Miami always got more money" (interviewed on July 31, 2001). Yet Hudson County spent a considerable amount of resources on Cuban exile assistance. In November 1975, refugee aid totaled more than half a million dollars, $639,335, an increase of 12 percent over the preceding month, and 91.4 percent more than in the same month in the previous year.[10]

Besides the government, the Catholic Church was key in helping Cuban exiles adjust to their new life in Union City and West New York. The Church administered the Cuban Refugee Program, which distributed the funds through Catholic Charities. Two major parishes, St. Augustine and St. Joseph of the Palisades, assisted the refugees with basic needs as they arrived. They helped them find jobs and apartments, facilitated translation of documents brought from Cuba, and provided many other services to the migrants.

Who were the exiles? Like most Cubans coming to the United States at the time, they were older than the typical immigrant. In their study of West New York in 1979, only a few years after the major refugee flow, Rogg and Cooney reported that the median age for Cubans was 38.9. The great majority of them were married (58.7%). A significant number of Union City exiles came from small towns or cities (42.2%) rather than from large cities (39.7%). They were mainly from Villa Clara (32.8%) and Havana (37.1%). The high proportion of refugees from Villa Clara confirms a chain migration effect, as many of the original Union City Cubans were from that area. Only 36.3 percent of the refugees were high school graduates, a figure dramatically lower than the national average (66.3%) and that for Cubans nationally (44%). Most exiles were white. Only 1.9 percent were nonwhite in Union City and West New York, lower than the figure for 1960s Cubans nationally (3%).[11]

Among Union City exiles there were owners of small farms in Cuba and workers from rural and semi-rural areas. Many of these were joining their relatives from the provinces, who had been residing in Union City for years. Others were small entrepreneurs, blue-collar or service workers from urban centers, notably from Havana, and others were professionals and white-collar workers. Overall, when compared with the Cuban exile population of the 1960s and 1970s nationally, Union City was always more of a "working-class" enclave.[12] Most Cuban exiles who came to this area did so after 1965, during the second wave of migration, which brought less affluent, less educated Cubans to the United States. Ideologically anti-communist, they wanted to escape communism in Cuba, but they were also motivated by economic reasons. The late 1960s brought increasing economic difficulties for Cubans. The Ofensiva Revolucionaria of 1968, a government measure that nationalized all remaining private businesses, even the smallest ones, made everyday life in Cuba very challenging. It is understandable that this group of exiles chose to relocate in an area of the United States where industrial jobs were abundant. Nevertheless, many Cuban exiles who were resettled in Union City had wanted to go there to join relatives in the first place. Family and community support were far more important in their adjustment than government and other institutional aid.[13] Aleida Durán, a well-known Cuban journalist in Union City told me: "Most Cubans did not like to depend on government aid. Families would help one another. When the exiles arrived here the change in this city was extraordinary" (interviewed on June 19, 2001).

Pre-1959 Cuban immigrants, most of whom had relatives coming as refugees, assisted the newcomers in countless ways. They also recount how their standing in the city changed. Manuel Pérez, a well-respected entrepreneur in Union City said:

> Once the stream of exiles began to settle in the area, and they started to maintain their neighborhoods and paint previously unkempt houses and apartments, Americans began to respect Cubans. Now there were many of us in the town. We were noticeable! Before then, there was not a good opinion of those of us who had lived here for years. We were often discriminated against. (Interviewed on August 29, 2001)

One Cuban immigrant woman noted somewhat resentfully, "Those of us who were here before went through the worst. We were not accepted automatically as legal immigrants or exiles, and we didn't get any help from the government" (interviewed on June 25, 2000). Although prerevolutionary Cuban immigrants received their relatives and friends and helped them start new lives, a few resented their privileges. Yet, together, immigrants and exiles would build a community that was a dynamic and active Cuban enclave in the heart of northern New Jersey for over twenty years.

Mariel

By the time the Mariel flotilla took place in April, 1980, there was a sizable and established Cuban community in Union City. Bergenline Avenue flourished with Cuban entrepreneurial activity. Cuban women there had the highest rate of labor-force participation in the country, surpassing that of other Hispanic, African American, white, and Cuban women nationally. Union City even had a young Cuban American serving on the state Assembly who had been the town's mayor for two terms. Cubans felt proud of their accomplishments. One Cuban man watching the annual Cuban Day Parade on Bergenline Avenue expressed this new-found pride: "Cubans have to be taken seriously for what they did to this community from the 1960s through the 1980s. They accumulated economic and political power. This city was destroyed when Cubans got here. They worked hard and they rebuilt it" (interviewed June 3, 2001). A Cuban immigrant woman recalled how most stores on Bergenline Avenue did not have windows before Cubans started opening businesses. "Windows in Cuban stores, especially clothing boutiques, were decorated beautifully, and jewelry shops displayed charming accessories, especially for women" (interviewed September 15, 1999).

The Union City Cuban community was very supportive of Mariel refugees. Upon learning about the events in the Peruvian embassy in Havana, Cubans rushed to donate money. "They contributed heavily to the $2 million collected in a telemarathon broadcast over the Spanish TV network. Refugee centers were set up by a Roman Catholic church, the Union City Baptist Church, and the Union of Cubans in Exile. In addition, an ad hoc committee of businessmen founded the Cuba-Peru Crusade and raised $125,000 in a couple of days."[14] All this money was collected for emergency aid. The refugee centers had few resources, and by mid-year, they could hardly offer any help to the migrants.

In July, 1980, the Caribbean Relief Program of the International Rescue Committee (IRC), a nonsectarian aid organization, opened an office in Hudson County. This voluntary agency helped primarily with refugee resettlement and sponsorship, housing, jobs, English language lessons, medical help, and assistance with legal documents. Over 3,000 refugees requested assistance from IRC. In a sample of 1,500 that the organization analyzed to obtain demographic information, the mean age of the refugees was 31.7 years, 70.3 percent of the migrants were white, 26.4 percent were black, and 1.1 percent were of Chinese origin. Males were 76 percent and females 24 percent of the sample. The average number of school years completed was eight.[15]

The IRC's involvement during Mariel was pivotal since "[i]t was not until the month of January, 1981, that a more orderly process for public assistance for refugees started with the centralization of all aid to Cuban refugees in the Cuban Refugee Program office."[16] Since the Cuban Refugee Program was being phased out, Mariel and future refugees were covered by the Refugee Resettlement Program (RRP) and the Cuban-Haitian Entrant Program. In all cases, the length and scope of aid was being reduced.[17] As referred to in Chapter 1, the RRP (which addresses the concerns of refugees from all countries), and the Cuban-Haitian Entrant Program, intended "to bring U.S. policy into line with international practice, which defines as a refugee anyone with a well founded fear of persecution or physical harm, regardless of the political bent of his or her country's regime."[18]

The first and second waves of Cuban exiles who came to Union City in the 1960s and 1970s could stay on CRP assistance for as long as they needed it. Older Cubans who could not work were given SSI benefits. But under RRP, help was only available for eight months. As a Hudson County Cuban Refugee Program caseworker told me,

> When the first exiles came, the government was really committed to help them, but things were not so easy for *marielitos* or the *balseros.* I guess there are so many more people coming to this country now and there are not as many resources as before. Despite the reduced help, both *marielitos* and *balseros* left public assistance rolls very quickly. They were interested in finding a job. (Interviewed on August 22, 2001)

Iraida Iturralde, who worked with the IRC office in West New York recounts how Mariel immigrants would tell her, "yo lo que quiero es pega," or, "what I want is a job" (using the Cuban slang for job; interviewed on April 5, 2002).

Mariel refugees encountered a great deal of prejudice. After being received as heroes, the new immigrants were discriminated against, even by earlier waves of Cuban exiles. The presence of dark-skinned, homosexual, delinquent, and criminal migrants defined society's attitudes toward the whole group. Some events, such as a violent prison hunger strike in Atlanta during May and June, 1981 after the refugees' resettlement, seemed to justify these feelings, albeit the majority of the group, as time has proven, had come to the United States in search of a better life. Guillermo Estévez writes about some of the difficulties Union City experienced in the resettlement of Mariel refugees:

> [Many sponsors] reneged on his/her verbal commitment to house, feed and otherwise support a refugee until he or she was self-sufficient. [Also] most tragically, the job offers that began to come into the [IRC] office at the beginning were gradually stopped coinciding with the widespread media coverage regarding the criminality of the new arrivals. Housing was a major problem, and the perception of this group as problematic did not help: [There were] 96 [refugees] sponsored by a local Union City church. They were more or less demanded out of Miami by the New Jersey Cubans eager to do something about the matter. . . . This group of refugees consisted of one woman and 95 young, single males, mostly black, whose manners left a lot to be desired. Very soon the parents of the parochial school children complained and the refugees had to be moved out. The only building that the St. Anthony refugee center could find was an abandoned one on 48th Street, perhaps the worst street in Union City. The owner agreed to let them in if they fixed the premises. With funds and labor from the Cuban community new floors were put in, pipes were fixed, electricity was installed. The city of Union City, however, did not give the occupancy permit and closed it down on July 1. Fourteen of the men who had been at the building went on a hunger strike [in a nearby park]. They were, of course, led by locals, a park demonstration was not part of the mentality of the new arrivals; such a thing is not tolerated in Cuba. The mayors of the two towns were squabbling as to who was responsible for what. Representatives of the governor came in person. IRC went to the scene and offered to put them up in a hotel. They were housed at the YMCA until apartments could be rented for them.[19]

At the time, unpleasant and sometimes serious incidents involving Mariel refugees obscured the majority of law-abiding, hard-working, and talented individuals who came. There were many writers, painters, and graphic artists who are referred to as *la generación de Mariel*, or the Mariel generation. A great number of Mariel refugees had to struggle hard against the stigma carried by the label *marielito*. As one of the writers who came in the 1980s clarified: "I am an exile and I came through the Mariel flotilla, but I am not a "marielito."[20] These negative feelings have subsided over time, and at present many Mariel immigrants are becoming as successful in many areas just like the early exiles.

The 1990s Migration

Ever since regular migration became difficult after 1959, there have been Cubans coming to the United States illegally by boats or rafts. Yet the number of these arrivals throughout the years pales in comparison to the *balsero* crisis of 1994. Economic adversity, the political discontent created by an atrocious economic situation, and a decision by the Cuban government to let people venture out to sea sent hundreds and thousands of people to the Florida coasts. A total of 37,000 rafters were rescued at sea at the close of the 1994 crisis.[21] Some of the *balseros* intercepted by the U.S. Coast Guard, who were taken to Guantanamo and later brought to the United States, made it to Union City, although the great majority wanted to stay in Miami. About 2,000 registered with the RRP in Hudson County. They received the same assistance given to Mariel migrants before them. Job training, health care aid, and cash were among the benefits offered to these Cubans for eight months after their acceptance as parolees by the U.S. government. The IRC, which had been opened during Mariel, continues to offer services to Cuban refugees. Another agency that opened in 1981, the International Institute of New Jersey, also helps Cubans and other migrants with English lessons and computer training.[22]

The majority of Cuban migrants to the United States now come through the lottery system. After disembarking, generally at the Miami airport, they receive form I 94, which grants them parole status. Those traveling to Hudson County have to report to the RRP office to register before obtaining the benefits described earlier. Among these immigrants are many professionals. The RRP refers them to agencies that can help them with job training in their professions, if possible, and especially in English language education, which is the main gateway to finding jobs. Other migrants of the 1990s are those who overstay their visas when they come as visitors or students. In all these cases, through the Cuban Adjustment Act of 1966, they are eligible for permanent residence status after one year and one day of continuous residence in the United States. This is the major advantage that Cubans enjoy, since, in all other cases when some immigrants are accepted as "refugees," "parolees," or "asylees" (e.g., from Colombia, Venezuela, Serbia, Egypt), they do not have the automatic option to become permanent residents after a period of time.[23] While there are current concerns about granting amnesty to illegal immigrants, U.S. law has already been doing that for years for Cuban migrants who overstay their visas.

Many of the *balseros* who came to Union City went back to Florida. Others went elsewhere, like Las Vegas, Nevada, where they saw opportunities for jobs in the casino industry. According to Lourdes Méndez from the RRP, about 25 percent of the *balseros* who registered with the program have stayed in Union City. Overall, about 35 percent of all the refugees since the Mariel boatlift have stayed. The reason that more migrants in these last two waves moved away from Union City than in the previous ones was their age. Recent migrants have been younger and in many cases single, while exiles of the first two waves were older, married, and tended to settle down with their families. Also, the economic opportunities in Union City were far greater when the first refugees came. It is natural that new immigrants go to other places to find the jobs that are now difficult to find in Union City.

The diversity of current migrants from Cuba translates itself into an amalgam of experiences and attitudes. Although in most cases they prefer to live in the United States, the differences between the social, economic, and political systems they grew up in and those of their new country are shocking and makes adjustment very difficult. Luis, a *balsero* who left Cuba with his wife and daughter told me: "If I only knew how difficult it was going to be . . . I wouldn't have come. Sometimes I feel that if I could find a boat, I would head back to Cuba" (interviewed on July 22, 2001). Others feel very satisfied with their decision to leave Cuba. Omar and Elsa, a *balsero* married couple who were detained at Guantanamo for eleven months, told me: "We love to live here. We came to New Jersey because we have family here. We especially love to live close to New York. We don't like Miami. We only go there to visit relatives" (interviewed on July 22, 2002).[24] María, a Union City woman who came through the lottery system confided: "The exiles that were here before don't like that we go to Cuba so often because 'we give money to Fidel,' but we don't care about politics, we want to help our families" (interviewed on July 2, 2001). Manuel, who came from Cuba in 2000, complained about the injustices he sees here too: "I was promised a promotion at work. I recognize that I've earned it. But the deal was that they were going to make me the boss for two departments and were going to fire the other two managers. They (the owners) were 'buttering me up' to convince me to take the job, but I felt that wasn't fair to the other two guys who have families to support. In the end, they were doing that to save money! I didn't take the position. Luckily, I found another job" (interviewed on July 11, 2001). Humberto, a young Cuban student who overstayed his visa, said that "a great number of young immigrants from Cuba now are professionals. These were the people who were promised a better life by the Revolution and for whom everything crumbled with the *período especial,* or special period in Cuba. But these immigrants are not so politicized. They are much more in contact with the Cuban reality; they maintain family, professional, and cultural ties" (interviewed on March 22, 2002). The majority of 1990s immigrants, like their predecessors, will likely find their place in their new communities. In the meantime, many of them ache for the country and the family they left behind.

Cuban Union City in the 1990s and 2000s

Union City is a community that has attracted many different nationalities, especially from Latin America. The proportion of Cubans in the total population began to decline gradually. In 1980, 32 percent was Cuban compared with 26 percent in 1990.[25] The 2000 census revealed an even greater decline of Cuban residents in the city and an increase in the suburbs. Cubans "are moving from urban environments and long-time Cuban enclaves such as Union City and West New York, and settling into more suburban places like Rutherford and Ridgefield Park."[26] Most Cubans moving to New Jersey suburbs go to Bergen County, a more upscale, residential area. The number

TABLE 2.1 CHANGES IN THE COMPOSITION OF THE HISPANIC POPULATION IN UNION CITY, 1990–2006

	1990	2000	2006	% of Hispanic population in 2006
Cuban	14,709	10,296	7,840	14.9
Puerto Rican	7,834	7,388	7,199	13.8
Dominican	5,281	7,688	9,259	17.7
Central and South American	15,060	19,286	27,998	53.5

Sources: U.S. Bureau of the Census, PO11 *Hispanic Origin,* 1990 Summary Tape File 3 (STF 3) Union City, New Jersey; U.S. Bureau of the Census, Census 2000 Demographic Profile Highlights, *Hispanic or Latino,* Union City, New Jersey; U.S. Bureau of the Census, B03001 *Hispanic or Latino Origin by Specific Origin,* Union City, New Jersey, 2006 American Community Survey.

of Cubans living in Bergen County "jumped from 6,984 in 1990 to 9,381 in 2000, a 34 percent increase. In Hudson County, the number of Cubans fell from 44,115 in 1990 to 33,901 in 2000, a 23 percent decrease."[27] The 2006 American Community Survey of the U.S. census revealed that the number of Cubans in Union City was 7,840, only 14.9 percent of the total Hispanic population. In contrast, there were 9,259 Dominicans and 27,998 Central and South Americans.[28]

Who is leaving? Who is staying? The migration to Bergen County seems to be related to socioeconomic status. Cubans who came in the first and second waves are more likely to be able to buy houses in the suburbs. Age is also an important factor determining where Cubans go. Many retirees go to Florida while most younger Cubans stay in the Northeast. Among younger Cubans, Miami is less popular than with older ones. Luisa, now a Hoboken resident who came from Cuba in 1961, when she was seventeen years old, said very firmly: "I don't like Miami. My worst punishment would be to have to live there! When I go on visits I ask my family: Are there any other radio stations here that are not obsessed with Cuba and with Fidel? Miami is very provincial. It remained frozen in the 1950s" (interviewed on September 20, 2003). Other interviewees shared their views about the changes in the community. Lourdes Gil thinks "that older Cubans move to Miami and the younger ones move to suburban New Jersey. But in many cases, the older Cubans return because of their children" (interviewed on July 9, 2001). Julio and Deisy Bello experience the opposite: "Our parents live here, that is the only reason we stay. We would like to move to Florida or Georgia . . . but for us, it's important to raise our children close to their grandparents" (interviewed on July 22, 2001).

Most Cubans I interviewed were careful to make a distinction between the "first exiles" and the "new Cubans." Many praised what they saw as the "hard-work ethic" of the first exiles as opposed to the "feelings of entitlement" of recent migrants. Many exiles feel that the new Cubans want things easy. Yet some Cubans did not agree with these generalizations and seemed disturbed by what they saw as discrimination among Cubans themselves. Chapter 7 will further discuss the relations among the different waves of Cubans and between Cubans and other immigrants in the area, especially other Latin Americans, in the context of community change.

3

Building Community

Economic Growth and the Rise of Local Organizations

When I arrived in Union City in 1968, I found a predominantly European American community. My first job was as a billing machine operator for a textile company, and at the time I was the only Hispanic in the office. I still remember Janet, a very kind German American woman, who helped me learn the ropes during my first months. I also remember Dawn, a young Armenian woman who, like me, had immigrated to the United States very recently. Another co-worker was Mary, an Italian American who did not feel comfortable with my foreign accent, and who often found an opportunity to complain about the Spanish (Cuban) invasion that was afflicting the town.[1] I had to work full-time to help my family settle in a new country. While working during the day I attended school at night. After a couple of years, I was able to quit that job, take part-time work, and go to school full-time.

There were already some Cuban businesses in the area before the massive migration of the 1960s. The prerevolutionary immigrants had opened at least two bodegas or grocery stores. One was on 26th Street and Bergenline Avenue (the main commercial thoroughfare) and was owned by Guillermo Labrada. The other was located on 48th Street and Hudson Avenue and was owned by a Spaniard who had lived in Cuba for many years before emigrating to the United States. Bodegas are mom-and-pop

FIGURE 3.1 *Bergenline Avenue at 48th Street facing downtown Union City.* (José Hernández)

stores that sell mostly food, but also some home conveniences. In immigrant communities, it is typical to see these establishments emerge as a result of social networks and the human capital that immigrants bring with them. Before the existence of the bodegas, Cubans had to go to New York City to find some of the products they consumed, such as black beans and plantains.

In addition, there was a Cuban restaurant, Hernández Restaurant, on Bergenline near 28th Street. And Manuel Pérez started a travel agency, Pérez Travel, at Bergenline and 24th Street. The pre-1960s immigrants formed the first social club, the Liceo Cubano, which was open until the early 1990s. But the Cuban immigrant community was small, and when the exiles started to come en masse in the 1960s, they still found a predominantly ethnic European enclave. Real estate was owned by European Americans or by European immigrants. For example, our landlord and many of our neighbors were Greek. Bergenline Avenue was dominated by white European American commerce. Mainstream stores like Woolworth on 35th Street, Schlezinger's, an upscale clothing store, and A. Holthausen, were flanked by small enterprises.

Most Cuban exiles came without money or possessions. They were allowed by the Cuban government to carry only essential clothing and other basic personal items. As many interviewees shared with me, and as I remember myself, Cubans could only bring a change of clothing for three days. When they arrived in Union City, they needed a lot of support. They received help from three major sources: (1) the Cuban Refugee Program in Jersey City's Hudson County Department of Social Services, (2) relatives already residing in the area, and (3) existing organizations such as churches that began to serve the needs of Cubans. A full discussion of the benefits under the Cuban Refugee Program can be found in Chapters 1 and 2. The role of religious organizations will be explored in Chapter 5. Here I would like to discuss ways in which the institutional structures of the city responded to the Cuban presence, in particular the commercial and educational structures.

As Cubans continued to flow into Union City, many small businesses began to cater to them. One example is Anthony's Pharmacy, owned by Anthony Inguaggiato, an Italian American who learned Spanish to perfection. This pharmacy is located on Palisade Avenue and 43rd Street. Tony served as half pharmacist, half folk doctor for the community, giving advice on how to treat a range of maladies from simple colds to muscular aches and pains. Waiting lines were long since he provided services in Spanish as well as medicines.

There was also a furniture store on New York Avenue and 37th Street. The store was referred to as *El Manco,* or "The Maimed One," because its owner was a former soldier who had lost one arm during War World II. This second-hand store furnished many Cuban homes during the early exile influx. One of my interviewees told me that El Manco employed disabled workers. Another second-hand furniture store, Manito, was started by a Cuban man, Jesús Pérez in the late 1960s. At the time of this writing this store still exists. In addition, Manito has become a social service entrepreneur. He built a center for the Hispanic elderly, which offers services on a daily basis. Clients go during the day, have breakfast, lunch, engage in activities there, and then return home.

Not only small stores helped the Cubans. Some large enterprises, especially furniture and electrical appliance stores, offered credit. The demographic impact of the migration must have been powerful enough to make some financial and other institutions in Union City respond favorably to the exiles' needs. The banks needed the business, and Cubans had a good reputation for being hard workers and for paying back loans. Many Cubans, in turn, were grateful. According to a member of the Federación Mercantil Hispana, or Hispanic Mercantile Federation, an organization created to advocate for the interests of Cuban businesses, a man named Bill Hunter, who worked in the credit department of the Commercial Trust Company Bank in Union City, was committed to assisting Cuban entrepreneurs in the 1960s and was named an honorary Cuban. On *Nochebuena*, or Christmas Eve, an important holiday for Cubans, a group of them presented Bill Hunter with a Cuban flag as a symbol of their appreciation for his generosity, in contrast to the lack of interest and even hostility of others.[2]

The educational needs of Cuban children were supported by sympathetic school officials. The bilingual education program in Union City started in 1968, during the peak of the Cuban refugee migration to the city. Federally funded by Title VII, the program employed some Cuban professionals. After working as a teacher's aid for a year, Dosinda Pérez joined the bilingual program in 1970. She became director of bilingual education for a few years and later coordinated the adult education program. Now retired, Dosinda recalls those early years: "When Cuban refugees arrived, they confronted problems with their small children. There were discipline problems that were aggravated by the fact that Cuban children didn't know English. This created many tensions with monolingual teachers. To resolve this situation, the district adopted the bilingual education program" (interviewed on July 19, 2001).

Not everyone agreed with the objectives of bilingual education. Many teachers believed that total immersion in English would help kids learn the language faster. There were clear divisions among teachers, principals, and superintendents about the value of bilingual education and the English as a second language program (ESL). Eunice Europa, a second-generation Italian American woman who taught fifth and eighth grades for twenty-eight years at Washington School in Union City, shared her thoughts with me:

> It all started with the government grants. There was the opportunity to get the money and there were people who firmly believed in bilingual education. A woman named Catherine La Rosa was very influential in setting up the bilingual program. She was a teacher at Roosevelt School, where the program was started. La Rosa eventually became director of bilingual education in the early years. I guess I didn't feel the same way. Though I supported

> ESL as a transition, I thought the children would be better served if they were exposed to English only. There were many of us who felt that way. And even some of the parents. Would you believe that some parents forged their addresses so that their children could attend nonbilingual education schools? (Interviewed on November 8, 2002)

Schooling in the groups' languages had been typical of the immigrant experience in early U.S. history, but resentment against this practice by the native population led to its abolition. When the Cubans came to Florida after 1959, there was a rebirth of bilingual education and a strong program was created in 1963, though not without opposition. Even in contemporary times, an "English only" movement has adherents in Florida. An even stronger antibilingual atmosphere exists in California, where voters ordered their schools to stop instruction other than in English in 1998.[3] Yet, national and local forces in the 1960s demanding bilingual education combined to make this program and ESL programs dominant in Union City schools. In 1978 both programs became compulsory. These projects were not only helping Cubans but also other Latin American groups that were starting to arrive in the area.

From the middle of the 1960s on, Cuban exiles began to develop their own institutions. They built an ethnic economic enclave and procured a civic space for themselves by creating numerous social, educational, religious, and political organizations. The rest of this chapter will be devoted to internal ethnic community building, beginning with economic development and followed by a discussion of some of the most important Cuban associations.

Cuban Economic Development

There is a body of theory in sociology and immigration studies that addresses the formation of ethnic enclaves.[4] The emergence of concentrated areas of immigrant entrepreneurship "has depended on three conditions: first, the presence of a number of immigrants with substantial business expertise acquired in their home countries; second, access to sources of capital; third, access to labor. The requisite labor is not too difficult to obtain because it can be initially drawn from family members and then from more recent immigrant arrivals."[5] Koreans and Cubans are often given as examples of entrepreneurial minorities in the United States.

Miami is considered to be the true Cuban enclave. Understandably, the concentration of the Cuban population in Miami as compared to other regions in the country helped in creating a strong, self-sufficient entrepreneurial area. However, in Union City, from the late-1960s to the 1980s, the just-mentioned factors for the development of an ethnic enclave were also present. There was a numerous Cuban population, a group of immigrants with sufficient experience in business, reasonable access to capital from local institutions that trusted the "hard-work ethic" of the refugees, and access to labor. Not all Cuban entrepreneurs in Union City had prior business experience. Some had been professionals or students in Cuba but opted to start a business in the United States once they could gather the resources. Others were practically illiterate people who came from rural or semi-rural areas. Among these were the owners of many bodegas and food-related enterprises. Family members helped run the businesses. Members of the Federación Mercantil Hispana told me that: "Women and grown children participated in family businesses. It was better for women to work in their husbands' enterprises than to go work in a factory. Children helped when they could, many times after school, although the majority of them preferred to do something different than their parents' occupations" (interviewed on August 21, 2001). The most recent waves of Cuban immigrants always provided labor power for the already established businesses in the enclave. This was particularly true of the 1980 Mariel migrants.

Cuban enterprises were concentrated on Bergenline Avenue. By the late 1970s, almost every need of the community was being met internally by the group's own economic and professional growth. There were Cuban doctors, lawyers, engineers, public accountants, and piano, arts, and dance *academias* or schools. A funeral home, Necker-Sharpe, previously American-owned, was purchased by a Cuban American and is now called Morgado Funeral Home. Luis Morgado, who came to this country when he was ten years old, had worked part-time at the funeral home while completing his engineering studies at the New Jersey Institute of Technology.

FIGURE 3.2 *Cuban restaurant/supermarket Bandera on 32nd Street near Bergenline Avenue.* (José Hernández)

Among the typical businesses were supermarkets, bakeries, restaurants, clothing stores, furniture stores, jewelry stores, travel agencies, florists, pharmacies, cigar manufacturers, and construction companies. Cubans no longer had to go to New York City to buy products. Now many Cubans came from New York and other parts of the region to shop in Union City, in Spanish, where everything Cuban could be found.

As mentioned before, not all Cuban businessmen had previous experience. I met Dionisio Villanueva, Juan L. Martínez (Kiko), Miguel Miqueli, and Félix Barrera from the Federación Mercantil Hispana, who were professionals in Cuba and later owned furniture and jewelry stores and an insurance agency in Union City. In many cases, it was easier to obtain the capital necessary to start an enterprise than to try to reestablish their professional credentials here. We talked about the early days of the Cuban enclave:

> Cuban businesses mushroomed. We used to help one another. Besides, the banks were very open to lending money to the Cubans because they realized how serious we were. When they

> arrived, Cubans needed furniture; that's why there were many furniture stores. Among the first ones were La Casa Tony, owned by Antonio Ibarria, and Continental Furniture, owned by Carlos Ugalde, which was the first Cuban-owned furniture store in New Jersey. Another pioneer business was Union City Building Supply, owned by Aracelio González and Elio Pérez. There were many shoe stores; the best one was La Defensa. One of the fanciest Cuban stores on Bergenline Avenue was Mr. Rojas, owned by Nené Rojas, an architecture student in Cuba, which specialized in fine women's clothing. There were also many jewelry stores and (door-to-door jewelry vendors). Cubans like jewelry, but the main reason for having so many jewelers was that people needed an additional source of income. They had their jobs, maybe in a factory, and sold jewelry on the side. When they could afford it, then they would open a jewelry store. (Interviewed on August 21, 2001)

Cuban business owners organized to mutually support each other and to establish good relations with community authorities. A Cámara de Comercio or Chamber of Commerce was created and represented the businesses. Later on it became the Federación Mercantil Hispana. In its new form, the association brought together business owners as members, as opposed to the enterprises, and professionals could also join. Manolo Pérez, owner of Pérez Travel, had requested the formation of the Federación because he recognized the need for an organization to protect Cuban business interests. Cuban owners experienced extortion and discriminatory attitudes from some government officials. Ernesto Gras, a journalist with extensive experience in collective bargaining in Cuba, contributed his skills to the leadership of the Federación. Though the headquarters of the Federación were in Union City, Gras envisioned the creation of delegations in Elizabeth, Newark, Paterson, Hoboken, and West New York. Gras engaged in a very active campaign among merchants, explaining to them the many benefits that the Federación could bring about. He wanted to convey "the importance of forming a body which, through the influence of its members and its community, could make a substantial impact on New Jersey State affairs."[6]

FIGURE 3.3 *Manolo La Cachita Restaurant on Bergenline Avenue in Union City.* (Ana Meseguer)

Given the political history of Cubans, anti-Castro motives were pivotal in the activities of the Federación. Even though the organization's immediate objective was to protect local businesses, various anti-Castro political movements sprang out of, or were supported by, the Federación. The association often took a leadership role in organizing protests against the Castro government on special patriotic days and mobilized its merchants members to participate. Other nonpolitical, Cuba-related activities also emerged from the Federación. The Beca José Martí, or José Martí Scholarship, named after the noted Cuban patriot, was created to help Hispanic high school graduates to acquire a college education.

The members of the Federación whom I interviewed told me how the organization has changed. As an almost exclusively Cuban association, it has been stripped of a large part of its membership by the exodus of the Cuban community from Union City. Many of the older members have passed away, others have moved, and today the membership is very small. The organization has few of its original functions left, since the population that it served has changed so dramatically. Now, the Federación rents its building on 41st Street and Palisade Avenue to other groups for social events and also for private parties. These changes have also diminished the association's anti-Castro militancy. Fewer members and changing times mean fewer Cuban causes to struggle for. As one Federación member pointed out with nostalgia: "Our members were all Cuban. In the early years, there was only one Puerto Rican guy who was considered an 'honorary Cuban.' And now a young non-Cuban man is the president. That tells you how much we have changed, how many of us are gone, how much Union City has been transformed."[7] On a more positive note, some members feel that a non-Cuban president may rejuvenate the organization and incorporate the city's new, diverse Latin American business sector.[8]

The informal lobbying by Union City area Cuban business owners has been important in the expansion of state programs for Hispanic entrepreneurs. Among other things, Cuban American and mainstream business, civic, and political leaders alike wanted to contain the flight of Cuban American–owned businesses away from Union City and surrounding areas, which was already visible by the 1980s. For some time, Hispanic leaders had been claiming that the New Jersey state government's various programs aimed at assisting ethnic minority businesses were not fully responsive to the expanding Hispanic business sector's special needs. In 1986, Governor Thomas Kean (1982–1990) created the New Jersey Bureau of Hispanic Enterprise (BHE), the first state-sponsored agency in the United States that promoted Hispanic entrepreneurship. Rolando Alum, a sociocultural anthropologist by training, was brought in as BHE administrator (1986–1989). The agency was not directly involved in financial or credit aid. Instead, it provided technical assistance and referrals; coordinated business, educational, and networking conferences (in conjunction with state universities); distributed bilingual information; and taught Hispanic clients to navigate the intricate bidding process for lucrative governmental contracts at all levels, as well as with certain regulated industries (such as casinos and energy). Although there was already a noticeable presence of Latin American and Puerto Rican immigrants in the state, a large number of the Bureau's initial clientele was of Cuban origin, especially from Union City and other Hudson County points.[9]

Changes in the Union City Cuban business sector are well documented. The 1977 *Survey of Minority-Owned Business Enterprises* listed 705 Cuban-owned businesses in the Jersey City Standard Metropolitan Statistical Area (SMSA) of the U.S. census. Union City and West New York, where most of the Cuban population was concentrated, is part of the Jersey City SMSA. In 1987, the number of Cuban-owned businesses rose to 1,998. This increase makes sense since the 1970s and 1980s were peak years of Cuban concentration[10] In 1992, the number of Cuban-owned businesses in the Jersey City SMSA decreased to 1,746, corresponding to the decline of the Cuban population in the area.[11] The 1997 *Survey of Minority-Owned Business Enterprises* listed 2,270 Cuban-owned firms.[12] The significant increase in Cuban-owned firms in 1997 is puzzling since the total Cuban population in the Jersey City SMSA declined from 45,719 in 1980 to 33,901 in 2000. It could be that, even when Cubans have moved to the suburbs, they continue to open businesses in Union City. However, that is not the impression that I have and that is not what my interviewees reported. Perhaps this upsurge is the result of Cubans investing in other, less visible sectors, for example real estate, even when they do not live in the community. This increase in Cuban-owned businesses may also respond to a change in census data collection techniques for that particular year.[13]

As the old Cubans leave, and Latin Americans from other countries and new Cubans arrive in Union City, Bergenline Avenue changes. Now, besides the Cuban cafeteria known for its *sandwich cubano*, there is also the *pupuseria* restaurant, where Salvadoran *arepa,* or soaked maize flour, is sold. As one Dominican man told me: "Years ago, all the bodegas were owned by Cubans, but now not even a few. Most bodegas in Union City are owned by Dominicans." The old Cubans respond to the changes on Bergenline with nostalgia. Benito, who is now a sales worker at a baby furniture store, previously owned a jewelry store, which he recently sold. He attributes his decision to sell his business to deteriorating economic conditions in the area. According to Benito,

> The competition from the nearby malls is making it difficult for small businesses to exist. It's not like in the 1960s and 1970s when Bergenline was full of Cuban stores. In the 1970s there were sixty-five Cuban-owned jewelry stores, now there are only

> five. The economy was strong then and small businesses thrived. This place has changed a lot. Many new immigrants from other countries have arrived and they are setting up their businesses. But the economy is very unstable and one day you see a store on the avenue, and the next day it's closed down and replaced by a different one! (Interviewed on June 8, 2001)

Other interviewees shared how, in the 1970s, local white American merchants in the area, who until then had seen Cubans as "the other," accepted their participation in a joint effort to contest competition from the emerging malls.

Longing for the old days is not exclusively characteristic of older Cubans. Alberto, a young Cuban American, remembers Bergenline's restaurants during his childhood:

> When I was growing up, we went out to dinner every Sunday. Of course we went to a Cuban restaurant. Bergenline was full of Cuban restaurants. The owners were Cuban; the workers were Cuban. In many of those places they knew my parents by name; they knew my name too. I particularly remember how funny most waiters were. They told these Cuban jokes! I live in Rutherford now, but I come with my wife to the few Cuban restaurants that are left in Union City. It's not the same. The owners may be Cuban, but the workers are all immigrants from other countries. I'm glad that these workers are able to find jobs, but it's not a full Cuban experience anymore. Even the food has changed to satisfy the taste of other nationalities. (Interviewed on November 4, 2003)

Manuel, who is selling his Cuban-style cafeteria to move to Miami, thinks that the changes in Union City are typical of cities that receive successive immigrant waves:

> Before Cubans there were Germans, Italians, and many others. Now many Latin American and other groups are arriving and Cubans are moving out. Many Cuban businessmen, like me, are retiring and leaving, and others who stay have to adapt to a new

> population. For example, in the last few years I hired Dominican cooks because there were more Dominicans available to work than Cubans! Besides, there are many Dominicans in the area now and they expect restaurants to cook their own dishes too. (Interviewed on September 24, 2003)

Many former Cuban entrepreneurs are investing in real estate. Miguel Miqueli told me: "I decided to sell my jewelry store the day I was mugged. It was obvious to me that the area was not safe anymore. Since then I have been active in the real estate business. It is ironic that Cubans are now the landlords of the new immigrant store owners" (interviewed on August 21, 2001).

A number of Cuban-owned businesses have opened outside the Union City–West New York area. Oscar, the owner of a drapery business used to work from his home in West New York, but after he moved to Ridgefield, he opened his own store. As he commented, "I had saved enough capital to start a business that has a general appeal. Most people need draperies!" (Interviewed on November 28, 2003.) Some of the enterprises outside of the Union City area, especially restaurants, are owned by younger Cubans who want to combine entrepreneurship with Cuban identity pride. The late Teresa Pérez told me that she and her husband Nick had opened their gourmet restaurant Azúcar in Edgewater, New Jersey, "to show the American public how good Cuban food is. [We] always had a dream to open a restaurant with all kinds of Cuban memorabilia on the walls . . . [we] saw the place in Edgewater and fell in love with it. [We] try very hard to maintain our *cubanía,* or cubanness, and to transmit it to our children" (interviewed on October 30, 2002). Azúcar's gift certificates clearly state this philosophy:

> Since coming to America in 1960, we've learned that maintaining strong cultural and family values are priceless testaments of heritage. We've also learned that a strong work ethic is a key virtue to accomplishing one's goals, especially in this land of opportunity. It is in this spirit that we created Azúcar, so that we could share with you the essence of our Cuban culture. Our recipes are prepared with only the finest and most authentic ingredients, bringing you the true flavors of our native dishes. Bienvenidos.

New businesses in the Union City surroundings facilitate transnational ties between Cubans living in the area and those in Cuba. Marazul Tours, a Cuban-owned travel agency with headquarters in Miami, is the largest of a few travel agencies specializing in travel to Cuba. It is located in Weehawken and Cuban Americans go there to arrange the necessary paperwork for travel to the island. Marazul's New Jersey office opened in 1994. Travel to Cuba by Cuban Americans has been allowed by the Cuban government since 1979. Up to the time of this writing, travel to the island is severely restricted by the U.S. government. Before Marazul came to Weehawken, local Cuban Americans had to use the company's New York office and other smaller businesses to get their travel documents. Other establishments, like El Almacén El Español, provided services to Cuba for years. Cubans were able to send medicines, other selected items, and remittances to their relatives on the island. El Almacén closed for business since the Bush administration strengthened the embargo measures against Cuba in 2004. Another establishment, Caribe Express, is still open. They mainly send remittances and medicines to Cuba.

There are a few Cuban-owned businesses in Union City that have opened up recently. These are owned by second-generation Cubans and by recent Cuban migrants. Havana Bay Coffee, a coffee house, and La Esquina Habanera, a club, are examples.[14] Havana Bay Coffee is owned by two young Cuban Americans. One was born here, and the other came to this country when he was very young. They see themselves as Cuban and as American and they consciously want to create a space where Cuban culture can flourish. They hold exhibits and sponsor concerts, poetry readings, and other cultural events. These functions are predominantly, but not exclusively, about Cuban art and by Cuban artists. La Esquina Habanera is a club owned by an Afro-Cuban *balsero.* This recently opened establishment has become a gathering place, especially for Afro-Cubans of all generations in the area. David Oquendo, director of the group Raíces Habaneras, says with pride:

> There is no other place like La Esquina Habanera. When I met Tony Zequeira (the owner), I said to him, "we have to do something, we have to open up a place where we can promote the rumba. We have to transmit our cultural roots to Cubans in the

> United States. I am not a businessman, I am a musician, but if you want to go along with this idea, let's start this club." Tony agreed, and it's been three years already! We have a group, Raíces Habaneras (Havana Roots), which plays wonderful music there. When new musicians come from Cuba, they visit this place and immediately feel at home. The rumba was always discriminated against in Cuba, even now. It was the music of poor people, of black Cubans. Not many people valued it. For that reason, our job is to educate Cubans here to appreciate the rumba, which is the mother of all Cuban rhythms.[15]

While the development of an ethnic enclave in the 1960s, 1970s, and much of the 1980s in Union City was the logical outcome of a numerous entrepreneurial and professional Cuban presence, the small upsurge in Cuban businesses in Union City and surrounding towns since the 1990s reflects a desire among younger and second generation Cubans to hold on to their Cuban roots, even though most of the owners of these enterprises do not live close to Union City. Recent immigrants, on the other hand, may want to establish themselves in the new environment in a very different way. Their life histories have little in common with those Cubans who came before them. For example, race had not been an issue discussed by the early Cubans. One of the reasons was that the majority of the exiles were white.[16] As more dark-skinned Cubans came to the United States since 1980, Afro-Cubans may be developing ways to assert themselves within the Cuban community. La Esquina Habanera provided an example of a space specifically serving the Afro-Cuban population.

Cuban Associations and Organizations

From the very beginning, Cubans began organizing themselves. The small prerevolutionary immigrant community met at a restaurant every Saturday evening to have dinner and discuss issues related to Cuba. These meetings led to the formation of the Liceo Cubano, a social club that served the community in various ways. Cubans acquired a building, which they rented for social and community events at a very reasonable price. They held benefit concerts and other functions for specific purposes, especially political causes. They collected money for efforts to free Cuba from Castro. The Liceo also provided social and community services. When the exiles came, they benefited from the work of the Liceo, and when the Mariel boatlift took place in 1980, the organization raised a considerable amount of money for a telemarathon to help the Mariel migrants. As a result of the Cuban flight from the area, the Liceo building was sold, and most of the board members have left.

Historically, civic associations have been a prominent feature of the immigrant experience in the United States. The literature on voluntary or ethnic associations demonstrates how these groups provide a space for immigrants to negotiate their new, generally urban environment. For example, ethnic organizations of Italian, Irish, and Jewish immigrants served as the primary mechanism for the articulation of these groups with political and economic institutions in New York City.[17] Among recent Hispanic immigrants, Dominicans have a highly developed associational structure. Most Dominican associations here are in direct contact with their hometowns in the Dominican Republic. In New York, Dominicans began to create "extensive organizational life within their own communities in the 1960s and 1970s, [first] in cultural, recreational, and professional activities. Beginning in the early 1980s, a cohort of Dominican-born and U.S.-educated leaders emerged who were intent on claiming resources and vying for power within New York City politics."[18]

Some segments of the Cuban community in Union City were highly organized politically, but their involvement was mainly in anti-Castro politics, at least until a new interest in local and national politics emerged among younger Cubans around 1980. Nevertheless, many other associations flourished. Because of the political situation, Cuban associations could not be in direct contact with their hometowns as Dominicans and other migrants could. During times of heavy concentration in Union City, Cuban organizations played an instrumental role in the adjustment of Cubans by providing a variety of services. As Eleanor Rogg suggested in her study of West New York, Cuban spatial concentration delayed acculturation but facilitated adjustment. Following is a description of some important social groups and organizations that helped Cubans adjust and served as vehicles for cultural transmission. The important topic of political organizations will be discussed in Chapter 6.

Social Clubs

Besides the Liceo Cubano, other social clubs began to emerge. Municipios, or hometown clubs, were formed by individuals and families from particular cities and towns. There were six municipios in Union City, including Camajuaní, Caibarién, Sancti Spíritus, and Güines, named after cities mainly located in central Cuba. The most notable of the municipios was El Club Amigos e Hijos de Fomento, founded by a medical doctor, Dr. Julio Rodríguez Fariña. Fomento was the birthplace of a significant number of Cubans in Union City, so this municipio was the most popular. Municipios celebrated hometown traditions. Families from the same region got together to have a good time, and to organize charity and community projects. Like U.S. Cubans elsewhere, they participated in anti-Castro activities. Most of these municipios became less active by the late 1990s with the notable exception of El Club Amigos e Hijos de Fomento.[19]

The needs of the elderly in the community were addressed by some organizations. Community social workers and psychologists have combined counseling and social activities. Tertulias de Antaño, or Gatherings of Yesterday, is an example. This club was started by Lidia Gil-Ramos, a social worker with the former Hudson County Cuban Refugee Program, as a response to one important need in the Cuban community: the mental and emotional health of the elderly. A 1973 study by the Cuban American Planning Council revealed that older Cubans were facing serious problems, especially in areas outside of Miami. Loneliness, depression, and a general feeling of social disconnection were reported by the study as one of the most salient problems.[20] Ms. Gil-Ramos started Tertulias on October 13, 1974, with thirteen older Cubans. By Christmas there were sixty members. At first, they used a small meeting room at Saint Joseph of the Palisades Church in West New York, but this place soon became too small for the growing membership. The church facilitated another meeting place in North Bergen, and today Tertulias owns its own hall at 6110 Hudson Avenue in West New York. West New York's late mayor Anthony DeFino was very instrumental in the development of Tertulias. The town provided transportation for all those who came from distant locations. There are some members who come to Tertulias's social events from Elizabeth, Newark, and New York City.[21]

Members of Tertulias de Antaño get together every Sunday and they hold four major parties a year. They pay $3.00 a month to cover expenses for coffee and pastries. Those who live in New York only pay $10.00 a year since they have to spend more money on transportation. One of the yearly parties is a contest where the entire membership decides who will be elected "King" and "Queen" of Tertulias. Sometimes married couples are elected and other times those who are unrelated form a relation and even get married! The winners receive the recognition of the community in a very special celebration that includes entertainment by well-known singers and artists.

I attended one of the parties of Tertulias de Antaño. Gradually, the program has incorporated many other Spanish-speaking nationalities. I noticed that there were Cubans from different migration waves, white Cubans, Afro-Cubans, and other Latin Americans. About the change in national composition, Ms. Gil-Ramos told me that "this is a place where the elderly come and dance, eat, and have a good time. It doesn't matter if they are from Cuba, Colombia, or the Dominican Republic. We even have a woman from the Philippines! Tertulias began as exclusively Cuban because this community was Cuban, but now we are very mixed." She added, "You know, I don't recognize races or nationalities, everybody is the same for me."[22] While at the party, I was able to speak to some members. An Afro-Cuban man came and warmly welcomed me (I had been introduced by Ms. Gil-Ramos). He said, "I have a great time here. I look forward to Sundays to come to Tertulias. But I can't understand why I have a good time and cry at the same time," expressing the complex feelings of the immigrant experience combined with older age. People were clearly having a wonderful time, they seemed to be connected to one another, and they obviously admire and love Ms. Lidia Gil-Ramos.[23]

Academies

Cuban *academias*, or schools, served very specialized educational needs in the Cuban community. From English to piano to dance lessons, the proliferation of these academias reflected the presence in the migration of Cuban professionals in those fields. Academia Amador was one of the first ones. Antonio Amador started this school, which was licensed by the state of New Jersey, to offer bilingual classes. There were also kindergarten and after-school programs. At night, the school offered English and typing lessons for adults. Amador's daughter Teresa told me that many white Americans enrolled their children there so that they would learn Spanish. However, other informants contradicted this view, saying that many Americans did not want to learn the language of the "inferior other." Examples of other academias are those owned by Dalia Condis (painting), Justica Docampo (music), Miriam Pellicer (music), and Oneida Quevedo (dance). Two other dance academias are Amarilis and Yolanda Studios.

Most Cuban academias have survived the Cuban flight from the community. There are still many of them, probably because, no matter what group comes, there will always be a clientele for these specialized schools. Many parents, regardless of nationality and even social class, want their children to learn music, dance, or other art forms.

The Press

The development of the Cuban press in the United States is intricately connected to political exile. After the 1959 Revolution, many disaffected Cuban journalists left, and, as the Cuban community settled in Miami and elsewhere, these journalists went to work in Cuban radio stations or they started publications. Understandably, New Jersey became, after Florida, the state with the largest number of publications by Cubans. Cuban journalists formed the Colegio de Periodistas Cubanos en el Exilio, or Association of Cuban Journalists in Exile in Union City, West New York, Elizabeth, and other New Jersey cities. The *periodiquitos,* or small newspapers, devoted most of their space to anti-Castro news and opinions, and, as some New Jersey Cuban journalists have said, they were created "to convey to Cubans and other Hispanics in the area the truth about Cuba's present slavery conditions."[24] These publications were weekly, or appeared sporadically, and most supported themselves financially through advertisements. According to some interviewees, there were newspaper owners who practiced extortion by pressuring businessmen to place ads and slandering the businesses if they did not.

Manuel Pérez shared with me the names of various Cuban journalists who were active in Cuban newspapers: Maná, Don Galaor, Yiyo Jiménez, and Rodolfo Rodríguez Zaldívar, who was one of the most respected Cuban journalists in Cuba. Pérez proudly told me that he cofounded the first anti-Castro newspaper in Union City, *El Heraldo de la Semana,* or the *Weekly Herald,* but the publication did not last long.[25] Other sources list *La Tribuna,* or *The Forum,* founded by Carlos Bidot, as the first Cuban newspaper edited in the Garden State. Other titles included *El Clarín (The Trumpet), Información (Information), Guerra (War), Nuestra Cuba (Our Cuba), Reportaje Gráfico (Graphic Report), Avance (Advance), Última Hora (The Last Hour), El Independiente (The Independent), La Voz (The Voice),* and *La Razón (Reason). El Especial,* or *The Special,* was published by the late Bienvenido Madán and Rodolfo Rodríguez Zaldívar. As Pérez had mentioned to me, and in the eyes of his colleagues, Rodríguez Zaldívar "was, perhaps the most sagacious reporter in the big era of Cuban journalism . . . [He] did outstanding reports for the popular magazine *Bohemia,* or Bohemia in Cuba. Those reports, filled with the author's sophisticated style and fine irony, were a landmark in Cuban and Latin American journalism."[26]

As their titles indicate, the main objective of these newspapers was to foster and maintain the anti-Castro fervor. As journalists have aged or died, and as the Cuban community is no longer predominant, the number of exclusively Cuban periodiquitos in Union City has declined significantly. The emerging Spanish-speaking publications are generally supplements of locally based English newspapers. For many years, *The Hudson Dispatch,* which for a long time was the main English-speaking newspaper in Union City, published a Spanish supplement which was directed by the well-known Union City Cuban journalist Aleida Durán. *The Hudson Dispatch* was later absorbed by *The Jersey Journal,* which also publishes a Spanish weekly, *El Nuevo Hudson.* Durán is retired and the contributions to *El Nuevo Hudson* are now more broadly Latin American.

Cuban Lions Club

Cuban Lions of New Jersey recalls the strong Lions Club that existed in prerevolutionary Cuba. As one of the first countries to obtain membership in the Lions Club International in 1927, Cuba had, at one point, more members than any of the other participating international chapters. It is this proud trajectory that Cuban Lions followed into exile, and that played a role in their decision to organize a club here. As with other Cuban organizations, anti-Castro sentiments served as the galvanizing force for the Cuban Lions:

> We formed the Leones Cubanos en el Exilio, or Cuban Lions in Exile club, in 1963, but the Lions Club International did not accept us because we were too political. All we wanted in the beginning was to depose Castro, no matter the means. Eventually, the strategy about Cuba evolved. It was evident that "Fidel no se iba a caer" (Fidel wasn't going to fall), as we thought in the early days. Finally the LCI accepted us in 1979. Now we are called West New York Leones Cubanos de Hudson, or West New York Cuban Lions from Hudson.[27]

The Cuban Lions Club has been a vehicle for cultural preservation. The members and their families and friends celebrate patriotic and other holidays, and organize charity events, a literary contest named after Cuban patriot José Martí, dances, and picnics. The organization's membership has increased "to levels never dreamed by the original founders, and, today, [we] are the largest Lions Club in the Garden State, the fourth in the United States, and the eleventh in the world. [We] have among us men and women of different nationalities which makes us a truly international Lions Club."[28] The inclusion of non-Cuban members seems to account for the growth of this club, a trend that differs from that of other exclusively Cuban clubs in the area.

National Association of Cuban American Women of New Jersey

The Asociación de Mujeres Cubano-Americanas de New Jersey, or Association of Cuban American Women of New Jersey is part of a national association, the National Association of Cuban American Women (NACAW), founded in Washington in 1972. This nonprofit organization describes itself as nonpartisan and devoted to promoting the rights of women and minorities. The New Jersey chapter was founded in 1978. According to their official magazine, "no person will be denied admission into the organization because of color, gender, or religion."[29] Nevertheless, although the association is inclusive, in reality the majority of the membership is Cuban.

The Asociación de Mujeres Cubanas de New Jersey is very active, sponsoring a variety of social services,, for example, immigration services, translations, counseling, and a day care center, which operates in their premises on 38th Street in Union City.[30] Asociación members visit hospitals to offer gifts to children and the elderly. There is an annual raffle to collect money for the association's expenses. Two events are noteworthy on the Asociación's calendar, an annual banquet and the celebration of Three Kings Day, or Epiphany, a Catholic feast widely celebrated in Latin America when children are given toys.[31] The purpose of the banquet is to raise funds for the Three Kings celebration on January 6th every year. That day, needy children in the community receive gifts. In addition, there is a cultural program featuring the city's Cuban dance and music academies in choreographed allegorical productions.

One of the most salient activities of the Asociación is the Elena Mederos Award, named after a Cuban feminist woman who participated in the women's struggle to obtain the vote in Cuba. Mederos came to the United States and continued to be active in social and political causes, especially in the Washington, D.C., area. The Premio Elena Mederos is conferred at the Asociación's annual banquet upon an Hispanic woman who has distinguished herself in the community.

I interviewed Siomara Sánchez, president of both the New Jersey chapter and the National Association. A lawyer in Cuba, Siomara came to the United States in 1961, shortly after the revolutionary government took over. She talks passionately about the Asociación and the work it does to help the community and to maintain a vibrant Cuban culture. Although our conversation was not focused on Cuba, it was evident that anti-Castro feelings were the driving force behind Siomara's decision to leave Cuba. She told me that she had been in jail after the Revolution because "Fidel did not like lawyers. He believed that we were a threat, maybe because, since he is a lawyer, he saw us as competing with him."[32]

Like many other Cubans, Siomara earned her Master of Education degree at Montclair State College. She worked at East Side High School in Newark as a guidance counselor until she retired in 1998. She is very proud of the Cuban community in the United States and claims that "Cubans have a special drive that helps them succeed everywhere they go." She admits that this ethnic pride was somewhat shattered when the *marielitos* came because

> many of them did not have a work ethic. Some were delinquent elements that Fidel put on boats and sent to the United States. They were very different from the Cubans that had immigrated before. When the Marielitos came in 1980, the Asociación organized cultural events to teach them cultural traditions that they had never learned in communist Cuba.

Siomara's comments reflect the middle-class pride, especially of the early Cubans. She stressed the importance of education in attaining success:

> The main objective of the Asociación is to promote education for Cuban women and others. If Cuban exiles have been successful in this country it is because there were a remarkable number of professionals and educated people in the group. I also think that Cubans work hard to institutionalize community work. We go beyond a show of superficial love of country. We know that we've gotten ahead because of our educational background. Now we have to make sure that we provide the same education to our children and the generations born here. We also have to transmit the Cuban cultural traditions to them. Otherwise they would die!

Siomara Sánchez also pointed out that, even though Cubans are leaving Union City, many hold positions of power, especially young Cuban Americans. For example, "most of the Board of Education members are Cuban, the judges in the Union City municipal court are Cuban, and there are Cuban city commissioners. Another example is Palisades Medical Center, with its high proportion of Cuban and other Hispanics on its board of directors."[33]

In their passage through Union City, Cubans, like many other ethnic groups, developed economic and civic institutions to serve their community needs. Yet the blueprint of most Cuban associations has been a strong anti-Castro fervor and militancy. From social clubs to lodges, to the Lions Club and to the women's association, these organizations were marked by the experience of the Cuban Revolution and by exile. The leaders of these groups are aging and the community has changed significantly. For the most part, younger Cubans are not as interested in anti-Castro politics as their parents were. As will be discussed in Chapter 6, those politically inclined tend to become involved in local politics. It will be important to see if new and younger members (if they are recruited) refocus some of these organizations' objectives, thus, redefining what is Cuban in Union City and its surroundings.

4

Women Leave Home for the Factory

Gender, Work, and Family

The first time that I saw my mother go out to work was when she became employed at a coat factory after we arrived in Union City in 1968. In Cuba, before marriage, she had briefly held a job as a leaf stripper in a tobacco factory. Even before Cuban independence, working-class women were incorporated into certain sectors of the workforce. One was the tobacco industry. Women—both black and white—were employed there supposedly because tobacco production required "delicate hands," which only females could provide. Once my mother married, she left the factory. Later, she became a very well regarded seamstress in our town, but she worked at home. Staying indoors, even when making some money as in the case of my mother, conferred respectability on most Cuban women. The present chapter will briefly trace the history of women and work in Cuba. This account is necessary in order to understand the employment and other behaviors of Cuban women after they emigrated to the United States and to Union City in particular. Subsequently, I will relate the findings of a study on Cuban women and work that I conducted in Union City in the late 1970s and early 1980s. I will also report on a follow-up to the first study in the 1990s. The end of the chapter will discuss the situation of Cuban women who arrived in Union City since the 1990s.

Women and Work in Cuba

Traditionally, there was strong disapproval of outside employment for women in Cuba. The norm placing women at home was the result of a complex set of cultural codes originating in Spain (and Mediterranean Europe, generally) that regarded female virginity and virtue as the main components of the family's status and ultimately of the male's dignity. Working outside the home was perceived as dangerous and, unless absolutely necessary, only done by women of questionable reputation.[1] A division developed between "bad" and "good" women that depended, among other things, on who could stay home and who had to labor outside. As happened with working women elsewhere, including immigrant women in the United States in the early 1900s, Cuban women expected that once they married they would no longer have to go out to work. Even if they helped the household financially by earning money at home, the husband would be the formal provider. That was the case with my mother and with many other working women of her generation and class.

These norms corresponded with the structural characteristics of the Cuban economy from the very beginning of the island's development. Starting early in the colonial period, the country's economic structure was that of a plantation enclave producing sugar for the world market. Plantation economies occupy all available land for large-scale production of agricultural products—sugar, coffee, bananas—and require a labor force that engages in intense but seasonal work. In Cuba, the white spouses and daughters of plantation owners had little choice but to live up to the domestic norm because there were no jobs for them within the formal economic system. Their place was at home, keeping their honor and virtue intact. On the other hand, black female slaves cut and loaded cane alongside male slaves. Beginning with slavery, the female division of labor along race lines was a marked characteristic of Cuban society.[2]

One of the features of plantation economies is that they create seasonal unemployment for a substantial part of the population. In Cuba, the peak of economic activity occurred during the sugar harvest, which lasted for less than half a year. When the harvest time was over, about 25 percent of the labor force was unemployed. Most of these workers were men, but some were women who could not find any other jobs. Often they migrated to the cities to become domestic servants or prostitutes.[3]

In short, the nature of the economic structure reinforced norms about female work behavior, the end result being that black and poor white women who needed to work took what jobs were available and most upper- and middle-class women did not take part in public life. They did not have to do so because their husbands could support them. However, having a provider did not mean that women in the middle- or upper-classes did not obtain an education. There were thus many women professors, architects, and artists, working in their fields, but most, even with the education, did not work.

In the late 1940s and 1950s, women from the lower ranks of the middle-class joined the workforce at a time when U.S. investments in Cuba underwent an upsurge after a period of stagnation. The new investments were not predominantly in sugar but were concentrated in utilities, communications, oil refining, and tourism-related industries. Along with investment came the growth of the banking and finance sectors. Mushrooming bureaucracies needed more white-collar workers, which meant an increase in employment opportunities for women, especially lower-middle-class females with the required education. The 1943 Cuban census reported 1,253 women as typists and stenographers. That number rose to 5,420 in 1953. Similarly, in 1943, 77.5 percent of all elementary teachers were female; by 1953 the proportion of female teachers had gone up to 84.3 percent. An increase also occurred in the percentage of women professors, from 53.6 percent in 1943 to 67.8 percent in 1953.[4] In addition, there was considerable growth in service categories such as waitress and janitor, in part due to the development of the tourist sector. The high proportion of black women working as domestic servants and washerwomen shows the continuation of the racial division of labor begun in slavery. In 1953, the major occupational sectors containing a significant number of women workers were domestic service, teaching, clerical, the clothing industry, and tobacco, with working-class women concentrated in domestic service and industrial jobs, and middle-class and some working-class women in teaching and clerical positions.[5]

By the 1950s, the norm that women belonged in the home was weakening, especially in the big cities.[6] Changes in the structure of the economy contributed to making female employment more acceptable. Even when staying home was seen as preferable, many women needed to supplement their husbands' income. The jobs that middle-class women did were labeled as "decent" because they were not manual. However, in most cases working was seen as temporary, and the goal was to come back to the home, which was still the place for the majority of women, especially middle-class women, in prerevolutionary Cuba.

The changes in the situation of women in Cuba after the 1959 Revolution cannot be separated from the general transformation of all sectors of society. The Cuban revolutionary government had a conscious strategy from the beginning to massively incorporate women into production as part of the national development plan. In 1973, 26.7 percent of Cuban women of working age were actively working (an increase from 13% in 1953).[7] The most striking changes after 1959 were in occupational structure. For example, the category of domestic service, which had employed about a quarter of all women who worked in 1953, virtually disappeared. Other occupational categories such as "patrons," "non-remunerated family worker," and "private worker" were eliminated due to the nationalization of property. On the other hand, in the 1970s, the category of "state worker" constituted almost nine-tenths of the economically active population.[8] This last figure points to the predominance of the state as the main employer. Even when Cubans work for foreign enterprises today, the Cuban government arranges their employment. The companies pay workers' salaries in dollars to the government, which pays the workers in Cuban pesos. Sometimes the government allows a fraction of the salaries to be paid in dollars directly to the workers.[9]

In 2003, 47.5 percent of Cuban women of working age were in the labor force.[10] A great number were concentrated in the fields of health and education. Women benefited from sweeping improvements in those areas after 1959.[11] They were also represented in the social services, nursing, clerical work, the garment industry, and elementary education, which indicates that they continued to do jobs that are viewed as extensions of the household. However, it must be pointed out that the proportion of women in formerly typically male occupations such as medicine and engineering has also risen dramatically since 1959. One of the problems that Cuban women, as well as men, face today is the devaluation of their professions after the legalization of the dollar in 1993. A woman working in the tourism industry who receives tips in dollars can earn more than a professional. A taxi driver who is paid in dollars makes more money than a medical doctor.[12] For that reason, many Cubans have left their professions to work in tourism and other dollarized areas of the economy, while many others have migrated.

Cuban Women in Union City

Perhaps seeing my mother go to work at a factory was what motivated me to study Cuban women's labor-force participation in Union City. Between the late 1970s and the early 1980s, I interviewed 107 women in Union City and West New York. Most of them had arrived in the mid- to late 1960s. Only a couple of the interviewees had migrated through the Mariel exodus of 1980. At the time, my main focus was to discover the reasons behind the high rates of labor force participation among Cuban women when compared with all other groups in the country, including white women. The study was both quantitative and qualitative. Demographic and labor-force data were collected and analyzed statistically, and in-depth interviews were done with the women to explore gender and family dynamics. I looked at both the conditions of the labor market in Hudson County and the social-class origins, aspirations, and class belief systems of the women and the impact of these factors on their economic behavior here. In 1980, Cuban women had the highest labor-force participation rates in comparison both with other Hispanics and with the general U.S. female population. Fifty-five percent of Cuban women worked outside the home compared with 40 percent for Puerto Ricans, 49 percent for Mexicans, and 50 percent for the total female population. In New Jersey, the rates for Cuban women were even higher. Fifty-nine percent of Cuban women participated in the labor force compared with 43 percent of Puerto Ricans, 52 percent of Mexicans, and 50 percent of the total female population.[13]

Research on Hispanic women conducted in the 1980s revealed similar results. Rosemary Santana-Cooney and Vilma Ortiz compared the labor-force activity of females among Mexican Americans, Puerto Ricans, and Cubans. They found "dramatic ethnic differences . . . among foreign-born Hispanic females, with Puerto Ricans showing the lowest participation, Cubans the highest, and Mexican Americans falling in between."[14] Similarly, Helen Safa noted that Cuban and other Hispanic women in the New York City area had higher labor-force participation rates than did the total population. She also found that Puerto Rican women had the lowest employment rate. Safa documented a shift in second-generation Puerto Rican women from blue-collar to white-collar employment.[15] Present studies confirm Safa's findings that, in general, second-generation Caribbean women out-perform female immigrants and young men in educational attainment, which has a favorable impact on their work experiences.[16]

Going back to my sample, it was divided almost equally between formerly professional middle-class and formerly working-class women. Ninety-eight percent of the interviewees were white, reflecting the racial composition of the early exile waves. The median age in my sample was 49.7 years old, compared to 40.0 for Cuban women nationally, 27.8 for all females of Latin-American origin and 33.8 for all women in the United States. The significantly higher median age of Cuban exiles when compared to other groups lies in the nature of the Cuban immigration of the 1960s. Most exiles migrated in their middle years with already established families. Perhaps the older age of my interviewees and of Cuban women workers in general, when compared to other women, contributed to their active participation in the labor force. Also, about half of the participants in my study had worked in Cuba, contrary to what the general norm prescribed.[17] However, what I found back in the 1980s is that U.S. employment for these women was primarily aimed at helping the family achieve or regain a middle-class status that was lost when they left Cuba. Paid work was viewed as an extension of family obligations rather than as a means for sexual emancipation.

There is abundant literature on immigrant working women and the family in the United States in the nineteenth and twentieth centuries. Most studies conclude that women's employment outside the home was often adjusted to the immigrants' cultural values. For example, Virginia Yans-McLaughlin maintains that strong cultural traditions in southern Italy conferred great authority on the male in the family. Even though the wife and children worked outside the home at harvest time in Sicily, the father's dominance in family affairs remained unchallenged. Thus, in the Sicilian community that Yans-McLauglin studied in Buffalo, very few women worked in manufacturing. They worked as migrant laborers with their husbands and children on farms and canneries near the city. In this way, the family maintained its old world character, and women could work in a sheltered environment.[18]

The adjustment to traditional family norms was not always possible, as the nature of the labor market shaped the type of work participation of immigrant women. A study by Miriam Cohen found that Italian females in New York City went to work in factories in great numbers. In 1911, Italian women comprised 68 percent of the female work force in the garment industry in New York. There is no doubt that the city provided enormous employment opportunities for women, offering many jobs in small-scale industries, traditional employers of women throughout the world.[19]

Seeking an education was important for many immigrant women. Interviewing older Jewish immigrant women in New York City, Sydney Stahl Weinberg did a first-hand analysis of their experiences with family, work, and education. Jewish women sought an education, worked when young, and then retired from the market place, at least temporarily, when they married.[20] Just as they are today, women's experiences were marked by the diversity in migration and women's relations to class, race, ethnicity, and nationality. A comparative study of Jewish and Italian women in New York from 1870 to 1924 by Kathie Friedman-Kasaba concluded that immigrant wives and mothers at the turn of the century found themselves living in a paradox. On the one hand, "migration to the United States promised the fulfillment of old world dreams in a new land, or at least a degree of emancipation from old world hierarchies and greater self-determination. At the same time . . . migration had the potential to intensify existing subordination [and to subject women] to new forms of control and domination."[21]

Regardless of their working traditions in their countries, it is obvious that the work of women has been central to immigrant families in the United States since the beginning of immigration. Consequently, I asked myself many times when starting my study in 1979 what was so unique about Cuban women's high rate of incorporation into the labor force in the United States. Looking back, there were many factors that contributed to their intense economic activity at that time. These included a need to help their immigrant families, a vital drive to regain or attain a middle-class status, and a labor market that offered many job opportunities.[22] Are these factors no longer present? Some are and some are not. Later on in this chapter I will come back to this discussion when I report on the new realities of more recently immigrant women. However, the social class base of at least the first waves of Cuban exiles influenced their economic behavior, and Cuban women's insistence on "making it," "helping the family move up socially and economically," revealed the beliefs of middle-class and aspiring middle-class Cubans. Cuban women's work was essential to achieving social mobility objectives. As one participant shared:

> I think that in this country women have to work. It is the only way for the family to improve. We Cubans are very determined to succeed. I work because we want to give our children a good education. We are also saving to buy a house in Miami. This country has given us so much; refuge from communism, work, and the opportunity for our children to move ahead." (Married white woman, 31 years old, middle-class with some secondary education in Cuba, from Pinar del Río).[23]

There is a significant difference among Hispanic females' labor-force activity in the figures released by the U.S. Census Bureau in 2000. There has been a major shift in labor-force participation rates for the women of the three major groups at the national level since 1980. After an increase in their rates in 1990, Mexican American women's labor-force participation dropped in 2000. Puerto Rican women saw their levels increase quite dramatically in 2000, while that of Cuban women began to decline. The same trend is evident for Hudson County. Puerto Rican women's labor-force participation rates are significantly higher than those of Mexican American and Cuban women. (See Table 4.1.)

TABLE 4.1 LABOR FORCE PARTICIPATION RATES FOR MEXICAN AMERICAN, PUERTO RICAN, AND CUBAN WOMEN IN THE UNITED STATES AND IN HUDSON COUNTY, NEW JERSEY

	Mexican American	Puerto Rican	Cuban
U.S. 1980	49.0	40.1	55.4
U.S. 1990	52.8	42.8	55.9
U.S. 2000	46.6	52.3	50.4
Hudson County, 2000	40.2	53.6	44.2

Sources: U.S. Bureau of the Census, Census of Population, 1980, *General Social and Economic Characteristics*, Vol. 1 Series, PC 80–1-C1; U.S. Bureau of the Census , Current Population Survey, data transcribed from *Employment and Earnings*, 1991; U.S. Bureau of the Census, , *Sex and Age by Employment Status, Racial or Ethnic Groupings*, 2000; U.S. Bureau of the Census , *Sex and Age by Employment Status, Racial or Ethnic Groupings*, Hudson County, New Jersey, 2000.

The variations in labor force participation over time reflect a host of factors: demographic changes in each group, with younger immigrants, for example, filling more available jobs, and those who are older retiring or leaving the labor force. This is likely to be the case with Cubans, an older population than the other two, and with fewer steady, younger migrants coming in. Regional differences also respond to different migration patterns. For example, Dominicans are gaining in numbers compared to Puerto Ricans in New York. The latter population in New York fell 12.8 percent between 1990 and 2000 as Puerto Ricans moved to the suburbs or other states, or went back to Puerto Rico. At the same time, the Dominican population almost doubled during the 1990s and the same growth rate continues.[24] As Patricia Pessar has amply documented, Dominican women's work has been crucial for family survival. However, she and Pamela Graham contend that there is a substantial gender gap in earnings between Dominican men ($15,088) and women ($11,347). Also, the high number of female-headed households (almost 40% of all Dominican households) contributes to the high poverty rates in the community.[25] It may be that Dominican women now occupy the place in the labor market that Puerto Rican women did years ago in the New York City metropolitan area, and Puerto Rican women, perhaps second-generation suburbanites and white-collar workers, are more active and better remunerated in the labor force.

In addition to labor-force behavior, studies about Cuban and other Hispanic women, including my own, have addressed questions of gender, gender roles, and gender ideologies.[26] Research on Cuban women has discussed the adjustment of cultural values and practices after migration. An article by Myra Marx Ferree on the early experience of Cuban women in Miami concluded that employment for the first generation of Cuban women who worked outside the home might not have been particularly emancipating. As in the old country, male participation in the domestic sphere was almost completely absent.[27] Similarly, M. Patricia Fernández-Kelly and Anna M. García, in a comparative study of Mexican and Cuban women, concluded that Cuban women accepted patriarchal norms at home and saw garment-industry jobs as a transitory experience aimed at recovering or attaining middle-class status.[28] I found similar patterns in my early study. Work for women was geared toward improving the standard of living. Women worked outside the home in great numbers, but they were still responsible for all household tasks. Yet, men were clearly the decision makers and overseers of household affairs. In many instances, when I was interviewing women, husbands were present even though all the questions were addressed to the women. However, work outside the home seemed to confer independence on women. When asked if she would stay home if the family did not need the money, one of the women said, "Absolutely not."

Follow-Up Study

In 1990, I went back to the community to do a follow-up of my earlier study.[29] This second time I was primarily interested in gender dynamics in the family among Cuban immigrant women, their daughters, and men. When socially constructed ideas about gender confront a totally different environment (as happens with migration), migrant men and women may resist, change, or adapt their old beliefs to the new situation. My interviews focused on the results of this confrontation and were conducted in-depth (each about three hours long) with as many women from my original study as I could find. I also interviewed their daughters, boyfriends, and husbands, when applicable.

Work

Did the discourses of Cuban women regarding work alter significantly between the 1980s and the 1990s? Was there a marked generational change? What did the men in their lives think? Employment outside the home for women was still seen as necessary to help the family, but one striking difference was that, for most of the women, work had acquired an intrinsic value. Women had also developed a greater sense of independence through outside employment: "I love to work. Work makes me feel satisfied, genuine. Work is central to my life." (Eva, 47, widow, who owns a hairdressing salon) Another woman, said:

> You know, work gives color to life. In Cuba, it was not common that women worked, although I was a teacher myself. But things have changed here. Most Cuban women work and are very active.

> I am not saying all these nice things because I have a good job. I worked in a factory many years ago when I came to the United States and I still would say that work, no matter what kind, is good for human beings. (Marina, 59, divorced and the Spanish-language editor of a publishing house in New York City)

Work was seen as good for women's minds. Eva, who was quoted above, commented: "It is good for women to work. They keep their minds occupied (at the same time that they earn money). Besides, idleness is bad company. It is better for a marriage if the woman has a job, because an idle woman at home is no good."

Other women emphasized that work confers self-respect, family and community recognition, and money. "A woman needs to work," Marta told me. "She feels better and more in control of herself. She doesn't have to ask her husband for money. It seems to me that if a woman has a job, she is given more respect by her husband and her children" (Marta, 56, married, sales worker).

How did the daughters feel about these issues? Even though the second generation of Cuban women and men had to endure the difficulties of growing up in two separate cultures, for the most part they did not face the painful consequences of deeply rooted, old beliefs that clashed with those of the new society. They never saw recovering the status the family enjoyed in Cuba as their main motive to work or to choose a career in the United States. Many were too young; others were born here. All the daughters had high levels of education. Older ones were professionals, while younger ones were in school pursuing qualifications. All the daughters assumed that women should work and have careers. Even more than their mothers, they emphasized self-actualization as the main reason for this. One of the daughters, Graciela, holds a degree in mathematics with a minor in physics from the New Jersey Institute of Technology (NJIT). After graduation she worked at various places, ranging from an insurance company to New Jersey Bell. It was at New Jersey Bell that she learned to work with computers. By that time, Graciela had a strategy:

> I wanted to learn a skill that would help me become independent because I had realized that what I wanted to do was write, and

> if I became an independent computer consultant at home that would give me enough money to contribute to the household and great flexibility with my time. And I'm doing it! I get enough jobs while I can write my poems, my plays. I just finished a play on the Cuban family! (Graciela, 35, married, self-employed)

Susy, who was in high school at the time of the interview, wanted to be a pharmacist. She had worked as a cashier at a pharmacy during summers and other vacations. What does a career mean to her? "I love to work," she reported. "I feel independent. It is not so much the money that I care about, you know. It is the pleasure that I get out of it" (Susy, 16, high school student).

How do the men feel about women working? Of those interviewed, Roberto is of the younger, U.S.-raised generation; the others are of the first generation. Most had high levels of education, and all except for one were professionals or business owners. The majority came from Cuba during the first or second wave of migration after 1959, and they fit the type of middle-class or middle-class aspiring Cuban refugee who came to the United States at the time. The men were much more reserved than the women in expressing their opinions. José, a small business owner from West New York, summarized how he felt about women working outside the home in the United States:

> I think that women should like the home. But I recognize that they have to work here. They have to help the family financially, so there is no choice. That's why men have to accept that helping women with the chores at home is not only good, but also necessary, because women also work outside. To help each other is good. We have to put yesterday's "machismo" behind. (José, 49, married, small business owner)

Pedro, a factory foreman, preferred to have his wife do only housework while he goes out to earn a living:

> I don't think it's a question of being "macho." It is the traditions we grew up with. I think that if I can keep my wife home, if she does not have to work, I am ensuring her dignity as a woman. If

> there comes a time when we really need it and my wife has to get a job, she'll have to do it, but not while I can provide for the family. (Pedro, 59, married, factory foreman)

Roberto, much younger than the other men, said that he "had no problems with women working and having their careers." However, even though he considers women's participation in public life to be normal, there is part of him that still sees women at home as "natural," perhaps from the values learned at home. When asked directly about the contribution of Cuban working women to family and community, he stated:

> About Cuban women? Oh yes, they work a lot. The work of Cuban women is very important for the community. The Cuban economic success is, in part, due to the participation of females. My mother has always worked. Every woman in my family works. I expect my wife to work. But I would like my wife to cook for me . . . I'd like to find her home when I come home from work. (Roberto, 24, single, electrical engineer).

Family

Family is very important to Cubans, as it is to other Latin Americans. Some have argued that Cubans' relative economic success in the United States is directly related to the strength of the family unit. Even though the incidence of divorce in Union City was visibly higher to me in the 1990s than when I went to the community in 1980s, many Cuban families are still cohesive units organized around realizing aspirations for economic achievement. Everyone pools resources for the benefit of all in the family.

Some authors have proposed that the three-generation family is a distinctive feature of Cuban Americans.[30] This family form includes parents, children, and grandparents, since there is resistance among Cubans to placing the elderly in nursing homes. Instead the elderly remain at home, where they also contribute economically, mainly with the care of the grandchildren. More recently, however, the resistance to placing the elderly in nursing homes may be weakening. Like many other groups before them,

Cubans have to struggle with the heavy demands of work and the complex organization of an industrialized society, a very different society from the one they left behind.

The Cuban family in the United States is small. This is partly explained by the low level of fertility among Cuban women.[31] Cuban women had low fertility levels even in prerevolutionary Cuba, especially among the urban middle class. The fact that the postrevolutionary migration to the United States had an overrepresentation of individuals and families from the middle-classes may explain the continuity of that trend among Cuban women here. However, low fertility is also a characteristic of Cuban women on the island at present. The reasons may be obvious; material difficulties in the everyday lives of Cubans may make couples decide not to have many children.

According to the 2000 U.S. census, Cuban American households had 2.7 persons compared with 3.9 for Mexican Americans, 2.9 for Puerto Ricans, and 2.5 for the general population. Household size in Hudson County is even lower than the national figure at 2.4.[32]

My earlier Hudson County study (1979–1980) confirmed the predominance of the small, mainly nuclear family type among members of the sample. The majority of the women were married and living with their spouses (73.8%). The rest were widows, divorced, or single women. This was not the case when I returned in 1990. There were more divorced, single females heading families than in 1980. As in the rest of society, singlehood and divorce are factors gradually affecting the shape of the Cuban family. In 2000, the percentage of Cuban families in Hudson County headed by women was 21.1, much higher than it was in 1980 (14.9).[33] However, even though some of the interviewees in 1990 had experienced disruptions in their family lives, such as divorce or the death of a spouse or parent, the image of the ideal family that always surfaced in the interviews was the married couple with two children at most. This was also expressed by the daughters who, regardless of their commitment to pursue their careers, clearly stated that they wanted to get married and have a family (two daughters were already married but also shared these views).

I wanted to explore how much the respondents acknowledged the existence of conflict within the family. Many comments referred to family economics. While most of the older interviewees told me that the economics of the family should be based on common interest, and that resources should be pooled, younger respondents favor economic independence between partners. One second-generation daughter, who is married, said, "Yes, my husband and I have separate checking accounts. This arrangement allows us to keep our individuality. That's the main reason we did it" (Graciela, 35, married, self-employed).

Increasing rates of divorce definitely influence ideas about family economics. Ana, who had participated in my early study, noted:

> Many marriages stay together, but many are breaking up. There is no doubt that divorce is on the rise. In some cases, men start making separate financial arrangements when they are getting ready to make a move. For example, many leave their wives for younger women. But Cuban women are very alert, and when they smell something they prepare themselves. Women are also keeping their financial resources separate (mainly savings, checking accounts). As soon as they realize that something is going on, women protect their interests. I have a friend in that situation right now. (Ana, 53, married, garment worker)

A common trait among the daughters I interviewed was their admiration for their mothers, whom they view as strong individuals. Some daughters recalled how important their mothers were when they were growing up and how hard they worked. In many instances these memories referred to the early years in the United States. Mothers were also pleased with their daughters' lives, their relationship to the family, and their seriousness about education.

Alongside admiration, many daughters expressed criticisms of their mothers. For example, Evelyn stated: "My mother is an exceptional person. She has devoted herself to her children. My mother has been a driving force. I admire her a lot. She always encouraged my brother and me to get a profession. But she is very strong-willed and controlling. She can be suffocating" (Evelyn, 36, divorced, lawyer). Adriana, an admirer of her mother, did not think she should put her on a pedestal: "I think a great deal of my mother and I have a great relationship with her. However, I look at my mother as a human being, with her good qualities and her weaknesses. I think that admitting that is better than trying to put her on an altar. I don't like altars" (Adriana, 26, single, accountant).

Sexuality

My interviewees' attitudes about sexuality were rooted in the sexual scripts governing the Cuba where they grew up. There was a difference between mothers and daughters, as expected, in issues having to do with sexuality. But first, let me examine the sexual norms prevalent in prerevolutionary Cuba.

As discussed earlier in this chapter, Cuban (and other Latin American) attitudes and behaviors regarding sexuality had their origins in Spanish culture. Except for slaves and prostitutes, women were expected to be pure, chaste, respectful, innocent, and well behaved, and to serve as good housekeepers and model daughters, wives, and mothers. Men, on the other hand, were expected to become sexually active before marriage and could have sexual relations with any women they wanted even after they married. But these norms implied that there had to be two kinds of women in society: the virgins or future wives, and the bad women, those with whom men could have sex when they wanted to. Spanish patriarchal values emphasized the importance of honor and shame, cultural codes that regarded female virginity and virtue as the main components of the family's status and ultimately of the male's dignity. In Cuba, this sexual culture generally survived colonial rule, depending on race, social class, and the social status of women and men. Confinement in the home for those women who were expected to be "good" became a requirement for the preservation of the family's honor.[34]

As earlier quotes illustrate, the *la casa* vs. *la calle,* or home vs. the street distinction was a predominant theme in the 1990 Hudson County interviews. Another theme was the changes due to contact with American society and with the women's liberation movement. As expected, there were generational and gender differences in sexual attitudes. Even though views on sexuality have changed drastically in Cuba and among Cubans outside Cuba, the cultural legacy of placing women in the home to protect them from the "dangers of the street" still resonated, especially among older males. "A woman should like the home," said one man. Even one of the younger males who found it very natural for women to work and pursue careers asserted that, when he married, he would like to find his wife home when he comes back from work. Even when there is acceptance of the inevitability of women working outside the home, males liked the idea of maximizing women's time at home, which is indirectly a symbol of male sexual control.

The influence of the women's liberation movement, in particular female sexual liberation, was discussed in many instances. The issue of virginity was of great importance to most of the first generation. However, mothers were accepting, resigned, and convinced that living in the United States meant adjusting to new ways of life. They did not expect their daughters to be virgins until marriage. Almost all mothers said they tried to talk to their daughters and to exchange views about sex. They asked them to be careful about whom they went out with, especially in light of the risks of sexually transmitted diseases. Many mothers were not only resigned but were willing to change. When I asked María de los Angeles, one of the mothers, if she would have preferred to raise her daughter in Cuba rather than in New Jersey, she replied, "Yes, but she would have had to have been born hundreds of years ago, because the change is happening all over. The sexual revolution is not a question of Cuba or the United States; it is a question of these times. I am the one who has to change." (María de los Angeles, 57, married, housewife) The daughters were very candid about their views. "What do I think about virginity? It is an old concept! If you are a virgin, you are a nerd, you are an oddity. The old Cubans still hold to this view. It's very hard for them to deal with this issue." (Susy, 16, single, high school student) The different treatment of male and female children by their parents concerning sexuality bothers Mariela. "One day I overheard my mother reminding my brother as he was going out, 'Please do not forget to take condoms in these days of AIDS.' Why doesn't she ask me?" (Mariela, 19, single, college student)

The daughters reported increasing communication with their mothers on sexual matters, but not with their fathers. Susy told me, "My mother and I talk about sex. She understands the gap between the ages. My mother and I don't always agree, but we try to resolve our conflicts by talking to each other." (Susy, 16, single, high school student) Young Roberto gave an interesting summary of the gap between the generations regarding sexuality: "The older generation of Cubans has had no choice but to accept premarital sexual relationships. I think there is a silent agreement where the younger Cubans do what they have to do, have premarital sex, and the parents pretend not to know anything" (Roberto, 24, single, electrical engineer).

The subject of homosexuality came up on several occasions. In all cases, it was introduced by the interviewees, especially the daughters. They complained about the degree of homophobia existing in the Cuban community. In one instance, a daughter shared her concern because her boyfriend was very homophobic, and she did not think that was right. The only mention of homosexuality among the men was by one who expressed some anxiety that homosexuality had increased significantly in the Cuban community. In this, as in other issues, Cuban women seemed to have changed their views at a much faster pace than Cuban men.

Cuban Women Migrants in Union City: Mariel and the Migration of the 1990s

When I conducted my first study in Union City, the 1980 Mariel exodus was underway (which is why the sample included such a small number of women from that wave of Cuban immigration). Even though many of the Mariel immigrants were, demographically and sociologically, different from their predecessors in that there were significant numbers of single individuals, black Cubans, and some lawbreakers, a great number of the 1980 migrants were families who had wanted to reunite with their relatives here but had not been able to do so before. (See Chapter 1.)

The few Mariel immigrant women whom I interviewed did not seem very different from the earlier Cuban exiles. They had traveled with their families. They wanted to succeed, had a work ethic, and made plans for a better future in the United States. Elsa, a former bank teller in Cuba, expressed her satisfaction at finally being reunited with her relatives in Union City:

> We were planning to come to the United States for a long time, but for many years it was not possible to leave Cuba. When the opportunity came to leave through the Mariel boatlift we couldn't believe it. I have a sister and an uncle here in Union City, and they rushed to Miami to pay for a boat to get us out. We miss Cuba and the relatives that we left there, but we are happy to be here. I am working in a factory now, but I am also taking English lessons. I don't plan to stay there. It's so sad that people have such a bad opinion of the "Marielitos." The troublemakers are only a few. The

> great majority of us are hard-working people. (Elsa, 43, married, white woman, with secondary education, from Havana)

As discussed in previous chapters, most Mariel immigrants have adapted successfully in Union City and elsewhere and, after a couple of decades, they resemble many of the early refugees in their values and future plans in U.S. society. Undoubtedly, support from the U.S. government and from their families has played a great part in their adjustment.

The migration starting in the 1990s has brought a very diverse group of Cuban women to Union City. It is very difficult to obtain figures as to exactly how many have come and stayed. In the beginning of the *balsero* exodus, about 2,000 migrants—women and men—registered with the Refugee Resettlement Program in Hudson County, but of those, only 25 percent remained in Union City. Cubans also come through the lottery system (see Chapters 1 and 2), and some have settled in Union City.[35]

How do Cuban migrant women who arrived in the 1990s and after compare with earlier cohorts? According to my observations and several more recent interviews, the new Cuban women migrants are younger than their predecessors at the time of arrival. Most are from urban areas, in particular Havana. They are racially diverse and a high proportion are single or divorced. Many are single mothers. They seem to be very independent. Perhaps one of the most striking factors is that these women are not as political as earlier Cuban women were. That is, ideological and political factors were not high priorities in their decision to migrate, even when politics is intricately connected to economic difficulties in Cuba. A couple of them mentioned the lack of *horizontes*, literally *horizons*, or future hopes in Cuba as the main reason for migrating. This is the way Laura, a 45-year-old white woman from Havana, put it:

> My reasons for migrating to this country were mainly economic. Most people coming now feel that way. I don't care much about politics. I tell you, as a medical doctor, I couldn't be better respected. I liked my job. But I couldn't make it with my salary! People working in hotels and earning dollars made more money than I did. Life here is tough. I am studying to validate my credentials. I just have to go on and not lose hope. I miss Cuba a lot, but there were no future prospects for me there. (Interviewed on October 25, 2003)

Cuban women migrants of the 1990s find it hard to get jobs. The labor market in Union City and elsewhere in the metropolitan area has been shrinking since the 1980s. The booming economy that allowed Cuban women of the 1960s and 1970s to work in such high numbers is no longer there. Many of the new Cuban women work in the few factories that are left, in service jobs, and as teacher aides in bilingual and other programs, at the same time that they study English.

Since most are not as intensely political as the early exiles, the new Cuban women migrants do not hesitate to go back to Cuba to visit relatives. Some reported being criticized by early exiles for this. As discussed in Chapter 1, some of the early refugees feel that taking dollars to Cuba only helps to perpetuate the regime. The new migrants not only travel to Cuba, but they seem to be more in touch with what happens on the island on a day-to-day basis through telephone calls or electronic mail.

This divide between the early waves and those who arrived later is evident in almost everything that is talked about. The older exiles often feel that the new arrivals believe they are entitled to everything. New

FIGURE 4.1 *Jaclyn's handbag factory was a popular employment site for Cuban women who came in the 1960s and 1970s. Today it is closed, revealing the flight of manufacturing enterprises from the Hudson County area.* (Ana Meseguer)

migrants, earlier exiles say, do not understand that in this society people have to work hard, like they had to when they arrived in this country. For their part, new migrants feel that their own relatives are insensitive to their needs. Mariana, a black, single mother from Havana, came to the United States in 1995 with her two sons. At first, she went to stay with her aunt. After a few weeks, she moved out on her own:

> I never thought that my aunt would treat us that way. I had such an idealized notion of family when I was back in Cuba. But when we came, everything changed. She claimed that I spoiled my children, that I wasn't doing enough to get a job, and she pitted me against other members of the family. I was feeling so uncomfortable that I decided to leave. I've gone through such financial nightmares! I rented a very small apartment in a neighborhood that isn't too good. I'm concerned about my children. Now I am taking English lessons. All I want to do is to get ahead. (Interviewed on September 21, 2002)

Many of the women arriving after 1990 are professionals. Some are medical doctors, like Laura, or architects or artists. They benefited from the educational opportunities that were offered by the 1959 Revolution. Their levels of education are higher than those of earlier women exiles and prerevolutionary migrants, but they are facing a constricted labor market. As happened to early exiles and immigrants, they have a language barrier, which makes it difficult to validate their professional credentials. Despite the obstacles, the women that I spoke to are very determined to continue struggling.

My observations suggest that there is a better relationship between the new Cuban migrants and other Hispanic women than was the case with earlier Cuban women. In many cases new Cuban migrants share characteristics with other Latinas such as race or single motherhood. However, some of the women I spoke to also felt special about being Cuban. One of them told me: "I don't know why, but I feel that other Latin American women in the office are jealous of me. Maybe it is because Cuban women are more educated" (Mariana, 47, from Havana).

Many in the Union City community have a high regard for the new Cuban women arrivals. As Siomara Sánchez, president of the National Association of Cuban American Women (NACAW) told me:

> Cuban women have always been very *emprendedoras*, or enterprising. It doesn't matter if we are talking about the older or the more recent Cuban women migrants; they have always been an example for the community. New Cuban immigrants work even harder than the old ones. They want to move ahead. Many of them are professionals and they work and also study to validate their credentials. They struggle against all odds! (Interviewed on October 15, 2003)

Like their predecessors, new Cuban women migrants are strong and hard working. They are different from the early exiles in that politics and ideology are not so important in their motivation to work or get ahead. Most were raised with the revolution and have careers. Even though they are opposed to the Cuban government, they did not lose a class position or possessions that they wanted to regain in the United States, as was the case with many of the early exiles. They would probably have not migrated had the economic situation been better in Cuba. As some commented, the lack of horizontes suffocated them, forcing them to make the decision to migrate.

5

Saint Augustine Parish and Cuban Adaptation

Religion and Reconciliation

Before the 1959 Revolution most Cubans identified themselves as Catholic, and the devotion to the virgin of El Cobre, the island's patron saint, was widespread. However, the Church itself was weak, especially in the rural and poor sectors of society. Many of the clergy were foreigners, particularly from Spain, and popular religiosity was less tied to the institution than it was in other Latin American countries. The urban poor, especially black Cubans, venerated Catholic saints as African gods, in the syncretic practice of *Santería*, the Afro-Cuban religion. The social base of the Church was made up of predominantly urban, white, upper, and middle-class individuals and families. There were also a number of Sephardic (Spanish) and Ashkenazi (eastern European) Jews, with the latter making up the majority. Some Jews assimilated into Catholicism, but most continued to practice their religion. Although few in number, they formed active communities and associations, and built synagogues and cemeteries. It is estimated that the majority of Cuban Jewry left for exile after 1959. Protestantism came to Cuba via the United States around 1898. After a period of growth, Protestant influence significantly declined, especially after World War II. Like the Catholic Church, most Protestant denominations drew their membership from the middle-classes, although there were exceptions.[1]

Many prerevolutionary Cuban immigrants in Union City were from rural areas and thus were not practicing Catholics, but gradually, after they came to the United States, a good number became very devout.[2] As is the case with most immigrants, Cubans displayed a higher level of religious participation once in the United States than they did in their own country. For immigrants, religion often serves as a vehicle for integration into the new society. According to many scholars, religion is one of the important identity markers that help immigrants preserve individual self-awareness and cohesion in a group.[3]

After a brief overview of the activities of the early Cuban Catholics, this chapter will concentrate mainly on the role that one of the Catholic churches, Saint Augustine, played in assisting Cubans in Union City when they came in the 1960s and after. I will discuss my interviews with several individuals in the parish, where I also did participant observation. I will explore the recent changes in the composition of the congregation and their implications for Cuban and other Hispanic members. Also, I will review the relationship between Cubans and their native Church, and the impact that Pope John Paul II's visit to Cuba in 1998 had on Saint Augustine's Cubans.

Risking criticism from some social science methodologists who would advocate for more distance, I decided to focus on Saint Augustine church precisely because it was my parish for several years after I arrived in Union City from Cuba. Although I moved away a long time ago, having been an insider gave me a special perspective on the history, sociology, and general day-to-day interaction among members of the parish. I still know many people there, thus participant observation, or taking the role of an active member who wanted to systematically learn about the place, was not faked or unnatural, but instead, relaxed and unaffected. I explained to the pastor, group leaders, and many group members about my study. My sense is that they trusted me.

Early Cuban Catholic Activities in Union City

The first Cuban Catholics in Union City worshiped at Saint Michael's Monastery, run by the Passionist Order of priests. They also formed their own Cuban Catholic organizations and in 1957 they collected money to buy a statue of the Virgin of El Cobre from Spain. The statue was taken first to Cuba to be blessed by Cardinal Manuel Arteaga in Havana. After it arrived in Union City, it was briefly kept at the convent of the Dominican nuns at 14th and West Streets. From there, the statue was transported in a procession of about 1,000 people to Saint Michael's Monastery on September 30, 1965. The monastery closed in 1981 and the Church merged with Saint Joseph Parish, also run by the Passionists. Saint Joseph Church, now called Saint Joseph and Saint Michael's R.C. Church, is located on 13th Street and Central Avenue in Union City. The statue of the Virgin of El Cobre now resides there.[4]

I interviewed Father Joseph Fahey, C.P., who came to work at Saint Michael's Monastery in May,1962, as a seminarian. He was ordained priest in 1971 and left the area in the same year. Known as Father Luis among the Spanish-speaking congregants, he remembers the early Cuban community in Union City:

> There was a group of very devout Cuban Catholics when I got to the Monastery in Union City. I know that the first Spanish mass was celebrated around 1954. First, there was a Jesuit priest from St. Peter's in Jersey City who knew Spanish and came to say mass. Then, Father Richard Kugelman, a noted Passionist theologian and linguist, who also knew Spanish, celebrated the Spanish masses. From 1957 on, before I got there, Father Martin Grey took over. On September 8, the day of the Virgin of El Cobre, there was a procession with the Virgin along a few blocks around the church, and then back to the sanctuary. A commemorative mass would follow. But since the late 1960s, there was pressure from commercial and other groups that the mass should take place in Roosevelt Stadium. I was opposed to that because the event was no longer a strictly religious function, and I didn't think that was right.[5]

Another interviewee has a different version. She recalls that, as Cubans began arriving in great numbers, they worshiped in different parishes, which individually celebrated the feast day of the Virgin of El Cobre on September 8th. In time, they decided to unite on that day and take the procession from different parishes to Roosevelt Stadium. Patriotic fervor was also present in the procession. Gradually, an inter-parish association was formed, Asociación de la Caridad or Virgen de la Caridad Association, to try to find a place to worship the Virgin of El Cobre in Union City.[6]

In the late 1970s, some Union City Cuban Catholics initiated a fund-raising drive to build the Casa de la Caridad or House of Charity, also known as the Confraternity of the Virgin of El Cobre.[7] They designed a very well organized campaign. Cuban businesses in the area donated lots of money and contributed in many other ways. For example, Nené Rojas, the owner of the women's boutique Mr. Rojas, organized an elegant fashion show at Schuetzen Park, a fine, long-established German club in the city. Active in the Confraternity was the Unión de Cubanos en el Exilio (UCE), or Union of Cubans in Exile. This was a regional Catholic association with many members in New York and New Jersey that met regularly. They were inspired by the work of the late exiled Cuban Bishop Eduardo Boza Masvidal, who lived in Venezuela but visited the area on occasion. He counseled the founders of the House of Charity and helped them establish the organization's mission statement. A house was bought in an auction in 1978 and paid for in full. The membership of the board of directors was rotated among the different parishes. However, the decline of Cuban immigration to the area since the late 1980s affected the Casa de la Caridad. Membership began to dwindle, and the board decided to pass its ownership to the Archdiocese of Newark in 1990. Among other requests, they asked the archdiocese that the Casa continue to worship the Virgin, and that the annual celebration on September 8th remain unchanged. A new board is trying to revive the activities of the Casa de la Caridad. Now the Casa serves a mixed Hispanic population, although the leadership is Cuban. Currently, the Confraternity is involved in a renovation project for the house, which is located at 3333 Hudson Avenue. For that purpose, the board of directors has created a foundation led by many religious and community leaders.

When the exiles began arriving in great numbers in the 1960s, many religious organizations set up programs to help the refugees. Among the Catholic churches were Saint Michael, Saint Joseph of the Palisades, Saint Rocco, Holy Family, and Saint Augustine.

Saint Augustine Parish[8]

Saint Augustine Parish was established in 1886. This church served the German, Irish, Italian, and other nearby Catholic, Union City populations. (Saint Augustine also has a school.) In the late 1950s, some Puerto Rican and Cuban families began attending masses. A Latin American priest came to say mass in Spanish from time to time. In 1959, an Irish American priest, Father Michael Feketie, was assigned to Saint Augustine in a permanent position. Father Feketie became the pastor of the Hispanic congregation since both his Spanish and disposition to serve the community were excellent. He was revered by the Cuban parishioners, who claimed that Father Feketie spoke Spanish with a Cuban accent. At first, the Sunday Spanish mass was celebrated in the basement. With the high number of Cuban arrivals in the 1960s, however, it began to be very well attended and it was permanently moved to the temple. A community began to form. After Sunday mass, churchgoers would meet in the church basement for coffee and pastry, which were donated by Cuban businesses in the city. Religious organizations began to flourish. As Father Feketie shared:

> A key association was the Legion of Mary. We established a tradition by bringing the pilgrim Virgin to the houses of parish members. In the beginning of the 1960s, organizations like the Apostleship of Prayer would take the picture of the Sacred Heart to the houses also. Nobody would reject the presence of the Sacred Heart in their houses! The idea was to have families open their doors, their families to God.[9]

Saint Augustine's Cuban lay leadership contributed to the formation of a strong community. In Father Feketie's estimate, 95 percent of the Hispanic parishioners in the 1960s and 1970s were Cuban. Among them, there were educated and professional exiles who had been practicing Catholics back in Cuba. Many of them had been active in groups growing in strength in the 1950s. For example, the most active group was Acción Católica, or Catholic Action, which developed a catechesis for the countryside and the poor urban areas where contact with the Church was minimal.[10] Thus, the organizational skills that they brought with them

FIGURE 5.1 *St. Augustine Roman Catholic Church located on New York Avenue between 39th and 40th Streets in Union City.* (José Hernández)

were very useful in Saint Augustine. Working-class, Union City Cuban Catholics who worshiped at Saint Augustine also became active and benefited from the level of organization that their middle-class compatriots brought to this church.

Like other religious organizations, Saint Augustine assisted the Cubans who were arriving as refugees. In the basement of the church, an office was set up to help them find jobs, apartments, and furniture. They also received help with the translation and legalization of documents. This office, known as *la oficina hispana,* or Hispanic office, was financed by Catholic Charities, one of the organizations through which the Cuban Refugee Program channeled financial support for the refugees. While much of the work was done by local Saint Augustine's personnel, a representative from Catholic Charities visited the office twice a week.

As the Cuban community of Saint Augustine grew, the number of social and associational activities multiplied. The social events also took place in the church basement, which was known as *El Batey*.[11] For example, there were fashion shows and presentations of *zarzuelas*, or Spanish operettas. The fashion shows were organized by the Mr. Rojas store. The singers in the zarzuelas were Cuban. One of them, *Estelita Santaló*, was very famous in Cuba. To these activities were added annual fund-raising banquets for the parish.

Gradually, the proportion of Cubans grew larger than the white Americans. When I asked Father Feketie about the reactions of the old parishioners to the Cuban presence, he replied: "Some resented the newcomers, others accommodated. It was a normal reaction to dramatic social change" (interviewed on December 18, 2001). The first Cubans who became leaders in the parish organizations recall the resentment of the white Americans. Ernesto shared with me:

> There were too many tensions in the parish. The Americans claimed that the church was theirs. As more Cubans became leaders of different committees, such as those on education, liturgy, and social activities, strains were pulling the groups apart. I was the third president of the Parish Council since it was founded, and there was a lot of jealousy. I am sure the American members didn't like me. These resentments led to the temporary dissolution of the Parish Council. (Interviewed on September 15, 1999)

Saint Augustine now has the highest proportion of Hispanic Catholics in the Archdiocese of Newark, though the majority of them are no longer Cuban. Most activities take place in Spanish. Instead of the original single mass in Spanish on Sundays, now there are three. All these masses are very well attended. There is a bilingual mass on Sundays too. On weekdays, there are two masses in English, though most of the attendees are also Spanish-speaking parishioners. Among the many parish activities in Spanish are: the Apostleship of Prayer, Legion of Mary, Christian Youth Group, Adult Youth Group, Bible Studies, Marriage Encounters, Group of Charismatic Prayer, Prison Ministry, the Family Movement, and small discussion groups that meet four weeks before Advent and Lent. There is also a reconstituted Parish Council, a Spanish Parish Choir, and Sunday School classes from first to eighth grade. The church also hosts meetings for Alcoholics and Narcotics Anonymous.

The composition of Saint Augustine's Hispanic membership reflects the changes taking place in the larger community. Father Pedro Navarro, a former pastor, told me:

> There has been a radical change in this parish since I came here in 1978. About 20 percent of the congregation was American and the remaining 80 percent was Hispanic. Of the 80 percent Hispanic, 75 percent was Cuban and 25 percent Puerto Rican. Now 93 percent of the parish membership is Hispanic. Of those, 35 percent are Cuban, 40 percent Colombians, and the rest are from other South and Central American countries and from the Dominican Republic.[12]

Father Navarro noted that most of the leaders at Saint Augustine are Cuban even though most of the parishioners are not. He said that "Cuban leaders in the parish have the education and the initiative. Most have stayed at Saint Augustine because they are committed to helping their less fortunate Catholic brothers and sisters who are arriving in great numbers."[13]

According to Father Navarro, who clearly prefers pastoral work to other institutional tasks, there is a lot more work in the parish as more immigrants come into town. As he added:

> There is no break here. The doorbell and the telephone ring constantly. Saint Augustine fills a vacuum here. We try to help solve religious and human problems. With our scanty resources we try to do what we can. Saint Augustine is the largest parish of the Archdiocese and it is also the poorest. The average individual contribution per week is $1.25 compared to $6.00 for the Archdiocese as a whole. But it is wonderful to see the generosity of the people. The majority are poor and they give of what they have for those who have less. (Interviewed on October 1, 2002)

How have Saint Augustine Cubans responded to changes in their parish? The reactions are mixed. Berta, a longtime Saint Augustine Cuban parishioner, told me: "I attend the 11:45 A.M. mass now instead of the one at 1:45 P.M. Remember how most people were Cuban at that mass years ago? Well, not anymore. Nowadays, it's hard to find a Cuban. They are all people from other Latin American countries. Not that I have anything against them, but I feel better with my own people" (interviewed on July 19, 2001). Ernesto, the former Parish Council member mentioned above, shared his feelings:

> Cubans are leaving the parish. When the church was predominantly Cuban, there was more cooperation. Cubans worked very hard because they are perfectionists and very efficient. Cubans supported each other and always worked in a spirit of solidarity. Saint Augustine was a model parish then, not anymore. There is a lot of disorganization now. A similar thing has happened with the Casa de la Caridad. Many Cubans have left and now the place is not very well taken care of. For one thing, the original directors handed in the House to the Archdiocese with all expenses paid off. But change happens, and I understand that we Cubans have the obligation to help other Latin Americans, not only in religious terms, but also to find jobs and education, and meet other human needs. (Interviewed on September 15, 1999)

Lilia, a Cuban parish leader, thinks that the reactions of Cubans toward other Latin Americans in the parish resemble those of the white Americans at the time of the Cuban flow years ago:

> Cubans don't open themselves easily to other nationalities, especially the early exiles. That's why they are a difficult group to evangelize. Sometimes Cubans look down on others. They always come together by themselves and are not very inclusive. Most leaders in the parish are Cuban, and many times most of the members of their groups are Cuban too. There are exceptions of some very mixed groups such as the Catechesis and the Family Movement. Maybe the leaders of these groups are more conscious of the need to attract other nationalities. (Interviewed on March 1, 2000)

Juan, the director of the Catechesis for many years, believes that the transition from predominantly Cuban to a more mixed Hispanic parish is a positive thing. As he put it:

> Every nationality offers something good. I know that other Cubans do not agree with me. But I think that the more diversity we have in the parish, the more representative we are of Christian values. At this point, the majority of the leaders, both men and women, are still Cuban because they come from middle-class, professional backgrounds and are well educated. In many cases they attended Catholic schools in Cuba. Most of the other Latin American parishioners have the best intentions but they are not prepared to take leadership positions. In the future this will change because younger people from other non-Cuban nationalities will fill the leadership vacuum. Once this happens, there will be more diversity. (Interviewed on March 4, 2000)

Other Cuban parishioners agree that there are benefits to having a mixed parish. Maritza, a member of the Spanish choir told me:

> I like the diversity of this community. This is really what makes it God's flock. Everybody is included, regardless of color or nationality. I've been here for years, and I've seen this community change. I am convinced that, as we welcome difference among us, we are fulfilling our mission as a people of God. (Interviewed on October 30, 2000)

How do other Latin American parishioners respond to Cubans? It was difficult for me to ascertain the feelings of other Hispanics toward Cubans precisely because I am Cuban. Nonetheless, I asked several non-Cubans about how they felt regarding the relations among the different nationalities in the parish. In every case all I heard was praise for the Cuban leaders. María, an Ecuadorian woman stressed: "These Cuban leaders know so much. They are good leaders and good people. We are very fortunate to have them" (interviewed on December 14, 2001). Evelio, a Cuban Saint Augustine's leader, confided: "I think that if other Hispanics feel resentments, they don't say anything. From comments I've heard, my suspicion is that they look up to Cubans and their leadership skills" (interviewed on November 17, 2000).

The harshest criticism of Saint Augustine Church that I encountered was from a recently arrived Cuban immigrant. Dalia, a black woman, complained that she never received any answers to her phone calls and that, when she visited the church to look for help, she was treated unpleasantly (interviewed on June 2, 2002).

Perhaps the best way to understand intergroup dynamics is through the observation of group interaction. I have had the opportunity to facilitate the small Advent and Lent discussion groups several times from 1996 to 2000. The groups that I have led are mixed, though the Cuban presence is still significant. There is a predominance of women in their 50s and 60s, from Cuba, Puerto Rico, Dominican Republic, Colombia, Ecuador, Honduras, El Salvador, and Mexico. Some of the Cubans are recently arrived immigrants. At the beginning of the session each participant introduces her/himself, including country of origin. The working groups usually start with an educational video about the day's subject, after which there is a discussion. It is clear that the universal religious message takes precedence over the Latin heterogeneity of the group. The points made by the group members are always geared toward applying the message of love and peace in the Gospel, with much emphasis on improving the life of the community.

As a sociologist, I was also invited to lecture to the Youth Adult Group. The group's aims are: (1) to study and debate controversial issues regarding modern life from a religious point of view; (2) to share experiences for spiritual support and help; (3) to establish moral guidelines for attitudes toward life. This group is quite differentiated. There are many nationalities represented, and the persons with official leadership roles were born in Mexico, Cuba, and Guatemala. As is the case with the older group discussed above, the young men and women are concerned with issues that transcend their original countries, and when ethnicity becomes a topic of discussion, the members identify themselves more often as Hispanic Americans than as members of specific nationalities. They conduct their meetings both in English and Spanish. Clearly, younger age facilitates the successful integration of immigrants into a new society. In this case, as in the past, religious structures have provided an institutional base to help immigrants adjust.

Forming a strong community at Saint Augustine in the 1960s reinforced Cuban exile identity. Also, part of the reason why this community solidified was because, for Cubans, there was no return to their homeland. Deep roots in this New Jersey church compensated for the emotional distance most Cubans have felt toward their native Catholic church, which they often see as being too accommodating to the Cuban government.

The Catholic Church in Cuba, Revolution, and Migration

For the most part, the Catholic Church in Cuba embraced the struggle against the Batista government in the late 1950s. Many Catholics participated in revolutionary activities in the cities and others, including priests, joined the rebels in the Sierra Maestra mountains. Santiago de Cuba's Archbishop Enrique Pérez Serantes echoed the Church's approval of the revolutionary triumph in the first episcopal document of 1959, *Vida Nueva:*

> [T]he first stage of this heroic enterprise is concluded. Many never had faith in its success . . . [but] there are no weapons that can strip the ideals that live in the minds and hearts of people. . . . We have now entered the second stage, the most arduous, delicate, and laborious one, which demands robust arms and a right orientation of mind together with a healthy and powerful heart. (Translation mine)[14]

During a period when relations between the Church and the revolutionary government were referred to by many authors as harmonious, the Cuban bishops supported the Agrarian Reform, the first law promulgated by the Council of Ministers in 1959. The new government expressed complacency about the Church's support of this major law, and in a televised speech in June Fidel Castro called the Catholic Church in Cuba "a revolutionary church, the most revolutionary in Latin America."[15]

But the honeymoon did not last long. Even though the bishops supported the initial government measures, there was a degree of caution in most public pronouncements. As early as January, 1959, during the government's first month in power, as Archbishop Pérez Serantes was lending his support for the victorious rebels, he also advised: "A new order will be established over the ashes of the old one. . . . [But] this new regime will have to be better, because if it were not, there would have been no reason to have toppled the old one" (Translation mine).[16] In July,

1959, Pérez Serantes went further and clarified that, even though he had supported the Agrarian Reform in an earlier letter, he was concerned about the great affinity that he saw between this law and the prevailing ideas among "the faithful and disciplined followers of Moscow [in Cuba]." He added, "Dr. Castro, probably unaware of Moscow's orientations, surely knows that this does not at all favor the success of the Revolution" (Translation mine).[17]

During the first year of the Revolution, there were institutional efforts to reflect on how Catholics could play a positive role in the process of profound national transformation that was taking place. For example, the Catholic university of Villanueva included in its curriculum courses on the social doctrine of the Church, economics, methods of social research, labor relations, and Marxist studies. Another example was a meeting for priests and religious that dealt with issues of economic and social justice. This gathering, which received major input by the Juventud Obrera Católica or Catholic Working Youth, lasted a week. The most important concentration of Catholics during this period, however, was the Congreso Nacional Católico or National Catholic Congress, the largest event ever organized by the Church.[18] The Congress revealed the polarization that was taking place among Catholics themselves. Some saw the meeting as a place to challenge what they believed to be a growing leftist tendency in the government. Others thought that the Congress presented an opportunity to support the changes occurring in the country, which they saw as positive. Antagonisms continued to grow between believers and revolutionaries, and fears about communism loomed over many in the Catholic hierarchy and among most of the laity. Marked frictions about executions, the nationalization of Catholic schools, and a general atmosphere of mutual distrust in the context of accelerating conflict between Cuba and the United States, finally led to a dramatic breach between church and state, one that has proven very difficult to mend.

In August, 1960, the first pastoral letter by the Cuban bishops was released. The document began by praising the positive initiatives the Revolution had taken about social justice, but it expressed the bishops' "concerns and fears . . . about the growing influence of communism in Cuba."[19] A second document was published in December of the same year which expanded on this theme. The polarization between defenders and critics of the Revolution within the Church continued to grow as the process of radical social and political change inevitably required that people take sides. In time, however, the great majority of Catholics opposed the new government.

The breakup of diplomatic relations between Cuba and the United States, internal counterrevolutionary activity, and the failed Bay of Pigs invasion in April, 1961, were followed by Fidel Castro's declaration that the Revolution was a socialist one. In a March, 1961, speech denouncing sabotage activities in the capital, he said:

> Has the government done anything to the church?. . . . [What] kind of war are these priests waging against us? Of course, there are very honorable exceptions. There are some very revolutionary priests here . . ." [referring to Father Germán Lence, who defended the revolution]. (Translation mine)[20]

As these confrontations continued, being Catholic became synonymous with being counterrevolutionary, and being revolutionary meant being atheist and suspicious of anybody with religious beliefs, especially Catholics. Other religions also experienced conflicts during this period, but the Catholic Church, perhaps because it was mainly supported by the upper- and middle-classes, underwent the most dissension. This became a real class war. A number of Catholics, including priests, got involved in insurgent activities, and many were among the exiles who went to Cuba in the Bay of Pigs invasion. Conversely, revolutionaries chanted slogans in front of churches during masses, and in some extreme cases, desecrated temples.[21]

Priests and lay Catholics began to leave the country. Some of those involved in counterrevolutionary activities asked for political asylum in foreign embassies. Religious orders arranged for their personnel to leave Cuba, especially foreign priests and religious, many of whom taught in Catholic schools, which had been confiscated by the government. But the clash between the Church and the government in this period climaxed with the expulsion of 131 priests and religious in September, 1961, following a procession which turned into an antigovernment protest.[22]

The exodus of thousands of upper- and middle-class Cubans during the early years of the Revolution eroded church membership. Priests also continued to leave the country. Church authorities decided to close the seminary in Havana, and some seminarians were sent to study abroad. With a significant shortage of clergy and lay members, the Cuban Catholic Church experienced the most vulnerable moment in its institutional history. During this period, the Church's efforts were mainly directed at surviving, strengthening its scant membership, and trying to find ways to fulfill its pastoral mission.

Most Cubans who left during this first phase saw their journey as temporary. These exiles hoped, even after the failed Bay of Pigs invasion, that the United States would help in overthrowing Fidel Castro's government. As hopes for a prompt return vanished with the consolidation of the revolutionary government, a growing gulf developed between the Catholics who stayed and those who left. The latter expected the ones in Cuba to continue to voice strong public condemnation of the government. Many Catholics in exile felt that, with their silence, the Cuban bishops had betrayed the Catholic Church and the Cuban people.[23]

Meanwhile, in Cuba, there were signs of a rapprochement between church and state. Msgr. Cesare Zachi, who had extensive experience in eastern European countries as a papal envoy, came to Havana as a Vatican appointee in 1961. His mission from the beginning was to ease church-state pressures and to prevent a massive exodus of priests from the island. To achieve his objectives, Msgr. Zacchi openly maintained relations with government officials. Although his close dealings with the government displeased many in the church hierarchy, Zacchi's strategy bore some fruit. A few Cuban priests who had left voluntarily came back in 1962. Seminarians studying abroad returned after ordination, and even one of the expelled priests, Francisco Oves, returned to the island, became a bishop, and was later designated Archbishop of Havana. European missionaries were allowed in, three Cuban bishops attended the Second Vatican Council in October, 1962, and some priests and lay Catholics traveled abroad to represent the Cuban Church at conferences and other events.[24] A process of adjustment by the Catholic Church to the new Cuba was beginning. Difficult as it was, this new moment brought an opportunity for self-reflection.

In the early years of change and confusion, the Church, while not officially promoting emigration, approved of the exodus. Most of the clergy, like the exiles, viewed the flight from Cuba as temporary. For example, Operación Pedro Pan, though designed and implemented by the Archdiocese of Miami, was at least indirectly assisted by some in the Cuban Catholic clergy:

> Members of the Catholic church played an important role in the children's exodus, albeit not purposely arranged by the church as an organization, but spontaneously. As most of the children attended Catholic schools, nuns and priests were trusted persons sought out by frantic parents.[25]

At the same time, the sweeping changes taking place in the Catholic church elsewhere, especially in Latin America, had a direct bearing on the pastoral orientation taken by the Cuban bishops. In 1969, two documents by the Conference of Catholic Bishops in Cuba addressed to the clergy and laity clearly stated the essence of the new direction taken by the Church. Citing accords from the Latin American Bishops' meeting at Medellín, Colombia, in 1968, the Cuban bishops wrote,

> [A new morality requires] . . . a universal human solidarity . . . The attitude of the Christian person implies a reawakening . . . especially when s/he is immersed in a reality such as ours, whose fundamental driving force is the problem of development. [The basis] for a renewed "social morality" is part of the social teachings of the Church . . . in particular the acclaimed encyclical letter *Populorum Progressio* by Pope Paul VI." (Translation mine)[26]

The bishops' letter also openly condemned the U.S. embargo against Cuba:

> How many excesses are due to the isolation in which we have been living in recent years! Who among us could ignore all the kinds of difficulties that circumvent development? Isn't this the case with the economic blockade that our country has been subjected to . . . which brings grave inconveniences to our Motherland . . . especially to our children, youth, workers, the sick . . . the separated families? Considering the best interests of our people, and motivated by our faithful commitment to serve the poor, according to the teachings of Jesus Christ, and the newly proclaimed pledge at Medellín, we denounce this unjust situation of economic blockade

> which adds unnecessary suffering and makes the achievement of development more difficult. (Translation mine)[27]

Clearly, the Cuban bishops had changed course, and even if there were internal differences, they adopted a unified position where they encouraged the Church membership to "give living testimony of Christ in the concrete conditions of [our] national community, new in the Latin American context."[28] This was probably the most open statement that the Cuban bishops had made so far about the obligation of Catholics to stay in Cuba. After these pronouncements, many lay Catholics decided to stay, but many more left in the subsequent emigration wave of the late 1960s and early 1970s. Their departure represented another loss for the Church.[29]

Because these migrants had stayed in Cuba longer, they could better understand the position of their bishops, whose statements were viewed by the early exiles as an affront. Since the bishops' documents emphasized the issue of development and not political oppression, some early exiles decided to write letters of protest to the bishops. For many Cuban exiles, the idea that the prelates had become the government's spokespersons was finally confirmed.[30] The first wave of Cuban exiles had the strongest links with the institutional church and, for the most part, their attitudes about Cuba and the Church there remained fixed in the experiences of those early years.

Catholic exiles of the early 1960s became very active in their local parishes wherever they lived. Particularly in Miami, Cuban Catholics have influenced worship styles and administrative practices within the Church. Also in New Jersey and New York, Cuban Catholics have held high positions in church bureaucratic structures.[31] A couple of St. Augustine parishioners have held high-ranking posts in the Archdiocese of Newark. The same level of engagement in the Church applied to many refugees of the late 1960s and 1970s. As it became evident that a return to their country was not plausible, their daily lives here became increasingly distant from the realities of the Catholic Church Cubans left on the island.

For a long while, contacts between Catholics living in the United States and those in Cuba were few and mostly made on an individual basis. Then, in the late 1970s, a series of events led to a split in the Cuban community in the United States. In 1978, the Cuban government invited some exiles to engage in a discussion which was known as El Diálogo or The Dialogue, to discuss issues of mutual concern: family reunification, visits by Cuban Americans to the island, and freedom for political prisoners. Amidst extraordinary controversy in the Cuban community, a variety of people, including Catholics, accepted the invitation and went to Havana. Before these meetings, groups of Cuban American youth sympathetic to the Revolution had also visited the country. After 1979, more visits to Cuba were possible, and despite fluctuations, contacts between the U.S. Cuban community and the island have been fairly constant. In addition to family visits, there have been significant academic, artistic, and religious exchanges.[32]

In 1979, the Asociación Católica Padre Félix Varela, or Felix Varela Catholic Association, named after the Cuban priest who lived and worked in New York in the nineteenth century, organized religious pilgrimages to reach out to the Church and to the people of Cuba. Most members of the Association were from Holy Family Church in Union City. Regardless of the criticism it received from many Cuban exile Catholics, the group organized several trips to Cuba, where members made donations to churches and paid visits to bishops, priests, and small Christian communities. Later, the Northeast Hispanic Catholic Center of the Archdiocese of New York took a leadership role in the distribution of donations of money and medicines to Cuba. Other Cuban American groups, such as the Unión de Cubanos en el Exilio, or Union of Cubans in Exile, worked directly with the Center to help in this kind of work. Visits to Cuba by Cuban-born clergy living in the United States or elsewhere were no longer rare. For example, Bishop Eduardo Boza Masvidal, who had been expelled from Cuba in 1961, and Msgr. Raúl del Valle, who worked with the New York Hispanic Apostolate, returned to Cuba in 1988 for a visit at the invitation of the Cuban bishops. However, this new openness was not displayed in Miami. It was only in 1996 that the Archdiocese of Miami could, for the first time, publicly send help to the Cuban Church for the victims of a hurricane in the island. Although many Miami Cubans responded positively, loud dissenting voices disapproved of the effort.[33]

Increasing contact with Cubans in the diaspora created an opportunity for the Church on the island to call for reconciliation. A letter by the bishops of November 21, 1978, reminded Cubans abroad that "their baptismal vocation is linked, by the Divine Providence, to the nation where they were born. To this land they owe the best of themselves, because of their unquestionable Christian identity" (Translation mine).[34] This letter was a clear encouragement for a new, positive engagement of Cubans abroad with their native Church.

At the same time that a diversity of positions was developing within the Cuban community in the United States, the Church in Cuba was gradually gaining some space. Attendance at Catholic masses increased, the number of baptisms rose dramatically, parishes experienced modest, but visible growth, and cases of discrimination against religious people decreased. An increasing tolerance on the part of the government created a better atmosphere for believers to practice their religion. In a 1977 speech to the Jamaican Council of Churches, Fidel Castro stated that "there are no contradictions between the aims of religion and the aims of socialism."[35] In 1985, he openly talked about these issues in an interview with Frei Betto, a Brazilian friar, which was published as a book in Cuba. In 1991, it was decreed that believers could become members of the Communist Party. This had not been possible before. In 1992, a constitutional amendment changed Cuba from an atheist to a lay state.[36] All these changes contributed, directly or indirectly, to a growing exchange between Catholics on the island and those abroad.

As discussed in previous chapters, there were two massive migrations from Cuba after the 1970s. One was in 1980 through the port of Mariel, and the second one was in the 1990s, bringing thousands of *balseros* or rafters. In both cases, the circumstances of these flows were chaotic. Many of the 1980s refugees were disillusioned revolutionaries who had espoused atheism, but others were believers. The Church in Cuba publicly expressed its position about the new exodus:

> We must encourage all [Christian] communities, as we face this exodus, to double their missionary concerns, as the Lord expects from us. . . . The Church exhorts its members to take a personal decision that is illuminated by the Gospel . . . and their commitment to their faith and their homeland . . . not only by human criteria. (Translation mine)[37]

Msgr. Pedro Meurice, Havana's Apostolic Administrator at the time and signer of this statement, outlined what has since become the consistent stand of the Cuban Church on migration: the Church encourages its members to stay in Cuba, although it will respect individual decisions to do the contrary. The final document of the Encuentro Nacional Eclesial Cubano (ENEC), or Cuban National Ecclesiastic Encounter, an unprecedented national project of reflection that took place among Cuban Catholics in 1986, also referred to the Church's concern for those outside of Cuba:

> [The Church] must reach out to those Cubans living abroad permanently, in a mutual and respectful acceptance of the different realities in which each group lives. Reaching out must go beyond family reencounters and material interests. We must aim at a moral and spiritual communion, which is supported by a common cultural heritage, including the Catholic influence. (Translation mine)[38]

At the same time that the Church encouraged Catholics to stay in Cuba, where it believed their missionary responsibility lay, the institution clearly called for dialogue and reconciliation with those who had left. The church made its position about reconciliation explicit in the 1993 pastoral letter *El Amor Todo lo Espera*, or Love Hopes for All Things. The document was drafted after the tumultuous events of the summer of 1994, when thousands of Cubans took to the sea, and it urgently called for dialogue among *all* Cubans, including the diaspora, to try to find solutions to the national problems. The government expressed its dissatisfaction with the pastoral letter, arguing that it promoted divisions by favoring U.S. influence in national affairs. The bishops reiterated their desire to engage in dialogue about issues of national concern, but asserted that the government did not want to talk about anything other than institutional matters.[39] This period brought back new tensions between Church and state. However, a long road had been traveled since the early 1960s, and despite the crisis, the Church's expanding voice and the government's softer stand toward the institution converged to make continuing conversations possible. These accommodations contributed to the successful joint planning of the visit by Pope John Paul II to Cuba in 1998.

Pope John Paul II's Visit to Cuba[40]

After the increased contact beginning in the late 1970s, some sectors of the Cuban diaspora were in support of an internal dialogue between

Church and state, and between Cuban Catholics on the island and those abroad. In 1994, three Cuban bishops met in Mexico with three Cuban-born bishops who lived outside of Cuba to talk about humanitarian help to the island through Caritas, the international humanitarian Catholic organization, and to promote relations between the Cuban Church and Cuban exiles.[41] Also, a movement by Catholic Cuban Americans, Comunidades de Reflexión Eclesial Cubana en la Diáspora (CRECED), or Communities of Cuban Ecclesiastic Reflection in the Diaspora, mainly based in Miami, began establishing closer relations with the Church on the island. This group followed events in the Cuban Church, and though it focused mainly on strengthening the institution in a post-communist Cuba, the CRECED movement supported the positions of the Church in its present reality.[42]

When the papal visit to Cuba was announced, many exile Catholics welcomed the news with great joy. Some thought that the pontiff's visit would bring about rapid change in the country. They expected the pope to encourage dialogue among all parties concerned. Yet, others, including prominent Cuban business and political figures in Miami, expressed great dissatisfaction and even contempt. And these were loud voices. Some radio stations, such as Radio Mambí in Miami, blasted their disapproval of the trip. From their point of view, an accord between the Cuban government and the Vatican for the pope to visit the island only meant that the pontiff was going to legitimize the Castro government.[43] Controversy about the visit was also present in Catholic circles. For example, Miami's Auxiliary Bishop Agustín Román made strong statements against the journey and claimed that, as someone who had been expelled by the government of Fidel Castro in the early 1960s, he could not join the trip. The Archbishop of Miami, John Clement Favalora, gave in to the pressures of Cuban American community leaders and agreed to suspend a luxury cruise ship that was supposed to carry 1,000 people to Cuba for the event, though he later arranged for a one-day trip from Miami by plane to attend the last mass in Havana.[44] These pressures persuaded many Cubans in Miami who wanted to attend the visit, both among the clergy and the laity, to cancel their plans. Other Miamians joined pilgrimages that left from New York, Tampa, and Boston, where opposition to the trip was not as strong. Back at Saint Augustine in Union City, not much was said publicly about the pope's trip. Silence about this topic underscored its delicate political implications. No Saint Augustine parishioner went to Cuba for the pope's visit.

Who were the Cuban Americans who did go? What were their feelings, given that, for a long time, many had not had contact with their church of origin? Had some of the critics of the Church in Cuba changed their minds, or were they mainly curious? Was the work of some Catholic groups in exile wanting to reach out to the Church there succeeding? I can only offer some impressions and observations as a member of a pilgrimage organized by the New York archdiocese.

The group left in a chartered plane that flew from New York's John F. Kennedy Airport directly to José Martí airport in Havana the day before the pope's arrival. The delegation included 400 persons, two-thirds of whom were Cuban Americans from different cities in the United States. There were also clergy, press, and travelers of other nationalities. Cuban Americans in the group tended to be middle-aged individuals who had migrated to the United States soon after the Revolution, as the first wave of exiles. Most had never been back. Persons from middle- to upper-class backgrounds in prerevolutionary Cuba were overly represented in the group. A number of the pilgrims did not have any family left in the country, but as practicing Catholics they wanted to be there for the papal visit. This event made it acceptable for them to go back to Cuba.

The outpouring of warmth and emotion experienced from all Cubans was unexpected for the exiles. For different reasons, everyone, whether Catholic, non-Catholic, or Communist, expressed great joy over the pope's trip. A taxi driver in Havana told me, "It is so important for Cuba that John Paul II comes to visit. You know, it's good for the Americans and others to know that" (interviewed on January 21, 1998). In a different tone, a hotel chef who was standing in the crowd waiting for the pope stated, "For the first time, Cubans can be true to ourselves and others. No more masks. No more fear about having our religious beliefs" (interviewed on January 21, 1998).

The Cuban American visitors that I spoke to were particularly touched by the liveliness of a Catholic church that many had assumed to be too weak or compromising. They were moved when they saw the difficulties that Cubans experience every day. The pilgrims were exceedingly inspired by the degree of help given to people by the Church. Many Cuban

Americans visited their old neighborhoods, schools, and in many cases, friends and relatives. The pope's visit was an important moment for the Church in Cuba and for the Catholic diaspora, and once back in the United States, many of these pilgrims were never the same.

Upon their return, many made a commitment to help the Church in Cuba and to promote humanitarian aid to their compatriots there. These visitors talked to relatives, friends, and church, business, and political leaders to tell them about what they had seen. Through their parishes they started to forge bonds with Cubans on the island by sending medicines, school supplies, and other basic items. According to most pilgrims, isolation has not helped the Cuban people, and as Catholics, they subscribe to the pope's call for the world to open to Cuba and for Cuba to open to the world. A great number of them now oppose the U.S. embargo against Cuba, which they view as ineffective.

Cuban American priest Father Pedro Núñez, editor of the Spanish-language Catholic magazine *Mensaje*, wrote:

> Who could have imagined only a few years ago that the pope would travel to Cuba, especially because, for 35 years this country has been under an atheist regime? Tears came to my eyes when I saw the Holy Father kiss Cuban soil . . . but, as the Scriptures say, there is nothing impossible for God. . . . What has happened is irreversible. . . . Neither Cuba nor Cubans feel that they are alone . . . this is the beginning of a new era of hope for all Cubans. (Translation mine)[45]

Similar feelings were conveyed by lay Cuban American visitors. José Andreas Rionda, a corporate executive from Forest Hills, New Jersey, said about the trip: "The Cuban people are the same today as they were when I was there. They suffer, but they struggle, the same as we do. They treated us like brothers and sisters, without resentment or anger. That made me think that the solution to Cuba's problems has to be peaceful, not violent."[46] Clara Baloyra from Miami told me how moved she had been during her trip to Cuba. Since her return, she has been involved in a number of projects with other Catholics in Miami to help the Church and the Cuban people. Some of these projects include providing material

FIGURE 5.2 *U.S. Cuban pilgrims having lunch after the papal mass in Santa Clara, Cuba.* (Yolanda Prieto)

assistance (medicine, food, money) to the Sisters of Charity for the leprous and for disabled children.[47] José Manuel Hernández, professor emeritus from Georgetown University, believes that the pope's visit to Cuba will have a lasting influence in Cuba and among Cuban Americans. As he told me:

> Many thought that Fidel tricked the pope and used his visit for his own advantage. First of all, the pope is a very intelligent man and he knows what he is doing. Also, we cannot forget that his main purpose in going to Cuba was pastoral. By going there he helped open a wider space for the church. Catholicism in Cuba was a middle-class thing before the revolution, but now we are seeing a new phase where it is becoming more popular. The church in Cuba has worked hard for this and the pope's visit helped a great deal.[48]

After the pope's visit, individual Cuban Americans returned to Cuba to establish contacts with parish groups there. Sammy Díaz, a former member of the Juventud Católica Cubana, or Cuban Catholic Youth, visited the island with a delegation from Caritas. During his trip, Díaz confirmed that the Church in Cuba is vibrant and immersed in the reality of the country. He had traveled to the island during the pope's visit a year earlier. On his second trip, Díaz was very impressed with "the professional level, the dedication, and the commitment of Catholics in the different dioceses and parishes in the distribution of food to people."[49] Father José Joaquín Espino, a Cuban American priest from Miami, wanted to go back to serve the Church in his homeland. Since he was ordained, his dream had been to return to the Guantanamo diocese in Oriente province, where he was born. Despite the harsh realities that he found upon arrival there (scarcity of food and housing, and parishes and chapels with collapsed roofs), he felt that "this was a call from God."[50]

The enthusiasm of the returning travelers following the pope's visit did not generate much controversy in the Cuban American community, mainly because of the visit's extraordinary success. Some dismissed it as having been futile, others were embittered by what they perceived as the Vatican's slight of the exiles, but for the most part, the visit was seen as a breath of fresh air by Catholic Cuban Americans. Few, in Cuba or here, expected the display of appreciation, respect, and love the Cuban people showed John Paul II.

Reactions from church leaders quickly followed in the trip's aftermath. Bishop Eduardo Boza Masvidal had long favored reconciliation. Regarding the repercussions of the pope's visit on Cubans in the diaspora, he said:

> I think all Cubans in exile, to whom the Pope referred on various occasions, should feel very happy about this [visit] and about the fact that a group of us were there, representative of various countries. . . . I was saddened to read a press release that appeared here in Venezuela saying that some in the Miami media called the mural of the Sacred Heart (displayed in Revolution Square) and other things "part of the show." For the Cuban people this was not a show, it was an intense and profound experience lived with joy and happiness. If we maintain such negative attitudes and foment hatred and division, we can expect little. (Translation mine)[51]

Some of the critical voices that were heard before the papal visit subsequently became more understanding. Miami's Auxiliary Bishop Agustín Román celebrated masses at the Ermita de la Caridad, the Miami shrine of the Virgin of El Cobre, while the pope was in Cuba to pray for the visit's success. Later, Msgr. Román praised the pope's trip and invited all to reflect on it. In an emotional statement, he wrote:

> Regardless of any interpretation of the Pope's trip to Cuba, there are the words that we have heard, the expressions that we have seen, and the Spirit that has made itself palpable between the Pastor and his flock. These have been blessed days with the presence of the Pope in our motherland . . . and before all else, we must give thanks to God, Our Lord, who has allowed this to happen . . . Now, after these strong emotions, the challenge is to augment our solidarity with our church in Cuba in prayer, in help, and availability. (Translation mine) [52]

In Union City, I gave a slide presentation at Saint Augustine after my return from my trip to Cuba during the papal visit. The event was very well attended. The silence that had surrounded the pope's visit before it happened gave way to a very enthusiastic and open discussion. Very few of the parishioners there had traveled to the island, perhaps on family visits. Their curiosity had no limits. Many had videotaped the papal masses on television. I showed pictures of the different masses and sites. Emotional comments, questions, and even tears followed my presentation. Many of the questions were about how to help the Church and the people in Cuba. The pontiff's trip to the island helped to legitimize the Church in Cuba in the eyes of the exiles. The success of the visit showed how hard the Church had worked. Somehow, even the cooperation between Church and state in planning the visit did not seem to matter.

A number of years have passed since the papal visit to Cuba in 1998. Ever since then, there has been an increase in church attendance in the island and most parishes are very active. Yet, the euphoria of that moment could not wipe out a complicated history of Church-state conflicts. Although there had been progress before the visit, and a new level of understanding seemed to permeate relations after it, tensions still flare from time to time. The government claims that there is freedom of worship in Cuba, and that any complaints to the contrary are unfounded. The Cuban bishops agree that there is freedom of worship, but contend that the Church's role in Cuban society is very limited. They assert that many of the legitimate demands made of the government at the time of the pope's visit (access by the Church to the means of mass communication, right to reopen schools) have been ignored. For the government, the bishops say, the Church is either an ally or an enemy, which makes the pope's request for a serene social climate conducive to individual religious freedom very difficult to attain.[53]

With regards to the diaspora, the pope's visit to Cuba led to a critical mass of Cuban American Catholics who openly favored closer relations with their native Church.[54] Since reconciliation among all Cubans is high on the bishops' priorities, the Conference of Cuban Catholic Bishops appointed Msgr. Dionisio García, Bishop of the newly-created Diocese of Bayamo-Manzanillo, to be in charge of relations with Cubans outside of Cuba. Besides holding this position, Msgr. García is the Vice President of the Conference of Catholic Bishops of Cuba. Meetings between Cuban clergy from the island and those abroad have taken place regularly since 1998. Since 2000, lay Catholics from Cuba and those abroad have also begun to meet to discuss efforts at reconciliation.

A growing number of Cuban American Catholics are regularly in touch with what is happening in the Cuban Church. Members of Saint Augustine Parish in Union City distribute the magazines published by the Cuban dioceses to small discussion groups. A parishioner from Saint Augustine is a delegate to the lay Catholic group mentioned earlier. When parishioners visit Cuba, they come back and report on their activities, which generally include contact with their churches of origin. Among many Saint Augustine parishioners, there is a new openness about the Church in Cuba and about the way the exiles relate to it. The papal visit facilitated the strengthening of ties between Cuban Catholics abroad and those in Cuba. In general, the visit helped to relax attitudes about contact with Cuba, including increasing visits by Cuban Americans there.

New arrivals from Cuba to Saint Augustine may also present an opportunity for change. They may make a difference in the long run in terms of a more open attitude about the Cuban Church, Cubans on the island, and other Hispanics at Saint Augustine. The new refugees more closely resemble other Hispanics regarding social class. They also travel to Cuba more often because they have relatives there, which many of the earlier exiles do not. Saint Augustine, as a multiethnic parish, presents the possibility of reconciliation between Cubans here and in Cuba, and among different waves of Cuban refugees in a very diverse Hispanic context.

6

Exile, Ethnic Identity, and Political Culture

Politics is at the core of the post-1959 Cuban migration to the United States. Perhaps no other ethnic group in this country is as politically active as Cubans are. Their intensity is mainly related to the desire to overthrow the government they left behind. According to some authors, this is typical of immigrants who are fleeing dictatorial, especially communist, regimes.[1] Yet Cubans are active in U.S. politics as well. Their political participation in the United States thus takes place on two levels: one focused on Cuba, the other focused on politics at the national and local levels, wherever Cubans reside. These two levels very often intertwine: Cubans who arrived in the early 1960s formed countless anti-Castro organizations, and many Cubans became active in local and national politics to further anti-Castro policies. However, younger Cuban Americans, perhaps understandably, are more interested in U.S. local and national politics and are not necessarily involved in anti-Castro politics. For many of them, Cuba is not the center of their political activities.

There are precedents for the high level of political involvement by Cubans in the United States. At various moments in Cuban history exiles have played an important role in their homeland's political development and struggled to change the government on the island. One instance was during the wars of independence, when José Martí, the foremost father of Cuban independence, and others conspired in the

FIGURE 6.1 *Statue of José Martí at J.F.Kennedy Boulevard in West New York, New Jersey* (Ana Meseguer)

United States to liberate Cuba from Spain. Another moment was during the surge of revolutionary activity during the 1930s in Cuba. Later, anti-Batista activities were carried out in Cuban communities in the United States in the 1950s, organized mainly by July 26th Revolutionary Movement cells, the largest anti-Batista revolutionary force, and by various other groups.

Fidel Castro himself procured assistance for his movement when he visited New York while living as an exile in Mexico after being released from a Cuban prison in 1955. Several of my older interviewees told me of the visits that Castro had paid to Union City Cubans. He "used to come to a bodega on 26th Street and Bergenline Avenue and many of us met him there. This was when we supported his revolution!" said a man in his late 70s.

The story of revolution in Cuba is also the story of opposition. By the end of 1959, attempts at overthrowing Castro's government had already begun. Many members of two groups that had fought with the rebels of the July 26th movement, the Segundo Frente del Escambray or the Second Escambray Front, and the Directorio Revolucionario Estudiantil or the Revolutionary Student Directorate, had turned against him. They believed that Castro had betrayed the revolution's original objectives: to attain socioeconomic reforms, social justice, national sovereignty, and political stability, among other goals. The source of discomfort among many dissenters was what they saw as the increasing influence that communists were having in the government. More groups joined in the struggle: the MRR, Movimiento de Recuperación Revolucionaria or Movement of Revolutionary Recovery, and the MRP, Movimiento Revolucionario del Pueblo or People's Revolutionary Movement. Their goal was to destabilize the Cuban economy and, to that end, they engaged in acts of sabotage on the island, especially within the first couple of years after Castro's victory. In Havana, bombs exploded in department stores and movie theaters. The new rebels also fought in the mountains of El Escambray in Villa Clara province.

Other dissidents came into exile and immediately engaged in insurgent activities. They supported the rebels in Cuba clandestinely, smuggling armaments and other supplies by boat. The U.S. government was interested in getting rid of Castro too and, as Cuba-U.S. relations deteriorated in the period 1959–1960 and Cuba aligned itself with the Soviet Union, the Eisenhower administration officially approved a CIA plan to recruit an army of exiles to invade the island.

In 1960, the CIA began to train an invasion force of 1,500 called the Brigada 2506. This force trained in secret in Panamá, Guatemala, and Nicaragua. In Miami, the CIA chose a government in exile to replace Castro. After taking office in January, 1961, President John F. Kennedy continued Eisenhower's plan to invade the island, and his main goal was to create a provisional government that Cubans on the island would support. In March, 1961, the Cuban Revolutionary Council (CRC) was formed. The CRC represented a distinct shift to the left among Cuban exiles. The organization included many people who had fought against Batista, supported the Revolution in its initial stages, and felt betrayed by the course of events in the revolutionary process. The rationale for U.S. support of the CRC was the expectation that this organization would draw more support among Cubans on the island.

On April 17, 1961, more than two years after the rebels had entered Havana, the force of exiles landed at the Bay of Pigs. They were defeated by the Cuban military within a couple of days at Playa Girón and had to surrender.[2] Much has been said about why the invasion failed. One of the reasons given is that the invasion was given absolute priority and that the anti-Castro forces inside Cuba were virtually ignored. In Cuba, "no one would risk his life for an invasion that could not succeed because it was too small, or for an invasion that could succeed because it had the full backing of the United States—and the latter was the first impression."[3]

After the Bay of Pigs fiasco, the struggle against Fidel Castro continued. The CRC was kept on the U.S. government's payroll, and the Department of Defense enacted a program to enlist able-bodied Cuban refugee males in the U.S. armed forces for the day when they might be needed.[4] In 1961, the U.S. government designed Operation Mongoose, a program created to instigate open revolt in Cuba. Exiles participated in phases of this program, which included gathering intelligence as well as conducting raids and acts of sabotage in Cuba. But the CIA had to cancel the program in the wake of the Cuban missile crisis. At the height of the crisis, and to avert world annihilation, an agreement was reached between U.S. President John F. Kennedy and Soviet Premier Nikita Krushchev that the Soviets would take the nuclear missiles out of Cuba in exchange for a pact of American non-intervention in the island. After this, the Kennedy administration began to focus on provoking internal revolt in Cuba rather than an invasion. The U.S. government still wanted Castro's elimination, but Cuban exile groups were frustrated. Many blamed the American government for the Bay of Pigs fiasco. Some of them had wanted a full U.S. intervention after that failure and, since that did not happen, they felt betrayed. Equally significant was what the exiles saw as the American betrayal during the missile crisis, as they felt Kennedy had made a pact with the Soviets at the expense of Cuban freedom. Since then, many Cuban exiles see Kennedy and the Democrats as enemies of their cause. These events helped turn increasing numbers of Cuban exiles into loyal Republicans.

The exiles were still committed to freeing Cuba of Castro's communism and, in response, more organizations emerged. The United States continued to support some groups, especially the CRC, the most prominent among them. However, most exile groups began to act independently. Many of them conducted raids, established their own intelligence networks, and infiltrated their own guerrillas into Cuba.[5] Since these paramilitary operations violated U.S. neutrality laws, groups used other countries, such as the Bahamas, as bases for their operations and to avoid penalties. United States government agencies, in turn, approved some actions and not others, sending mixed signals to the exiles. Some believe that, ever since those early years, inconsistency toward Cuban exile groups has become the chief characteristic of all U.S. administrations.[6]

Cuba's Political Culture

Cuba's closeness to the United States has long been a factor in Cubans' political positions. It is not only proximity; it is the power that the United States has exerted on Cuba that has helped shape the internal politics of the country. From 1902 until its abrogation in 1933, Cuba-U.S. relations were mediated by the Platt Amendment, a clause in the Cuban constitution that allowed the latter to intervene in the former's affairs. This was a major cause of the deep ambivalence that many Cubans felt toward the United States. Some Cubans defined themselves for and others against the United States.

Social class membership was a good indicator of a Cuban's political leanings. At the time of the establishment of the republic at the turn of the twentieth century there was no economically dominant social class. What remained of the old planter class was overshadowed by foreign capitalists. As historian Louis Pérez says, "The interests of the surviving creole bourgeoisie became intimately identified with United States interests."[7] Postwar prosperity in the 1920s stimulated economic development and shaped a more complex social order. A new Cuban entrepreneurial class emerged and a nascent working-class began to mobilize. The first attempts at reform in this period were felt in different venues, especially on the university campus. Students demanded the dismissal of incompetent faculty, free higher education, and autonomy for the university.[8] These were years of rising nationalism in Cuba, much of which "derived directly from an abiding abhorrence of the Platt Amendment—a sentiment that translated quickly into revilement of the political elites and a revulsion for their U.S. backers, setting in sharp relief the feebleness with which the officeholders defended national sovereignty."[9]

Violence has been part of Cuba's political history since the nineteenth century wars of independence. Since the 1920s, and especially after the revolution of 1933 that overthrew Gerardo Machado's government, extremism became rooted in Cuban politics.[10] The Constitution of 1940, suppressed by the Batista coup of March 10, 1952, embodied a strongly democratic commitment to social justice, but the corruption of most republican governments before Batista impeded its full enactment.

The great majority of Cubans supported the Revolution of 1959. Their hopes for national sovereignty and social justice seemed about to be realized this time. The Constitution of 1940 "was the platform of the organized opposition to Batista, which meant a commitment to democracy, good government, and profound socioeconomic reforms."[11] But the polarization that had always characterized Cuban politics soon became evident. The struggle between reformist and radical sectors began shortly after the revolutionary victory, and this time, the nation suffered the greatest polarization in its history. The main point of contention for the opposition was the radicalization of the Revolution and what the reformists considered to be its totalitarian and procommunist tendencies. Thus many anti-Castro exiles were liberals in Cuba and in many cases fought alongside Castro and the rebels, which perhaps explains why some of their views continue to be liberal or progressive.

Some exiles have critically admitted their reliance on the United States to topple Castro. Rafael Quintero of the Brigada 2506 said in relation to the Bay of Pigs invasion:

> Cubans thought of the Americans in what I call the "John Wayne syndrome." What we thought about the Americans was what we have seen as little kids in the movies of John Wayne. We thought the Americans worked the way John Wayne worked in his movies. Of course, this was naïve, but this was the way most of us felt. I mean, the Americans hated communism, and, like John Wayne, they never lost—ever. That was important. In the beginning, defeat was never in our minds. And that worked against us. There was this attitude of, why do anything? The Americans will take care of it.[12]

Reliance on the United States has been one side of the picture. Contempt for it is another side. Some of my interviewees in Union City clearly conveyed their discontent at the changes in U.S. attitudes toward Cuban anti-Castro groups, from open support to complete neglect. For this reason, many anti-Castro Cubans expressed anti-American sentiments as well. It seems that, up until today, the presence and actions of the United States are still central to Cuban political culture, in Cuba and among Cubans in the United States.

Cuban Politics in Union City

In the wake of the Bay of Pigs failure, new organizations emerged, not only in Miami, but also wherever Cuban communities were located. Union City was no exception. Some of these organizations were the northern chapters of national groups like Alpha 66. Others, like Abdala and the extremely violent group Omega 7, originated in New Jersey.[13] There were other groups, such as CID (Cuba Independiente y Democrática), or Independent and Democratic Cuba, 30 de Noviembre, or November 30th, and Movimiento Nacionalista Cubano, or Cuban Nationalist Movement. Other groups with social or civic agendas cooperated with political groups. Examples are the Asociaciones de Presos Políticos, or Association of Political Prisoners, El Club Amigos e Hijos de Fomento, or Friends and Sons of Fomento Club, and the Asociación de Mujeres Cubano-Americanas, or the Association of Cuban American Women.

Some members of the political groups saw themselves as belonging to paramilitary and propaganda groups. Paramilitary groups were very active in New Jersey, where they got the support of many Cuban businessmen and professionals. A group of businessmen told me:

> We created the Movimiento Nacionalista Cubano, a secret organization that served as an umbrella for other organizations such as Alpha 66 and others. We would provide them with money when they needed it.[14]

As happened in Miami, politics and extortion sometimes went hand in hand. An interviewee told me that, in order to finance their activities, "many groups forced community members to give them money and to comply with the organizations' demands." A Union City political activist confided: "We used to close Bergenline Avenue when we wanted to hold a demonstration. Storekeepers knew that they'd better cooperate with us."[15] Also, many community leaders saw the members of these organizations as "patriots," even when they engaged in extreme violence. The Movimiento Nacionalista Cubano collected money clandestinely and established a network that would assign "taxes" to all segments of the community who were able to contribute, and then divide the money between the various groups they supported.

The late 1970s saw a period of reduced tension in U.S.-Cuba relations. During the Carter administration, the two countries established Cuban and American interests sections that allowed for a basic diplomatic relationship. A maritime agreement between the two countries was signed. Among other things, many scholars, artists, and scientists were able to travel to and from Cuba. At the end of the decade, a meeting between representatives of the Cuban government and the Cuban community in the United States, *El Diálogo,* (the Dialogue), took place (see Chapter 5). The purpose of the meeting was to negotiate the release of political prisoners and family visits. Around the same time, Cuban American youth organizations supportive of the Revolution, such as Areíto and the Antonio Maceo Brigade, visited Cuba. These organizations were made up of young Cubans who had been influenced by the social and political movements of the 1960s in the United States. They found it contradictory to reject Cuba's revolutionary program in light of their general worldview. Mostly, they encountered conflicts in going against their parents' anti-communist ideology.

Radical Anti-Castro Organizations

As a result of the late 1970s rapprochement, many exile groups grew frustrated, even desperate, about what they saw as further betrayal by the U.S. government, as well as by certain sectors in the Cuban community. Membership in anti-Castro groups very often overlapped, but it is hard to know with certainty who was active in more than one group. Some groups used extreme violence as tactics; others were not as violent; Among the violent groups were El Condor, Coordinación de Organizaciones Revolucionarias Unidas (CORU), or Coordination of United Revolutionary Organizations, Poder Cubano, or Cuban Power, Movimiento Nacionalista

Cubano or Cuban Nationalist Movement (CNM), and the New Jersey-based Omega 7. Some of these organizations bombed Cuban embassies and consulates around the world, murdered Cuban diplomats, and harassed and sometimes killed individuals who they claimed were supportive of the Cuban government.

Omega 7 derived its name from the fact that there were seven original members from different anti-Castro Cuban factions. The group was always small, believed to have always had fewer than twenty members, and many think that is why it was so successful. It is believed that the group was condoned and supported by the CNM, whose resources were considerably larger and which was accused of participating in the car-bomb assassination of the former Chilean Ambassador, Orlando Letelier. The CNM was very active in northern New Jersey and had some sympathizers in the Cuban community in Union City. One of my women interviewees, showing her positive opinions about the organization, said: "The CNM was the most important anti-Castro group here. Alpha 66 was 'soft' compared with CNM. The problem is that some of its leaders, Alvin Ross, Juan Pulido, and Guillermo Novo, were convicted of terrorism and the organization dissolved."[16] Armando Santana, the CNM's leader was also arrested.[17]

New York and New Jersey were the main areas of operation for Omega 7. The majority of its attacks were bombings, shootings, and assassinations. The terrorist attacks were well planned and executed. I was told by many of my interviewees that a number of the Omega 7 members were veterans of the Bay of Pigs invasion who had been trained in demolition, intelligence, and commando techniques. A U.S. government report indicated that their expertise, combined with the financial resources available to them through some sectors of the exile Cuban community, gave Omega 7 an almost unlimited potential for terrorist activity.[18] In addition to bombings, it was known to be responsible for two murders. On November 25, 1979, the group gunned down Eulalio Negrín in front of his son in Union City. Negrín had participated in the Dialogue meeting called by the Cuban government a few months before. On September 11, 1980, on the sixth anniversary of the founding of Omega 7, a Cuban diplomat, Félix García Rodríguez, was shot and killed in New York with the same weapon used to kill Negrín, a MAC 10 machine gun.[19]

In 1983, Eduardo Arocena, the founder of Omega 7, was arrested and prosecuted on forty-two counts of violating Federal statutes on conspiracy, explosives, firearms, and destruction of foreign government property. According to the FBI, there have been no Omega 7 attacks since that year.[20] Several Omega 7 members were prosecuted during 1984 for refusing to testify before a Federal grand jury. In 1986, three of the group's members pled guilty to conspiracy to destroy the property of a foreign government. Following his grand jury appearance, Arocena was urged by the FBI to cooperate with the government. At first he was reluctant, but he finally admitted to being the leader of the organization and provided solid information about the numerous bombings and murders it had committed. Arocena provided details about plans to assassinate Raúl Roa-Kouri, Cuban ambassador to the United Nations, and Ramón Sánchez Parodi, Chief, Cuban Interest Section in Washington, D.C. While funding for Omega 7 activities came, in large part, from some Cuban exile business owners in the Union City area, it also came, according to FBI investigations, from involvement with narcotics traffickers.[21]

Perhaps the most notorious of the extremely violent anti-Castro militants are Orlando Bosch Avila and Luis Posada Carriles. In 1968, Bosch was convicted of machine-gunning a Polish cargo ship in Miami harbor. Along with Posada Carriles, he is believed to have spearheaded the bombing of a Cuban airliner in 1976, killing all 73 people on board. Bosch obtained a presidential pardon from the first president Bush in 1990 and now lives in Miami. Posada Carriles, however, escaped to Venezuela, where he became a citizen. In 1985, while being tried in Venezuela for his role in the Cubana bombing, he escaped from prison and went straight to work with paramilitary forces in El Salvador.[22] Like many other Cuban exiles, Posada Carriles had been trained by the CIA to participate in attempts on Castro's life. In July, 1998, he gave an interview to *The New York Times* revealing some secrets. One of the most important of these was that his operations were financed by the Cuban American National Foundation (CANF), a powerful Cuban exile lobbying group.[23] Since then, however, both Posada Carriles and the Foundation have denied that the CANF had any role in financing his activities. According to *The New York Times* article, in a message sent to his Central American collaborators, Posada Carriles discusses payment for his activities. The money "would be sent through Western Union from New Jersey."[24] In the *Times* interview, Posada Carriles asked the reporters whether the men in Union City (whose names were listed in the message) could get in trouble for this.[25]

In March, 2005, Posada Carriles clandestinely arrived in the United States from Mexico. His goal was to obtain political asylum here, although the present Venezuelan government and the Cuban government both want him extradited to Venezuela. After arriving in the United States, Posada Carriles was taken to a luxury condominium on Brickell Avenue in Miami where he hid for a couple of months. He told two reporters from *El Nuevo Herald*, "At first, I used to be more careful, and I would hide more. Now I go out; people recognize me, in supermarkets, at doctors' offices, especially the older people. I don't think this government is really looking for me" (Translation mine).[26]

Posada Carriles was finally arrested in Miami in May of 2005. Later, on January 11, 2007, he and two supporters were indicted in Texas by a grand jury that accused Posada of lying about how he entered the country in 2005. He was subsequently set free on bail and returned to Miami.[27] For the United States, the presence of Posada Carriles presents a dilemma. At the same time that the country is engaged in a "war against terror," many do not understand how the U.S. government could think of granting political asylum to a "terrorist." From Posada's point of view, however, who sees himself as a "freedom fighter" no matter the methods employed, there is a great sense of betrayal by the United States. The same country that trained him to conduct these operations is now treating him as a criminal. It is important to note, however, that he is not considered a hero by many Cubans in Union City. Many of my interviewees confided that he is an embarrassment to the community. Many *periodiquitos* such as *Avance,* have written negative pieces about him and his activities.

Alpha 66

Alpha 66 is very active in Union City and other New Jersey localities. It is perhaps one of the better-known anti-Castro military organizations in the United States. In the past, it conducted paramilitary operations against the Cuban government and it appears that it did not resort to extreme violence on American soil. At different times in the early 1960s, numerous raids were carried out, Cuban ships were destroyed, and Russian ships were assaulted[28] (interview with Silverio Rodríguez, November 14, 1999).

I interviewed Silverio Rodríguez, who, at the time of the interview was the general coordinator of Alpha 66 in the northern U.S. region with its headquarters in Union City. He was very affable and seemed pleased to be cooperating with my study. Silverio was twenty years old when he came from Cuba in 1954. He described the history of Alpha 66 to me:

> At first Alpha was formed by members of El Segundo Frente Nacional del Escambray, which fought against Batista in the 1950s. El Frente was organized in the Escambray Mountains, in Las Villas Province, by comandante Eloy Gutiérrez Menoyo and others. After 1959, as many of the former fighters became disenchanted with the Revolution, they went back to fight in El Escambray again. Gradually, many of these fighters in El Escambray were eliminated by Castro, and many of the survivors escaped to the United States in early 1961. But those in Miami worked in coordination with those in Cuba who had escaped detection, and finally they reestablished El Frente inside Cuba. But Castro continued to eliminate El Frente fighters, and those in the United States were arrested many times by U.S. authorities because their actions violated the U.S.-Russian agreements. Finally, six months after returning from Girón [Bay of Pigs], we were sent to New York from Texas, where we had been sent after the Bay of Pigs invasion. There were some meetings in New York, and Menoyo announced a pact between El Frente and Alpha 66. Alpha was formally formed in Puerto Rico around the end of 1961. That's when I became most active. Later on, the group branched out to other parts of the United States. Alpha conducted many raids and commando operations in and near Cuba. Eloy disembarked in Punta Coleta, in Oriente province, and was arrested by the Cuban government. (Interviewed on November 14, 1999)

When I asked Rodríguez how the organization saw itself now, he replied:

> Alpha 66 is a revolutionary organization and it continues to strive for the downfall of the Castro regime. It is an organization oriented to action and to politics. We do accept criticism.

> This is what we expect to happen in Cuba after the country is liberated!

Rodríguez showed his frustration with the rapprochement period between Cuba and the United States. He feels resentment against Eloy Gutiérrez Menoyo, who was freed by the Cuban government following the Diálogo meetings after he had served many years in prison, and then took a conciliatory position. Gutiérrez Menoyo founded the pro-dialogue organization Cambio Cubano, or Cuban Change, in 1989, and subsequently returned to Cuba to promote his program of reconciliation there. On the other hand, Rodríguez also feels bitter about the U.S. government. Although Alpha 66 still maintains contacts with the State Department and the CIA, they feel they have been harassed and labeled as "terrorists" by these authorities.

Like many members of anti-Castro organizations in Union City, Miami, and elsewhere, Rodríguez once belonged to Castro's July 26th movement. His father was also heavily involved in anti-Batista activities, and was even a delegate for the July 26th movement. Rodríguez and his father met Castro and other revolutionary leaders when they visited New York. After the Revolution was victorious in 1959, Rodríguez's father returned to Cuba, but soon after that he became disillusioned with the direction the revolutionary government was taking, and he came back to the United States.[29]

A Shift in Anti-Castro Organizations: The Cuban American National Foundation

The 1980s changed the landscape of Cuban exile politics. Ronald Reagan's election in 1980 pleased the hardliners in the Cuban community at the same time that the Mariel boatlift crushed the hopes of those seeking reconciliation between Cuba and Cubans in the United States. Reagan's views were close to those of the exiles, who felt again that there could be a possibility for Castro regime's overthrow.[30] Cubans started becoming American citizens in record numbers and voted overwhelmingly for Republican party candidates. There was an exception to this trend. Cubans voted for Bill Clinton in 1996 after he signed the Helms-Burton

Act into law, a piece of legislation that tightened the embargo on Cuba. This conservative climate facilitated the emergence of what was to become the most influential Cuban American organization in the United States: the Cuban American National Foundation (CANF), founded in 1981 by a group of wealthy Cuban businessmen, including some members of the Brigada 2506. The CANF was set up as "a nonprofit organization whose principal goal was to help the Reagan administration formulate a 'realistic' foreign policy toward Cuba."[31] By "realistic" the CANF meant adopting new methods to hasten Castro's demise. For example, the administration funded Radio Martí, a project to transmit news to Cuba by radio. Powerful lobbying would take the place of paramilitary activities and violence. Both Republican and Democratic administrations have acknowledged the CANF and followed their suggestions carefully. The organization's first leader was the late Jorge Más Canosa, a charismatic man with a great pull in the Cuban community. The CANF is considered a powerful lobbying group, comparable nationally to influential Jewish lobbying groups from which it sought advice.

After Jorge Más Canosa died in November of 1997, his son, Jorge Más Santos, became the chairman of the CANF. Up until then, Más Santos, like many of his generation, had not been involved in anti-Castro politics. But his father's death inspired him to join the cause and to take charge of this powerful Cuban exile organization. Más Santos' leadership, however, along with the advent of younger cohorts joining the CANF in the mid 1990s, has created a deep rift in the Foundation. Many in the old guard believe that "he has softened the Foundation's hard line against the Cuban government."[32] But Más Santos makes no apologies for refusing to be his father's echo, and says the CANF must "look past Castro," to the future.[33] One source of conflict was when Más Santos supported having Miami host the Latin Grammy Awards in 2001 against criticism that pro-Castro Cuban artists would attend. He claimed that freedom of speech rights was more important than opposing the Awards. The Foundation would never have taken that position in the past. Also, the CANF bought a building in Washington, DC, to carry its lobbying mission closer to the government. That was seen by many as taking the power away from Miami. Another source of conflict is the Foundation's continued contact with Democratic leaders, especially after the Elián González saga under the Clinton administration. The conflict around Elián González showed the fissure evolving in the Cuban community. While the part of the community that supported the boy staying in the United States stood in contempt of U.S. laws and public opinion, other Cuban organizations, including the new sectors of the CANF, saw the need for negotiation and dialogue between the United States, Cuba, and the Cuban community in the United States. But Más believes that the real problem is that the old group in the CANF has a hard time passing the torch to the new generation. He thinks that "Fidel Castro's worst nightmare is that there is a younger generation here that has not forgotten Cuba, that will make sure to rebuild Cuba as a model for the world of freedom and democracy."[34]

The founders of the CANF in the early 1980s in Union City were Rodolfo Pardo and Aleida Durán. Durán was a well-known Cuban journalist with *The Hudson Dispatch*, a paper that has ceased circulation since. She talked about the changes the CANF had brought about:

> That violence of the 1960s and 1970s led to nothing productive; it had to change. The Fundación changed that. Lobbying is the answer. Más Canosa was an extremely brilliant man. He changed all that violent approach. Many of the old guys are very resentful against him because many still think that violence is the way. Más Canosa's son has other ideas, but that is fine. The new generation is different. For example, the whole debate about allowing the Grammy Awards to take place in Miami was a generational one, for the most part. Cubans over 60 did not want them in Miami, the younger Cubans did! I understand and support the approaches of the new generation. Change is inevitable. (Interviewed on June 19, 2001)

To my surprise, Durán also expressed her support for the Diálogo. She admitted that the meeting had been the best, peaceful way to free Cuban political prisoners. Since I had attended the Diálogo, I was often apprehensive when discussing political issues with my respondents. But Durán reiterated more than once that, under the same circumstances, she would have supported the meetings.

Pardo and Durán asked Remberto Pérez to be the leader of the CANF in the Hudson County region. Pérez came to the United States in 1967 from Victoria de la Tunas in Oriente, Cuba, via Spain through a program directed by a priest, Father Camiñas, called Pedro sin Pán or Peter Without Bread. This name is a play on words that refers to the lack of resources of this program when compared with the Peter Pan program for Cuban children in the United States (see Chapters 1 and 5). Pérez owns three insurance agencies and is an investor in a Hispanic bank that also sells insurance. Now in his 50s, he remembers how, as a younger man, he participated in anti-Castro politics. He was a member of CID. Although Pérez genuinely respects the older fighters in the anti-Castro organizations, he noted that there are tensions with many of them who feel isolated and left out. But this was inevitable, according to Pérez, because what the Foundation did was "to take the struggle out of the basements of Union City and Hialeah, Florida, into the public sphere" (interviewed on August 9, 2005).

I asked Pérez about his position on the recent divisions within the Foundation. "I tend to side with the old faction. However, I don't think that to promote and to dwell on that division is good at all. I think the late Más Canosa was one of the most brilliant, committed leaders in exile, but I don't think that Jorge Más Santos has done anything wrong. He didn't do anything to provoke that division. I think that we should strive to move from the *comparsa del 20 de Mayo* (the May 20th parade) to be a more efficient type of organization (Ibid.)[35]

During the 1980s, Cubans and Cuban Americans became more involved in local and national politics. The conservative ideology of the Reagan years served to integrate exile politics with Cuban registration and voting in the United States. Participation in the U.S. political system was actually an extension of exile concerns.[36] By the 1990s, Cubans and Cuban Americans were mayors of Miami, Hialeah, Sweetwater, West Miami, and Hialeah Gardens in Florida. The same was true of Union City and West New York. At present, there are three Cuban Representatives from Florida: Lincoln Díaz Balart, Mario Díaz Balart, and Ileana Ros-Lehtinen. From Hudson County, New Jersey, Cuban American Robert Menendez was elected to the U. S. Senate in November, 2006. Also, Albio Sires, former mayor of West New York became a Congressman in November, 2006. As Grenier and Pérez state, "Nowhere else in America, not even in American history, have first generation immigrants so quickly, or so thoroughly, appropriated political power."[37]

However, Remberto Pérez thinks that participation in local politics reduces the commitment to the Cuban cause. In many cases, he said,

Cuban politicians have to compromise, and their local aspirations may clash with the struggle to free Cuba. For example, Pérez does not think that party politics should interfere with Cuba work. He is a Democrat himself, perhaps because he has always lived in a heavily Democratic district. He regrets what happened when Más Canosa visited Union City in late October of 1993, during the Democratic administration of Gov. James Florio. Local Cuban Republicans protested in front of the hall where Más Canosa was to speak, with banners denouncing what they saw as the CANF's meddling with local and state concerns. Pérez thinks that the protest was manipulated by Cuban Republican leaders to advance their agenda. Pérez commented sadly, "That demonstration only made us look weak as a people."[38]

Cubans, Cuban Americans, and Hudson County Politics

New Jersey politics is often the subject of jokes and disparaging remarks. Typical among the latter is that New Jersey is ruled by political bosses and warlords of both political parties. The state is beset by scandals. In the summer of 2004, Governor James McGreevey surprised the public with his resignation because of his sexual preference. But there have been many other scandals. In 1954, "Harold Hoffman, who was governor between 1935 and 1938, admitted in a letter opened after he died that he had stolen $300,000 over the course of his career in public service. Senator Harrison A. Williams Jr. (1959–1982) was charged in the 1981 Abscam sting, in which FBI agents posed as Arab sheiks and offered bribes to members of Congress. Williams was convicted on nine counts and sentenced to three years in prison."[39]

Even two of the most previously unscathed Democratic New Jersey politicians in the 1990s and 2000s, Governor Jon Corzine and Senator Robert Menendez, have recently been the subjects of criticism. In 2002, then Senator Corzine gave a $470,000 mortgage to the president of a union that represents thousands of New Jersey state employees. He forgave the debt two years later to the union president, Carla Katz, who was Mr. Corzine's girlfriend at the time the loan was provided. According to Mr. Corzine, the loan was not illegal, and he claims that he "took care of the required gift tax on the money he ended up giving to Ms. Katz."[40] Since then, Governor Corzine has been cleared of any wrongdoing. Senator Robert Menendez has been criticized by some for using hardball tactics typical of party bosses. Gerson Borrero, former editor-in-chief of *El Diario La Prensa,* said that his weekday radio program had been taken off the air because he "had refused the requests of station managers to stop criticizing Nidia Velázquez, José Serrano, and Robert Menendez."[41]

Hudson County is considered one of the toughest political counties in the state. Similar to Chicago, where Mayor Richard M. Daley has run powerful Democratic political machinery, Hudson County has been generally governed by Democratic politicians with similar practices, though on a much smaller scale. Unions, especially the Teamsters, have controlled the labor movement, and organized crime has often been a protagonist in local politics. Frank Hague, mayor of Jersey City from 1917 to 1947, was perhaps the most powerful party boss. His administration was marked by a great deal of corruption, although he invested a lot in social services. One example is the construction of Jersey City Medical Center. Hague named the Maternity Hospital after his mother, Margaret Hague, but he also purchased privately millions of dollars in property, though his salary was only $8,000 a year. An investigation forced him to step down in 1947.[42]

William Musto served three terms as mayor of Union City. He was in city government for twenty-one years as a state legislator and as mayor of Union City.[43] A lifelong resident of Union City, he stepped into public life in 1946 when he was elected to the state assembly with the backing of Jersey City mayor Frank Hague. After three years in the assembly working alongside Hague, Musto allied himself with the John V. Kenny victory ticket and by 1953 became the Democratic minority leader of the state assembly.[44] In 1965, then Assemblyman Musto was elected to the State Senate. However, in 1970 he lost the city election to reform candidate William Meehan and did not return to the mayoral seat until 1974, where he remained until the 1982 election.[45] Meehan's political platform was based in large part on an anti-Cuban stance. He did not want any more Cubans to come to Union City. When Musto came back as mayor in 1974, Cubans again enjoyed a welcome in the community. Musto was called "father of the state lottery" because of his central role in getting it legalized. Musto's constituents supported him for that and for his populist appeal. He was a friend of ordinary people and made social services a priority. He did a lot for the Cuban community in Union City. On the other hand, however, he was on the wrong side of the law. In May, 1982, he was sentenced to prison following a bribery conviction for school construction kickbacks. His following was so extraordinary that he was reelected as mayor a day later. A Superior Court judge ruled that he had to step down, however, and Musto served three years in prison.[46] He died on February 27, 2007.

In the 1970s, a federal investigation was aimed at corruption within county machineries of both parties. The senior U.S. senator from the President's political party had the prerogative to appoint the federal prosecutor. The president was Richard Nixon at the time, and the prerogative belonged to Senator Clifford Case, a liberal Republican with few debts to local Republican organizations. It has been said that the senator's appointees in New Jersey were responsible for "virtually all of the prosecutions of political figures here. Almost singlehandedly they have destroyed the old Hudson County Democratic machine, and without concern for partisan interests, have at least wounded just about every other party boss in the state."[47] Although the investigations were presumably nonpartisan, they had the effect of severely damaging the Democratic machine in particular.

Political Succession

In the times of Frank Hague, the Irish dominated Hudson County. Then came the Italians. Ethnic political succession did not take place without upheaval. There was favoritism too. Often, a member of the dominant group would bring in persons from the next group in line. It was Musto, an Italian American, who brought the Cubans into Union City politics. Two of the best known examples are Julia Valdivia and Robert Menendez.

Now retired, Valdivia was an icon of Cuban politics in Union City. She came to the United States in 1957. She had finished university in Cuba and, as she has said, "my mother knew what was coming," referring to the political turmoil that preceded the Revolution. They came to Union City as economic migrants, since there were more job opportunities there than in Cuba. At first, it was very difficult, Valdivia said. There were very few

Cuban families in Union City and they used to get together in the Liceo Cubano José Martí, a social club that was formed in the 1950s (see Chapter 3). Valdivia began to work at the New York Telephone Company as an accountant. She was always a very active member of the Democratic Party. In 1970, she campaigned for Musto when he ran for mayor of Union City. He lost that year, but in 1974 he won, and she started to work with him. Valdivia became known as *La Alcaldesa* (The Mayoress), and people knew the influence she had earned, and the power she held:

> I owe Musto a great deal, not only because he was good to me and my family, but he was great to Cubans. He knew that Cuban immigrants were good people who had come here to work and get ahead. But many people discriminated against Cubans and other Hispanics. I worked for four mayors, and during all that time, I labored to end racial discrimination, especially in public offices. (Interviewed on September 22, 2003)

Robert Menendez was born in New York City of Cuban parents. When he was still a child the family moved to Hoboken, New Jersey, where they lived for a while, and then moved to Union City. When I interviewed him, he remembered his childhood:

> I went to elementary and high school in Union City. At first, the family spoke Spanish at home, but eventually we all switched to English. I have two siblings. My mother was a seamstress and my father a carpenter. I remember the tenement house where we used to live. And I remember growing up in Union City in the 1960s when the town was full of Cubans! (Interviewed on August 22, 2001)

Robert Menendez began his political career "fighting successfully to change an appointed school board to an elected school board in Union City. This turned around the city's schools, increasing graduation rates, attendance, and student performance."[48] He told me, "the reason I became interested in politics is because I was not happy with the education I received. I wanted to improve the system" (interviewed on August 22, 2001). As Raymond Hernandez from *The New York Times* says: "Menendez became the first Hispanic elected mayor of Union City. He was also the first Hispanic to serve in the State Assembly."[49] In 1993, he became New Jersey's first Hispanic Congressman. In November, 2006, Menendez was elected U.S. Senator, after serving for a few months as an appointed senator when Governor Corzine left his position. I asked Menendez whether it was difficult to deal with his diverse constituency. After all, Cubans have left in great numbers:

> It is a challenge. Cubans say that I don't pay enough attention to Cuban issues. Other Hispanics say that I only deal with Cuban issues. Nobody realizes that I've given the same amount of time to all groups. Take Vieques, for example, or the case of Elián González. Proportionally, I devote the same time to all groups. General issues that affect everybody. Otherwise, you can't get elected! (Interviewed on August 22, 2001)

Cuban political figures in the Hudson County area are mainly Democrats, but there are some Republicans as well. Nivio Martínez, a pre-Castro immigrant, was the first chairman of the Republican Party in Union City. Some interviewees told me that Martínez's goal was to fight corruption and "Democratic hegemony in Hudson County." Octavio Alfonso was elected as Hudson County freeholder in a district where Hispanic voters were numerically insignificant. He did not speak English fluently and had another freeholder, Nidia Dávila Colón, a Puerto Rican Democrat, translate for him at meetings. Alfonso had been a Democrat, but in the 1980s, coinciding with the Reagan era, he changed party affiliation. According to many interviewees, he did much to reorganize the Republican Party in the area. It was around this time that a number of other Cuban Democrats switched to being Republicans. Some Cubans were commissioners and some were running for the state legislature. For example, Cuban-born José Obdulio Arango was the first Hispanic Republican elected to the legislature by a Hispanic constituency. But there was a lot of in-fighting among Republicans due to generational differences, and that hurt their aspirations to attain power.

No matter what the Reagan rhetoric was, however, the Democrats continued to hold sway in Union City. Robert Menendez was elected as Commissioner in the 1980s. Manny Díaz, whom Musto had appointed as

Spanish liaison to his administration, had been friends with Menendez since the early Musto days. In the Republican Party there were defections too. Albio Sires, mayor of the neighboring town of West New York, first Hispanic speaker of the New Jersey Assembly from 2002–2005, and elected Congressman in 2006, was a Republican who switched to the Democratic Party. He talked about his party affiliation change:

> I was a Republican and switched parties because the Republicans were getting to be too conservative. I'm not like that. The romance of Cubans with the Republican party has to do with Kennedy and the Bay of Pigs. (Interviewed on August 21, 2001)

Sires was promoted by Governor McGreevey to be the Speaker of the Assembly. According to Representative Frank Guarini, a veteran Hudson County Democrat, "Sires just happened to be at the right place at the right time when the sun shone."[50] It should be noted that Sires had once tried to unseat Mr. Guarini.

Local Cubans have inherited the complicated and rugged terrain of Hudson County politics. For example, while Sires has introduced much needed reforms in housing, education, and other areas in West New York, many accuse him of rampant corruption. A federal investigation, which became public in 1998, resulted in convictions of, or guilty pleas from, thirty people, including fourteen police officers, among them the former chief, Alexander V. Oriente.[51] Sires said that he had no knowledge of any illegal activity and proceeded to ask local prosecutors to investigate the police. Chief Oriente, who pleaded guilty to racketeering charges and became the government's star witness, "testified during cross-examination by lawyers for other defendants that a portion of the bribes he received went to the mayor. . . . Mr. Sires, who did not testify at the trial, said Mr. Oriente's testimony was false and that he only wanted revenge because Mr. Sires had refused the former chief's demand for $315,000 in unused sick pay and vacation time when he resigned in 1997 before his indictment."[52]

In Union City, Cuban American mayor, Raúl (Rudy) García, resigned in 2001 under fire for his economic decisions and political ambitions. He was accused of ignoring the city's financial realities by granting raises to municipal employees and a tax cut to residents, which had contributed to a $12-million deficit—a gap that García contended was only $5 million.[53] García also found himself at odds with Representative Robert Menendez, who had been his mentor. Menendez was instrumental in defeating García.[54]

Cuban Political Culture in Union City, 1900s–2000s

Is there a unified Cuban political culture in Union City? Is the situation in Cuba at the center of the political discourse as it is in Miami? When I asked Remberto Pérez from the CANF if the anti-Castro groups still existed, he answered in the affirmative, but he also said that they were weak. Their members are old, many had died, and others had gone to prison. The CANF is still active in the area. Perhaps Pérez' concerns about Cuban ideals being compromised when people become involved in local politics are justified. In Miami, a Cuban local politician still has to address issues related to Cuba to be elected. The ethnic identity of Cubans is inextricably related to their condition as political exiles. In Union City, however, particularly among the younger generation of Cubans, candidates have to respond to a much more diverse population or they will not get elected. Their ethnicity is mediated through the complexities of changing demographics in a huge cosmopolitan area.[55]

Sires, who became interested in politics when attending anti-Castro meetings with his grandfather when he was a child, now says that the old guys are tired, although "they are still active, they write in the periodiquitos and can still cause an uproar if they don't like something you say or do. If you don't agree with them, they accuse you of being a communist. I respect them, but you have to move on and try other methods" (interviewed on August 21, 2001). When I asked Robert Menendez if there were two streams of Cuban politics—the old, anti-Castro groups and the younger Cubans involved in local and national politics—he said that in some areas there is a convergence between the old and the new. For example "my own position regarding U.S.- Cuba foreign policy is consistent with what the old organizations believe. But the younger generation is more focused on local politics. They have to get their job done locally. Their center of attention is not Cuba" (interviewed on August 22, 2001). Menendez himself often joins his Cuban Republican congressional colleagues from Florida in making pronouncements against the Cuban government. Nevertheless, his real focus is on his Democratic agenda.

Cubans in Union City overwhelmingly vote Democratic for local candidates. I asked Menendez why, and he replied:

> You vote for your "friend," and friends in Hudson County are mainly Democrat. If you need a *palanca,* or a favor, a Democrat is the one that will give it to you. There is ethnic loyalty too, and that is what happens with me. Also, Cubans in this area are less conservative than people think. Locally, they are very interested in supporting the "right side" of issues. Many are old and in need of social services. Social security is an example. They need a candidate who fights for that. The Presidential vote is different. Cubans are traumatized by what they see as Kennedy's betrayal and the Bay of Pigs. But party allegiance is slowly changing. Cubans voted for Clinton in great numbers in 1996 because he signed the Helms-Burton Bill. They vote for whoever they think is going to do something for Cuba. But the general perception is still that Republicans will do more. For example, Bush has followed the same policies toward Cuba as Clinton. He has not done anything different, but since it's "Big Brother Bush," Cubans justify it. I am getting a lot of flack in Miami for criticizing the "Bush/Cubans love affair." Is this patriotic or partisan, because Bush has not done anything different? (Interviewed on August 22, 2001)[56]

There are several reasons why Union City Cubans tend to be more liberal than those in Miami. Union City Cubans are predominantly working-class. They respond to working-class interests: job security and social services among others. Also, the community interacts with many other groups and, even during the times of Cuban concentration in the 1970s and 1980s, it was not an insulated enclave. Proximity to New York City facilitates exposure to a worldwide perspective. According to a 1995 poll, Cubans living in New Jersey were more likely to favor a dialogue with Castro's government than those living in Miami.[57] I remember that, during the Elián González saga, many of my respondents would reveal, very discretely, their opinion that the boy belonged with his father. This is not to minimize the passions aroused by this case, when perhaps a majority of Union City Cubans demonstrated in the streets, demanding that the boy stay in the United States. I asked Menendez about the difference between Union City and Miami:

> The difference between Union City and Miami, especially politically, is that, because of the concentration of Cubans in Miami there is a lot more pressure to conform. Spanish media is owned by Cubans. Here, although Cubans have influence, they don't control the media. In Union City there is less pressure to conform to the same views. Here, Cubans interact with many other groups. In Miami, even when there are so many other Latin Americans coming in, the Cuban pressure is too strong. (Ibid.)

Union City, Miami, and New Organizations

Part of Cuban political culture in the United States in recent years has involved the creation of organizations that support a dialogue between the Cuban government and Cubans in the United States. Their claim is that violence does not lead to problem solving. As noted earlier, the organization that was most openly supportive of the Cuban government was the Antonio Maceo Brigade, which consisted of a group of Cuban youth that, beginning in 1978, traveled to Cuba regularly to engage in manual labor and cultural exchanges. After the Dialogue meetings took place, other, more moderate organizations were formed. Examples are: Puentes Cubanos or Cuban Bridges, Cuban Committee for Democracy, Fundación Amistad or Friendship Foundation, Consenso Cubano or Cuban Consensus, and Cambio Cubano or Cuban Change led by Eloy Gutiérrez Menoyo. After the Elián González case, well-known members of the Miami Cuban community decided to use other tactics to deal with U.S-Cuba relations. Carlos Saladrigas and other wealthy Cuban business owners organized the Cuba Study Group, asserting that the time had come for exiles to act with more intelligence and finesse. Dialogue and reconciliation among all Cubans, including those on the island, was seen as the answer. In December, 2008, the Cuba Study Group cosponsored a survey done by the Institute for Public Opinion Research of Florida International University and the Brookings Institution. Surveys of this kind had been conducted by Florida International University in the past. The Cuba Study Group survey gauged changes in attitudes within the Cuban community in Florida about Cuba, national reconciliation, the embargo, and other issues. The responses showed, for example, that the majority of Cubans (55 %), no longer support the U.S. embargo against Cuba.[58] This percentage indicates that most Cubans favor a climate of distention between the two countries. It seems that strong anti-dialogue attitudes may be changing in Miami, too. Although no survey of this kind has been conducted in Union City, I can attest that most of my interviewees favored some kind of reconciliation between Cubans on the island and those in the United States.

Although ordinary Cubans in Union City are more liberal than their counterparts in Miami, no pro-dialogue organizations have formed in the area. In the past, the reason might have been fear. It is said that, proportionally, there was more extreme violence by anti-Castro groups in Union City than in Miami. Perhaps the nature of a complex metropolitan area allowed violent groups to be less visible and more active. Many of the radical organizations, such as Omega 7, were based in the area, and Union City residents felt a great deal of pressure from them. Perhaps the most important reason for the absence of pro-dialogue organizations is dispersion. Union City has fewer and fewer Cubans by the day. Also, most of the younger Cubans do not seem to be interested in Cuba one way or the other. Those who are involved in politics are focused on their local political concerns. Most Cuban migrants of the 1990s and 2000s are staying in Miami. Only a few are coming to Union City and new arrivals are not becoming involved in political organizations so far. They left a highly politicized society and when they arrive in the United States they want nothing to do with politics. Even when they want to maintain ties with the island, it is mainly to visit family. For the most part, newly-arrived Cubans look down upon political organizing.

Union City remains a predominantly working-class community. Most of the Cubans who became involved in anti-Castro politics were from rural, small town, working-class backgrounds in Cuba with not much education. Many of the younger Cubans involved in politics today also come from working-class origins and some of their parents were economic, not political, migrants. These young Cubans obtained an education and then started a political career. Although the social-class origins of the old and the new Cubans are similar, the generational divide is crucial in understanding the political culture of Cubans in Union City today.

7

Union City Cubans and Community Change

Some Theoretical Considerations

The preceding chapters have underscored a central theoretical claim of this work: the association between a supportive immigration policy and immigrant integration and economic success. This chapter will recap the book's main arguments in light of the changes in Union City.

Cuban Integration versus Assimilation

Sociologists have long tried to explain how immigrants become part of the larger society. A number of terms have been used to describe the process through which cultural differences among groups are reduced and a common set of values emerges. Terms such as *absorption, integration,* and *assimilation* have been used.[1] The assimilation model dominated sociological research on immigration for almost half a century. The assumption was that immigrants would become like the dominant group. As they adopted the values, customs, and language of the majority, immigrants would become *acculturated.* As the work of sociologist Milton Gordon suggested, *cultural assimilation* involves acculturation on the part of the immigrant. Cultural assimilation is the dominant pattern in the United States. Cultural assimilation may or may not lead to *structural assimilation*—the large-scale entrance of immigrants into the primary groups of the absorbing society.[2] Structural assimilation takes place when immigrants are completely incorporated into the main institutions of society, for example, the occupational, educational, and economic structures. Intermarriage is also an important indicator. Many second-generation Cubans have intermarried, some to white Americans and others to other Latin Americans, though the former is more indicative of assimilation than the latter. Religious intermarriage is occurring too. In the summer of 2007 I attended a Bat Mitzvah of the daughter of a Cuban American father and a Jewish American mother.

Recent scholarship on the new second generation of immigrants has proposed that "the current second generation may be characterized by a new "segmented assimilation," in which different groups experience either traditional assimilation and upward mobility, downward mobility by unsuccessfully competing in the mainstream economy, or upward mobility by living and working in ethnically homogeneous immigrant communities."[3]

Much of the criticism leveled against assimilation theories is that this process is not a one-way street. Immigrants may want to become part of the larger society, but the larger society may not accept them. Also, immigrants may want to accept some aspects of the general culture, but they may, at the same time, want to keep aspects of their own. That is why many scholars prefer the term *integration*, which allows for the incorporation of immigrants into the structures of the receiving society, but permits them to maintain characteristics of their own. In this case, it is possible to see that even second-generation immigrants, who are bilingual and bicultural often want to keep customs and values from their parents' culture. For example, in Chapter 3, the late, second-generation Cuban Teresa Pérez, owner of Azúcar Restaurant, represents integration. Living outside of Union City, educated in the United States, and part of the middle-class, she told me, "My husband and I always wanted to open a Cuban restaurant. We want to show Americans and others how good Cuban food is." In the same chapter, Oscar, who moved to Ridgefield, Bergen County, from West New York and who owns a drapery business, is quoted: "I love to live in Ridgefield. It is so quiet and we own a beautiful home. But every weekend we go back to Union City or West New York to eat Cuban food." Food and language are not the only signs of the native culture that immigrants may want to preserve. There are many other values related to family organization, religion, and politics that they may choose to maintain. Integration provides immigrants with the opportunity to choose the best of both cultures. This concept may be more applicable to immigration after the 1960s, when, given the climate of the times, the search for one's ethnic roots became legitimate. Early immigrants were under a lot more pressure to assimilate than contemporary ones. In the beginning of the twentieth century, assimilation was enforced, many times physically. Kids were beaten up in playgrounds for speaking languages other than English. As Sherry Gorelick explains, in the 1890s, teachers became professional Americanizers. This was the way "the dominant social class exterminated, via Americanization, the creative potential of the natural learning situation (of the classroom).... Civic lessons in the elementary schools were to emphasize American institutions and love of country. Teachers were urged to encourage children to be kind to immigrant newcomers, to help them adjust and 'learn our ways.'"[4]

Social class shapes assimilation or integration. Integration into the social and economic structures of society implies having the education and the skills to move up through those structures. Cubans, especially younger Cubans who have moved away from Union City into more affluent communities, are obviously upwardly mobile individuals and families. Most of those who do not have the skills, including English language skills, or those who are too old to start a new life, have stayed in Union City.

Challenges to assimilation theories have come from different quarters, especially since the 1960s. The internal colonialism model, first espoused by Robert Blauner, claimed that minorities of color, especially African Americans, had not experienced the kind of assimilation that European immigrants could aspire to in the United States. Proponents of this model argued that these minority groups had suffered internal colonization in their own country because of their color.[5] Other more recent models are transnationalism and diasporic citizenship. Since the 1990s, many researchers of immigration have pointed to new interpretations in the study of immigrants and their experiences. Transnationalism, as mentioned in Chapter 1, indicates that immigrants have lives divided between their countries of origin and their country of destination. Travel, remittances, constant communication with relatives, voting, and in many cases ownership of property and businesses in their countries of origin describe the lives of many of the new immigrants. Similarly, the concept of diasporic citizenship points to the membership of immigrants in more than one nation state.[6] Many of the newer Cuban arrivals, who are not as integrated into U.S. society, keep frequent ties with Cuba despite the antagonistic relations between Cuba and the United States.

Race and Ethnicity

The discussion of race is important when talking about Cubans because most of them see themselves as "white." They dislike any reference to them as people of color. Following, we will see how most contemporary scholars view race as a historically specific and socially constructed concept.

The 2000 census of the U.S. population allowed for a new "multiracial" category. For the first time ever, individuals could choose more than one racial classification. This option ended, at least officially, years of enforcement of the rule of hypo-descent, which stated that one drop of black blood makes you black. It illustrates "how the categories that we use to describe ourselves and those around us are the product of social rather than biological factors."[7] Difference in itself is not negative. It is the meaning that is ascribed to specific categories that creates a system of racist social stratification where some of the layers are considered inferior and others superior. Thus, in the white-black dichotomy, years of struggle, in which northern Europeans have imposed their dominance, have determined that white is seen as superior and black as inferior.

State institutions such as the Census Bureau play an essential role in constructing racial and ethnic categories. *Race* signifies a group of individuals who perceive themselves and are perceived by others as having distinctive hereditary traits. *Ethnicity* denotes a group of people who perceive themselves and are perceived by others as sharing cultural traits such as language, religion, family customs, and food preferences.[8] In creating and changing racial and ethnic categories, the census contributes to transforming the way in which groups perceive themselves and are perceived by others. Conversely, existing social forces shape the way the census creates categories.

Recent changes in the designation of census categories are due to the dramatic demographic transformation experienced by the United States. Immigration, especially Latino and Asian immigration since 1965, has altered the racial landscape of the country. The rule of hypo-descent is slowly giving way to a multiracial system of racial classification.

Some authors refer to the *Latin Americanization* of race relations in the United States. For example, Eduardo Bonilla-Silva and Karen S. Glover contend that:

> racial stratification and the rules of racial (re)cognition in the United States are becoming Latin America-like. . . . Specifically, . . . the United States is developing a tri-racial system with "whites" at the top, an intermediary group of "honorary whites," (similar to the "coloreds" in South Africa during formal apartheid), and a nonwhite group of the "collective black" at the bottom.[9]

They predict that the "white" group will include traditional whites, new "white" immigrants, assimilated Latinos, some light-skinned coloreds, and other subgroups. The intermediate racial group, or "honorary whites" will include light-skinned Latinos (most Cubans, and parts of the Mexican and Puerto Rican populations and most Asian Americans). The "collective black" will include blacks, dark-skinned Latinos, Vietnamese, Cambodians, Laotians, and perhaps Filipinos.[10] However, this classification still perpetuates racism, with whites at the top and darker and black groups at the bottom.

Whether the above predictions turn out to be correct or not in the future, the fact is that there is already a continuum of racial categorizations that have made the hypo-descent system defunct. Multiracialism is closer to the racial reality in the United States than the black-white dichotomy.

Do these changes imply an automatic improvement in the racial dynamics of the country? Clearly not. Many scholars have described new forms of racism. For example, Lawrence Bobo refers to *laissez-faire* racism as the "persistent negative stereotyping of African Americans, a tendency to blame blacks themselves for the black-white gap in socioeconomic status, and resistance to meaningful policy efforts to ameliorate U.S. racist social conditions and institutions."[11]

The problems of race and racism are also exacerbated by the complexities of perception, which is in turn shaped by power dynamics in different historical contexts. A group may perceive itself as white, while others perceive it as non-white. For example, many Caribbean immigrants who in their home are considered white are labeled as non-white once they arrive in the United States. This has been true of Dominicans and other Spanish-speaking Caribbean people.[12] In the case of Cubans, they most definitely see themselves as white: In the 2000 U.S. census, 88.2 percent classified themselves as white.[13] The majority of Cuban immigrants, especially before the Mariel exodus, came from the upper- and middle-classes, which were overwhelmingly white. Most dark-skinned Cubans began to arrive in this country after 1980. Some of my interviewees would point out, "That is what's different between us and other Hispanics; we are white." Many referred to the new immigrants coming to Union City as "blacks" or "Indians" (from Central or South America). The black Cuban exiles that I interviewed were very careful in making a distinction between themselves and African Americans. They considered themselves Cuban first, black second. National identity is more important than racial identity. In Cuba, blacks also define themselves as Cuban first. A strong sense of nationalism, rooted in the specific dynamics of Cuban history, often overpowers racial classifications. This practice may be carried from Cuba to the United States, however, in the U.S.context, where race and racism are so much part of the social fabric of society, black Cubans may attain additional gains by defining themselves as Cuban, rather than as black.

When I asked Doris, a light-skinned black Cuban woman if she had ever been discriminated against in Union City for being black, she said:

> Never. I came to Union City in 1968, and I was always accepted by both white Cubans and Americans. My children are darker than I am, and they got an education here and grew up here without any problems. Only once, my eldest son was the victim of a verbal racist attack. An Italian American student in school called him a "black spic" and they fought physically. I'm sure that among the students there were tensions, but maybe it was more tensions between the Cubans and the Americans, not specifically racial tensions. (Interviewed on June 8, 2008)

María Antonia also recounted how her black children excelled in school in Union City. One of them is a lawyer today. She told me that she did not feel any discrimination from the Cubans, and that, when asked what she was, she always insisted on being categorized as Cuban and not as black. María Antonia came to the United States in 1970. She was a university graduate in Cuba, and later worked for the board of education in West New York. However, she confided that:

> at the board there were tensions. An Italian American officer, who was in charge of distributing summer jobs among the students, always gave the best jobs to the white American kids. The worst jobs went to the dark-skinned students. One summer he gave my son a very bad job and I confronted the officer. I finally left the board. (Interviewed on June 8, 2008)

It appears that many of the black Cuban exiles of the 1960s and the 1970s were professionals in Cuba and some regained that status in the United States. Their class status or aspirations helped them blend into the large, mostly white Cuban community. They seemed to open up freely when talking to me.

Manuel, a thirty-two year old university graduate from Havana who came to this country in the 1990s told me: "I never think of myself as black or white. I think of myself as Cuban." This confirms that Cuban national identity is still very strong.

Ariel Fernández has a different perspective. He was born in the United States to Cuban parents. Raised in Union City, he remembers how, as a child, he often had to endure cruel racist remarks from white Cuban kids. He felt that he did not fit. As he put it:

> We were a minority within a minority. In addition, my parents were Pentecostals, so I was part of yet another minority. I didn't attend Catholic school, like many other kids did, or got to the procession of the Virgen of El Cobre. I felt that whites "tolerated" you. Very often they would make disparaging racist remarks which would pass as "jokes." I would say that I experienced attitudinal racism. For example, the idea of interracial dating was taboo. (Interviewed on July 11, 2008)

When I asked Ariel if he felt more Cuban than black, he said that he feels Cuban but in a different way. When older black Cubans choose to be Cuban first, he explained, they are trying to gain socially:

> That is how the old guard sees it. I am Cuban by choice, and my definition of Cubanness is very inclusive. It includes my African ancestry, the Spaniards, the homosexuals, the communists. I have acquired this identity through an intellectual process, by studying my history with all that it entails.

It seems that a new racial pride is emerging among young black Cubans. One example is the development of a Cuban rap movement on the island. I interviewed Yesenia Fernández-Selier, an Afro-Cuban woman who arrived in the United States in 2004.[14] Yesenia is, after only three years in this country, the marketing manager and audience development director of the Park Performing Arts Center in Union City. She is a psychology graduate of the University of Havana, where she wrote a thesis on racial identity. According to Yesenia, this racial pride is evident in Cuba as well as among many new black arrivals in the United States (interviewed on June 25, 2007). However, as Union City becomes more racially diverse by the day, most Cubans still view themselves as exclusive, that is, as white.

Gender

The role of gender in the immigrant experience is pivotal. In particular, the study of immigrant women's contributions to the family economy is central to the understanding of immigrants' social and economic integration. In 1986, sociologist Lisandro Pérez concluded that Cubans' economic "success," could not have occurred without the contribution of women. He also attributed this economic success to the organization of the Cuban family, where grandparents helped carry out family functions.[15] My own work on Cuban women in Hudson County in the 1980s revealed that family economic success, among other goals, was the main reason why so many Cuban women worked outside the home.[16] A married woman, thirty-one years old, from a middle-class background, who had completed secondary education in Cuba, told me in 1980: "In this country women have to work for the family to improve. We are saving money to buy a house and to pay for our children's college education. Besides, this country has given us so much! We have to pay back with our hard work." In the 1970s and 1980s, before the new Cuban arrivals, there was an emphasis on the political and ideological nature of hard work. Other interviewees at the time also stressed the importance of working hard as a way of showing gratitude to the United States. Cuban males, even if they did not like "their women" (as they defined them) to work outside the home, accepted that they should do it to help the family and to succeed in the country.

Years later, the situation has changed. The labor force participation of Cuban women in Hudson County has declined significantly. In 1980, 55.4 percent of Cuban women worked outside the home. That figure dropped to 44.2 percent in 2000.[17] The fact that the Cuban population is older now, and in-migration is relatively small, may indicate that many women are retiring. Also, this figure applies to women in Hudson County and does not include the women who have left and integrated themselves into the work force of neighboring counties. Many of the industries that employed these women have left the area and new arrivals from Cuba are finding it hard to get jobs. As discussed in Chapter 4, many work in service occupations, while others are learning English as they get government assistance in order to validate their credentials from Cuba. For the new Cuban women, work outside the home is not only a way to help the family, but a necessary component of their identity, especially since many of them are professionals who worked in Cuba. However, some of the more recently arrived women also saw themselves as "special." Mariana, a woman introduced in Chapter 4, told me: "Cubans are very special and very good workers. I want to work very hard to learn English and be able to contribute to my family and my new society. I think that Cubans have proven that they can do that." It is clear that the collective consciousness of Cubans, which involves being special, has also been absorbed by many of the new arrivals.

Religion

What has occurred in the Cuban congregation of Saint Augustine in Union City is a microcosm of the dispersion of the Cuban community and its integration into other localities. There has been a tremendous decline in membership in the Cuban congregation. While old age and deaths have also contributed to this decline, the major cause is out-migration and integration into surrounding communities. Many Saint Augustine's Cuban parishioners were middle-class in origin and had a better time integrating into middle-class communities in other places in New Jersey. Some have moved to Florida. Although the Cuban membership at Saint Augustine represents a minority at present, most group leaders are Cuban. Some of them come to worship there but live elsewhere.

Most of the new Cuban arrivals were not religious. Religion is an important vehicle for integration into the receiving society. It will be interesting to see if the new Cubans become involved in religious activities, as many other immigrants have done in the past.

Transnationalism

Many Union City Cubans maintain transnational ties with their native land, especially the new arrivals. Transnational theories of migration claim that migrants, especially post-1960s migrants, experience divided lives between their countries of origin and their country of residence. Instead of becoming part of their new home completely, new immigrants maintain regular contact with their home countries through visits, remittances, telephone calls, and electronic communication. For those Cubans who have been in the United States for a long time, the need to maintain contact with Cuba may not be so great. In most cases, the majority of their relatives are in the United States. For those who have arrived since the 1980s or 1990s, however, contact with their homeland and their relatives in Cuba is generally high. The offices of Marazul Tours, a travel agency specializing in travel to Cuba, are generally full of Cubans who want to visit their relatives on the island. There are other agencies, such as Caribe Express, that specialize in sending remittances and medicines. Their offices are usually full too. The main difference between Cubans and other groups is that Cubans cannot participate in their homeland's political process.

New Cuban arrivals resent that older Cubans often criticize them for going to Cuba. The old Cubans believe that trips and remittances benefit the Castro government, following the American government's logic on that issue. It is interesting, though, that even those who are critical of sending money do it themselves, which points to a contradiction between their strong ideological opposition to Cuba's government and their concerns about the practical needs of relatives on the island.

Another transnational connection has occurred through religion. Chapter 5 described how Cubans felt alienated from their native church until John Paul II's visit to Cuba in 1998. Talking about the Catholic Church in Cuba is no longer taboo, and many Saint Augustine parishioners have visited the island and their original parishes.

Identity and Politics

Immigrants spend most of their lives searching for, or "negotiating," their identities—the answer to the question of who they are. Identity formation involves a complex process. Choosing a social and cultural identity is not static. As Iraida López states, "Cultural identity is far from being an essence. . . . [Identity] . . . is not unidimensional, but a mosaic of identities, articulated from a specific position in a given historical moment."[18] Contemporary authors believe that, contrary to what the model of immigrant assimilation predicts, Spanish-speaking migrants from the Caribbean share the particular experience of a bilingual, bicultural existence. On the other hand, variables such as race, class, gender, nationality, and sexual preference further complicate the issue of biculturalism, fragmenting even more the social and cultural negotiation of identity.[19]

In the Cuban experience, the bilingual, bicultural existence is mediated by variables such as class and race. The Cuban migration to the United States brought many upper- and middle-class Cubans, especially in the first waves of the migration. Those Cubans brought knowledge and skills that allowed them to easily move up the social-class ladder. Even Union City Cubans, who were predominantly working-class in origin, have experienced a great deal of upward socioeconomic mobility. Cubans consider themselves Cubans first, not Latin American. Also, their racial self-identification is primarily white and their class self-identification is mainly middle-class, which varies from the way many other Latin Americans view themselves.

However, one of the most important variables involved in Cuban identity formation in the United States is politics, specifically anti-Castro politics. This is particularly true of the first exile waves and the first generation. As Portes and Rumbaut note, "Exile politics permeated . . . [patterns of settlement and economic incorporation] . . . and most other aspects of . . . [the group's] collective life."[20] As discussed in Chapters 1 and 6, until the Bay of Pigs invasion, exiles were convinced that they would return to their homeland as soon as Castro was deposed. But time proved those hopes wrong. In the missile crisis of 1962, President Kennedy agreed with the Soviets to stop the refugees' activities to topple the Cuban government in exchange for the removal of Soviet missiles from the island.

Early Cuban exiles saw themselves as different from other immigrants because they were political exiles. Most still think so. Many of my interviewees would say that they are different in that way and could not be compared with other immigrants. Very often these assertions implied that Cubans were better, they were hard working, especially because they were grateful for the refuge that the United States offered them. A friend's father claims that he "didn't come here to make money," but in "search of liberty." Members of anti-Castro political organizations strongly feel that they are distinct. In Chapter 6, Silverio Rodríguez from Alpha 66, noted how Cubans, especially patriotic Cubans, were special. Even when he expressed negative feelings about the United States due to what he sees as the American government's neglect of anti-Castro political groups in the country, he was also pro-American.

The hopes for return to Cuba in the early 1960s was based in the "dispossessed Cuban upper- and middle-classes, compelled to leave their country against their will. Although the passing away of the first generation will surely weaken this orientation, the trauma of departure and subsequent military defeat still tinges Cuban American politics today."[21]

As Portes and Rumbaut suggest, the intensity of the political identification seems to be subsiding among the members of the second generation. As Luisa said (Chapter 2), "My worst punishment . . . [when going to Miami] . . . is to hear all these radio stations that are obsessed with Fidel Castro. I always ask my family, are there any other radio stations here?"

New arrivals are, in general, very depolitized. As discussed in previous chapters, they left a very political environment behind, and do not want to get involved in politics. Also, there is a class difference; they did not go through the experience of losing possessions when they left. They are much more like the economic immigrants arriving from other Latin American countries. As time goes on, and as Cuban reality on the island changes, the anti-Castro component in Cuban identity formation will surely die down.

Union City in the Context of Contemporary Immigration Politics

If a preferential immigration policy based mainly on foreign policy considerations contributed to the economic success of Cubans, and the integration of many into American society, what are the implications of contemporary immigration debates for Cubans as well as for other immigrant populations today?

Immigration policy has often been a contentious issue in U.S. history. At the same time that immigrants are credited with "building the country," there is great ambivalence about receiving them with open arms. Fears about expenditure of resources on the newcomers, language, and the changing nature of American culture due to the presence of foreign groups loom large in the general population. These concerns are raised at some points and not others. It is clear that the debates on immigration are often manipulated by the power structures of society. Since 1965, when occupational skills, family reunification, and fear of persecution became the guiding criteria of U.S. immigration policy, a new wave of immigration has arrived in the United States, this time mainly from the third world, in particular Asia and Latin America. Although not as numerous as at the turn of the twentieth century, "when immigrants accounted for 13.2 percent of the American population, the impact of contemporary immigration is both significant and growing."[22]

The new migration is very diverse. Chapter 1 discusses its varied nature. Although European migration was not homogeneous, current migrants differ greatly in terms of ethnicity, social class, and legal status. However, despite this, the majority of them are economic, labor migrants. In many cases they are undocumented (though the issue of documentation is often framed by the nature of immigration law at any particular time).

The magnitude of undocumented immigration has prompted plans for immigration reform, which former President George W. Bush supported. In May, 2007, a comprehensive immigration reform measure was agreed to by Senate negotiators from both parties. The proposal would give twelve million people the opportunity to become legalized. They would have to pay fines and pass background checks. The bill proposed to crack down on employers who hired undocumented workers. It also created a guest worker program to allow foreigners to be here for up to two years. Skills and educational levels would be counted ahead of family ties in a new point system that determined who got a chance at permanent legal status. Spouses and minor children of U.S. citizens would be eligible for a green card under the proposal, but this would be difficult for adult children and other relatives.[23] The bill, which finally collapsed on the Senate floor in early June, faced criticisms from left and right. Many Republicans contended that the measure was just an amnesty for lawbreakers, while most Democrats pointed to the potential of an inhumane division in families. The Catholic Church, while indicating that the bill was a step in the right direction, was concerned about family reunification and the high fines immigrants would have to pay.[24]

How does the public feel about immigration and about this bill in particular? *The New York Times* and CBS conducted a poll from May 18th to 23rd, 2007. Surprisingly, a large majority of Americans want to change the immigration laws to allow illegal immigrants to receive legal status, and to create a new guest worker program to meet future labor demands.[25] Sixty-six percent of those polled favored the creation of a guest worker program, and 67 percent stated that illegal immigrants should get a renewable visa if they paid a fine, had a clean record, and passed a background check. Sixty-two percent thought that illegal immigrants who have been in the United States for at least two years should be allowed to apply for legal status.[26] Perhaps one of the reasons for these highly favorable views on legalizing immigrants is the creation of a guest worker program. Migrant workers who came to work in the United States in such a program would go back to their countries once their work was completed. They would thus not represent the threat of increasing immigration. The *New York Times* poll also found that Americans have mixed feelings about "whether the recent wave of immigration has been beneficial to the country. . . . Americans are sharply divided over how open the United States should be to future immigrants."[27]

How does the Cuban migration fit into this discussion? Chapter 1 examined this population displacement. The Cuban immigration from 1960 to the mid 1970s represented the largest refugee movement to the United States. The main reason for the acceptance of Cubans on

U.S. soil was political. The United States' opposition to the Cuban government was the driving force behind the formation of the Cuban Refugee Program. Cubans arriving in the United States during that period were political exiles. Besides its humanitarian component, U.S. immigration policy toward the Cubans was part of U.S. foreign policy.

Cuban exiles benefited legally from the status of refugees, or parolees, and did not face the legal hurdles that other immigrant groups encounter. As documented in Chapter 6, anti-Castro Cuban exile groups received, for a long time, support from the U.S. government to try and topple Castro's government. At the same time, Cubans came with few possessions and were not able to go back to their homeland. During the first years of exile, enduring a great deal of suffering, Cubans were convinced that their return to Cuba after Castro's demise was imminent.

Cuban exiles were welcomed by the U.S. government and by a large part of the American public. The fact that most were defined as white and middle-class made that acceptance easier. This situation changed in 1980 with the Mariel exodus. Ever since 1980, Cuban immigrants have not had such a favorable reception. As explained in Chapter 1, Cubans still enjoy legal privileges. Any Cuban or any person married to a Cuban can apply for legal residence after a year and one day of residence in the United States. Also, the "dry foot–wet foot" policy allows those Cuban escapees reaching U.S. shores to apply for political asylum. This literally means that if the escapee touches American land, he or she is considered for asylum. This policy is not applicable to any other immigrant group. However, continuing anti-immigrant concerns in the population cause a great many doubts about accepting more Cubans into the United States. These feelings in the population, and the difficulty of justifying spending so many resources, would make it impossible for the United States to finance another, large-scale refugee program for Cubans or for any other group.

Although many Mariel immigrants have adjusted well, the fact that many Cuban arrivals since the 1980s were dark-skinned and from the working-class in Cuba, has not helped their integration into American society. They have suffered discrimination and have changed the "image" of Cubans in the United States. Many pre-1980 Cubans also feel that they experience discrimination now because they are all put in the same category. Despite the results of the poll mentioned above, the public today is afraid that immigration is going to become uncontrollable. The mention of numerous waves of illegals or refugees is enough to press fearful buttons in the population, including among legal immigrants.

The Culture Wars

The *Foreign Policy* issue of March/April, 2004, published an article, *The Hispanic Challenge,* by Samuel P. Huntington. The article was part of his book *Who Are We? The Challenges to America's National Identity,* published by Simon and Schuster in May, 2004.[28] Huntington's arguments against Hispanic, especially Mexican, migration to the United States are very strong and reminiscent of previous, historical, anti-immigrant, nativistic, and xenophobic claims. Huntington begins his article by saying:

> The persistent flow of Hispanic immigrants threatens to divide the United States into two peoples, two cultures, and two languages. Unlike past immigrant groups, Mexican and other Latinos have not assimilated into mainstream U.S. culture, forming instead their own political and linguistic enclaves–from Los Angeles to Miami–and rejecting the Anglo-Protestant values that built the American dream. The United States ignores this challenge at its peril.[29]

Huntington goes on to say that contemporary immigration differs from past immigration due to a combination of six factors: contiguity, scale, illegality, regional concentration, persistence, and historical presence. That is, the United States is now confronted by a massive influx of poor people from a contiguous country. The scale of the migration is another major difference, with Mexican immigrants constituting 27.6 percent of the foreign-born population in 2000. A great bulk of these Mexican entrants are illegal, and they tend to concentrate regionally. Mexican immigration, as opposed to earlier immigration waves, persists over time. Lastly, no other immigrant group could assert a historical claim to U.S. territory.[30]

As Daniel Drezner notes, Huntington is hardly the first to make this kind of argument. During the colonial era, Benjamin Franklin complained that Germans immigrating to Philadelphia were "generally the most stupid of their nation. . . . Few of their children know English."[31] Joining other critics, Drezner points to inaccuracies in Huntington's argument about language.

For example, one study showed that 60 percent of third-generation Mexican American children speak only English at home. Another study revealed that 30 percent of second-generation Mexican Americans in Los Angeles spoke English at home, suggesting, "Mexican Americans, like other immigrant groups, are becoming more likely with each generation to adopt English as their primary language."[32] Nonetheless, even some proponents of integration would question why this is positive. Is forgetting one's native language a sign of progress or a sign of ignorance? Drezner also notes Huntington's assertion that today's immigrants keep closer ties with their countries of origin, ignoring that nineteenth-century immigrants did the same thing. Between 1870 and 1914, 30 percent of immigrants emigrated back to the country they came from. Among Italians, the rate approached 50 percent "because young Italian men went back and forth between the new world and the old country in search of work."[33]

Francis Fukuyama, in an excellent critique of Huntington's arguments, claims that it is ironic that Huntington is concerned about the loss of Anglo-Saxon values in American culture, when the actual Anglo-Saxon Protestants today are a very complex group. "The old mainline Protestant denominations—Congregationalists, Anglican, and Presbyterian—were at the forefront of liberal causes like multiculturalism and affirmative action."[34] Fukuyama believes that the United States can meet the challenge of absorbing Hispanic immigrants. For one thing, "they will help reinforce certain cultural values like the emphasis on family and work, and the Christian character of American society."[35]

Another criticism leveled against Huntington by many authors is the claim that new immigrants are concentrated in specific regions of the country. Huntington argues that Hispanic migrants are found mostly in the Southwest and in Miami. But he ignores the fact that Hispanics are starting to expand beyond their traditional locales. Union City Cubans are a case in point. The states experiencing the largest increases in Hispanic population between 1900 and 2000 were outside of traditional Hispanic enclaves: North Carolina, Arkansas, Georgia, Tennessee, and South Carolina.[36] Again, critics of Huntington could be blamed for arguing on his turf, implicitly accepting his values.

Though Huntington focuses on Mexicans, he generalizes about other Hispanics. With a mixture of admiration and indignation, he talks about Cubans in Miami:

> Miami is the most Hispanic large city in the 50 U.S. states. Over the course of 30 years, Spanish-speakers—overwhelmingly Cuban—established their dominance in virtually every aspect of the city's life, fundamentally changing its ethnic composition, culture, politics, and language. The Hispanization of Miami is without precedent in the history of U.S. cities.[37]

Huntington notes how the economic growth of Miami, led by the Cuban immigrants, made the city a magnet for other Latin American migrants. The "Cuban takeover," as Huntington calls it, had major consequences for Miami. Cubans in the early 1960s, unable to send money home, invested in the area. According to Huntington, Miami became an international economic dynamo where business was conducted in Spanish. In 2000, only 31.1 percent of adult Miami residents said they spoke English very well, compared to 39.0 percent in Los Angeles, 42.5 percent in San Francisco, and 46.5 percent in New York.[38] Huntington is right in claiming that the Miami case has no precedent in U.S. history. Mainly because a great number of middle- and upper-class Cubans arrived in Miami in the 1960s with no possibility of returning home, they formed an enclave and invested in the economic development of their new home. They did not need to speak English to do that.

Union City was similar between the 1960s and the 1980s, when Cubans were highly concentrated there. However, what distinguishes Union City now is dispersion. Contrary to what Huntington argues, Union City Cubans started to disperse in the 1980s. As other migrant groups began to arrive in the city, Cubans opted for leaving. Those Cubans who have moved away from Union City are fairly well integrated into U.S. society. Even when they maintain some of their cultural traits—love for Cuban food, art, religion, etc.—they are completely bilingual and bicultural, which means that they share in the values of American society as well. Dispersion, a sign of integration in many cases, is common among the Cubans who have left Union City. As mentioned in the section on assimilation, social class is central when considering integration. Those who have left Union City, especially the young Cubans, are professionals, speak English primarily, and think as Americans. Since the 1960s Union City Cuban migrants have had the dream of integration for their children. As related in Chapter 3, Eunice Europa, a second-generation Italian

American who taught fifth and eight grades at Washington School in Union City, told me: "Not all the parents liked bilingual education. Parents wanted their children to learn English. Some would forge their addresses so that their children could attend non-bilingual education schools." Maybe Huntington is right in that Hispanic migrants are not assimilating at the same rate that other groups did. But as years pass, integration is surely taking place among Hispanics. Clearly, assimilation or integration is a two-way process. As long as discrimination against the poorest and darkest Hispanics keep them marginalized, they will not be able, even if they desire it, to fully become part of American society.

Concluding Remarks

This community study has documented various aspects of the everyday life of Cubans in Union City. Every chapter has explored the origins, development, and transformation of Cuban Union City. Let us go back to the initial questions of this study: Who leaves Union City? Who stays? Who is coming? Where do Cubans go? It seems that younger Cubans, who are educated and have good jobs, are moving to the suburbs. Sometimes they take their parents with them. Some Cubans are also moving to Florida, although the number is not so significant. Many older Cubans who have businesses in Union City are moving to the suburbs and to neighboring counties and cities, but they still come to take care of their businesses during the day. North Bergen, a more upscale town than Union City, and Bergen County, a more affluent county than Hudson, are popular locations. Older and poorer Cubans, as well as new arrivals from Cuba have stayed in Union City. Incoming immigrants to Union City now come from practically every Latin American nation: Colombians, Ecuadorians, Dominicans, Mexicans, Peruvians, and many more. There are also East Indians who may or may not live in Union City, but who have businesses there. Also, there are white and non-white Americans who move to Union City to be close to New York City. Some European Americans whose parents immigrated to Union City in the past, and who had moved elsewhere, are coming back to their city of origin.

Were Cubans discriminated against when they came to Union City? Of course they were. I remember when Father Feketie, former Saint

Augustine's pastor, told me, "It was like with any other group. Some natives accommodated to the presence of the newcomers, and others didn't.

Many European Americans started to leave Union City when the Cubans came." As I detailed in Chapter 3, my own experience at my first job with the co-worker who made fun of my accent and treated me harshly is another example. In time, however, Cubans gained the respect of most in the community. As Delia told me, "When we moved into our house, an Italian-American neighbor came and told us, 'we are so happy that you are Cuban. Wherever Cubans move they fix and paint their houses so nicely. They keep their neighborhoods in great shape.' Of course we were happy to hear that."

The respect that Cubans received had a lot to do with their image as hard-working people who had left a dictatorship and had come to the United States in search of freedom. Partly because a number of them were middle-class, they fit into the American value system more than other immigrant groups. Even in the case of Union City, where there were many working-class families, this collective image applied.

For the most part, Cubans were admired. Jeffrey Tarallo, a social studies teacher at Memorial High School shared with me:

> Coming to teach at Memorial High School in the 1960s was an eye-opening experience for me. At first it was "culture shock." The language, the cultural differences. I remember how the girls had to date with chaperones. Generally, they married too young. I was so positively impressed by the parents' involvement. They really cared about their children. I was also so impressed by the "Cuban drive," which was surely reinforced by the anti Communist ideology. That is true even for the immigrants after the 1980 Mariel exodus. (Interviewed on August 31, 2006)

Tarallo laments that everything has changed:

> Now we are getting poor, uneducated immigrants, mainly from Central and South America. The pregnancy rate is very high. Poverty is the single most important reason why our students are not doing well. Also, the level of parent involvement is not significant, and that makes the biggest difference.

Is there conflict between Cubans and other Hispanics? The fact that Cubans are leaving means that they have the resources and do not want to live in Union City anymore. Their "turf" has been occupied by people who are different. Even among those who stay, they feel "superior," as Tarallo says of his Cuban students. Delia recounts nostalgically, "I go to Bergenline Avenue and I don't run into anybody I know. This place is full of strangers. Also, the city is so dirty now, and there is a lot of crime."

Are the new Cubans finding a welcoming environment? Do the old Cubans accept them? Yesenia still finds symbols in the community that remind her of Cuba. Certain restaurants, stores. Her husband was born in Union City. She claims that, even if the number of Cubans is low in Union City, the pressure to conform is high. She told me, "I'm anti-Castro, but I'm not conservative politically. Some Cubans here want you to be Republican, even reactionary. That brings conflict between the old and the new Cubans sometimes. We, the new Cubans have to find a voice politically, a voice that is representative of our own realities." At the same time, Yesenia notes how conflict with other Hispanics is contributing to the formation of an interesting alliance between the old and the new Cubans. She told me:

> The old stereotypes are fading. If there are problems between other Latin Americans and Cubans, the old Cubans will side with the new Cubans, just because we are Cubans. It doesn't matter that I am black, or educated under the Revolution. In the end, I'm Cuban. At the same time, being Cuban often generates conflict with other Hispanics who believe that Cubans see themselves as "superior."

Differences in political views among Cubans are the product of the different migratory waves. Generally, the exiles—or 1960–1970s migrants, known as the *históricos* or first arrivals—are the most conservative and anticommunist. After 1980 the Cuban community in the United States became more differentiated. Mariel migrants had lived much longer under the Revolution and were not as conservative politically. The same, and even more so, can be said about Cuban immigrants after 1990s. If post-1980 or 1990 Cuban immigrants find the voice that Yesenia is claiming, Union City Cubans will be a more progressive group, even if strongly anti-Castro, . At the same time, if we accept the association between higher social class and conservative political affiliation, upwardly mobile Cubans who have moved to affluent localities may become more conservative, despite their working-class roots.

Cubans are a minority in Union City today. However, Cubans are well represented in the city's political structures. As Tarallo and Yesenia told me separately, "most city officials are Cuban," even if they live elsewhere. The drive and hard-work ethic characteristic of Cubans is greatly responsible for their success, but it is clear that U.S. policy toward the Cuban immigration helped Cubans adjust. A generous immigration policy on the part of the U.S. can help immigrants and can benefit the country. This thinking may be very relevant in the 2000s, when debates about immigration policy are so heated in the government and among the public. The strength of the old Union City and its residents' eventual integration can be viewed as a social experiment in the supportive treatment of immigrants, which promotes economic success. This leads to the cultural integration of immigrants that mainstream Americans favor and support. The characteristics of migrants are important, but immigration policy is central in influencing adaptation patterns. Even working-class Union City Cubans benefited from a favorable reception on the part of the U.S. government and the American public.

FIGURE 7.1 *Forty Third Street in Union City was renamed Celia Cruz Way in honor of the renowned Cuban salsa singer.* (Ana Meseguer)

Although Union City is a very diverse place now, for many Cubans it continues to represent a "Cuban province." As José, a Spaniard who lives in North Bergen, told me: "Many of the old Cubans have left to other cities and towns with their children, but they still come to Union City to buy Cuban food, to play dominoes, and to hang out with old friends."

Union City was a strong, lively Cuban community and that is not easily forgotten. It is ironic that, as the Cuban community disperses, the Cuban presence can still be seen in monuments along the Hudson River and in the names of schools and some streets. Maybe, despite all the changes, Union City will remain, even if at some symbolic level, Cuba's northernmost enclave.

Abbreviations

BHE	Bureau of Hispanic Enterprise
CANF	Cuban American National Foundation
CBS	Columbia Broadcasting System
CIA	Central Intelligence Agency
CID	Cuba Independiente y Democrática (Independent and Democratic Cuba)
CNM	Cuban Nationalist Movement
CORU	Coordinación de Organizaciones Revolucionarias Unidas (Coordination of United Revolutionary Organizations)
CRC	Cuban Revolutionary Council
CRECED	Comunidades de Reflexión Eclesial Cubana en la Diáspora (Communities of Cuban Ecclesiastical Reflection in the Diaspora)
CRP	Cuban Refugee Program
ENEC	Encuentro Nacional Eclesial Cubano (Cuban National Ecclesiastical Congress)
ESL	English as a Second Language
FBI	Federal Bureau of Investigations
HIAS	Hebrew Immigrant Aid Society
IRC	International Rescue Committee
JUCEPLAN	Junta Central de Planificación (Central Planning Board)
LCI	Lions Club International
NACAW	National Association of Cuban American Women

NJIT	New Jersey Institute of Technology
ONE	Oficina Nacional de Estadísticas (National Office of Statistics)
PARAL	Program for the Analysis of Religion Among Latinos
PMSA	Primary Metropolitan Statistical Area
RRP	Refugee Resettlement Program
SDUSA	Social Democrats in the United States of America
SMSA	Standard Metropolitan Statistical Area
SSI	Supplemental Security Income
UCE	Unión de Cubanos en el Exilio (Union of Cubans in Exile)

Notes

PREFACE

1. Portes and Rumbaut, *Immigrant America.*

2. All these studies are included and discussed in Warren and Lyon, *New Perspectives on the American Community.*

3. Ibid., 107.

4. Ibid., 98.

5. According to some writers, spatial concentration delays assimilation or integration into the larger society. New immigrants do not have to learn the English language to get by. See Rogg, *The Assimilation of Cuban Exiles: The Role of Community and Class.*

6. For example, see Lowenstein, *Frankfurt on the Hudson: The German-Jewish Community of Washington Heights, 1933–1983, Its Structure and Culture.*

7. Kelly, *The Portable Kristeva* (Introduction). Some of these reflections, in particular the work of Julia Kristeva, delve into the role of the unconscious. For a more political approach to the usage of experience in social and historical research see Scott, "The Evidence of Experience."

8. Throughout this book, Cubans identified as the first generation are those who came from Cuba as adult immigrants or exiles. Cuban Americans of the second generation were born here or came from Cuba as children or adolescents 15 years old or younger.

9. For example, some interviews for Chapter 5 on religion preceded the 1999–2008 period because I conducted an ethnographic study of St. Augustine Parish before conducting interviews for this book. Similarly, in Chapter 4, on women, I include many interviewees' quotes from the 1980s, a period when I was

studying the labor force participation levels among Cuban women in Union City and West New York (Hudson County), New Jersey.

CHAPTER 1

1. Cubans have settled in various places in New Jersey, including Elizabeth in Union County and Newark in Essex County, but Union City has always been the center of the state's Cuban community. West New York, a smaller municipality next to Union City with an even higher proportion of Cubans, is viewed by many as part of the same concentration. The same is true of adjacent towns like North Bergen and Weehawken. But most people, especially those Cubans outside of New Jersey, refer to the whole area as Union City. A reason could be that the first Cubans who arrived in New Jersey settled in Union City. This book, at times, will incorporate information about other cities, even though its focus is on Union City.

2. Portes and Rumbaut, *Immigrant America,* 50.

3. *The New York Times,* "Newest Immigrants Head Straight to New Jersey's Suburbs," B1. Throughout this work, the terms *Latina, Latino,* or *Hispanic* will be used interchangeably.

4. See Portes and Rumbaut for a discussion of immigrant spatial concentration, 28–56. For studies on transnationalism see Glick Schiller and Georges, *George Woke Up Laughing: Long Distance Nationalism and the Search for Home;* Glick Schiller, Basch, and Szanton-Blanc, "A New Perspective on Migration," in *Towards a Transnational Perspective on Migration: Race, Class, Ethnicity, and Nationalism Reconsidered;* and the articles in Goldin, ed. *Identities on the Move: Transnational Processes in North America and the Caribbean Basin.* Also, see Pessar and Graham, Dominicans: Transnational Identities and Local Politics, 251–273; Smith, Social, Educational, Economic, and Political Problems and Prospects in New York, 275–300 in Foner, ed. *New Immigrants in New York.*

5. See Handlin, *The Uprooted: The Epic Story of the Great Migration that Made the American People;*Weinberg, *The World of Our Mothers,* 67–81.

6. See Portes and Rumbaut, *Immigrant America.*

7. See the works of Alejandro Portes, Rubén G. Rumbaut, Silvia Pedraza, María Cristina García, Lisandro Pérez, María de los Angeles Torres, Guillermo Grenier, Ted Henken, Jorge Duany, Rafael Hernández, Antonio Aja, and Félix Masud-Piloto, among others.

8. Haslip-Viera and Baver, eds. *Latinos in New York: Communities in Transition,* 8–9; Pérez-Stable, *The Cuban Revolution: Origins, Course, and Legacy.*

9. Prohias and Casal, *The Cuban Minority in the United States: Preliminary Report on Need Identification and Program Evaluation,* 15–18. This study concluded that the census underestimated the total number of Cubans by 9.3 percent. The figure used here is the corrected one.

10. U.S. Bureau of the Census 2000. Table DT-1, *General Demographic and Social Characteristics.*

11. Many social scientists agree that the concept of race is socially constructed. Throughout this work, terms such as *white* and *black* will be used to

denote phenotypical characteristics only. This topic will be further discussed in Chapter 7.

12. García, *Havana USA: Cuban Exiles and Cuban Americans in South Florida* 13–30. In addition to parole, there are other terms that connote a technical difference when assigning a legal status to a person who comes to this country to escape conditions at home. Refugees are persons who suffer persecution in their countries, especially prisoners; asylees are those who are oppressed because of their politics or ideologies; refugees apply for protection from outside the United States, while asylees from inside. Exiles are generally defined as those who are forcibly removed from their homeland. For the purposes of this work, these terms will be used interchangeably. (New Jersey Department of Human Services. *Public Assistance Manual, Refugee Resettlement Program,* Subchapter 10, page 1.) Also, interview with Angelica Harrison, Director, and Lourdes Méndez, Elsa Aguila, and Lourdes Miranda at the North Hudson County Department of Human Services, Jersey City, New Jersey, July 31, 2001.

13. Conde, *Operation Pedro Pan,* 98. Torres, *The Lost Apple,* 88–93.

14. Torreira Crespo and Buajasan Marrawi, *Operación Peter Pan,* 92–117.

15. Masud-Piloto, Félix, "The Mariel Boatlift of 1980: Consequences of a Politicized Migration Policy."

16. See U.S. Department of State, *A Report of the Cuban-Haitian Task Force;* Prieto, *Reinterpreting an Immigration Success Story: Cuban Women, Work, and Change in a New Jersey Community.*

17. Prieto, 67; For a detailed discussion of the demographics of the Mariel migration from a Cuban perspective see, Hernández, "La política de los Estados Unidos hacia Cuba y la cuestión de la migración" and Hernández and Gomis, "Retrato del Mariel: el ángulo socieconómico."

18. Ojito, "You Are Going to El Norte," *The New York Times Magazine;* Pedraza, "Cuba's Refugees: Manifold Migrations." Also see Bach, "The New Cuban Immigrants: Their Background and Prospects."

19. Pedraza, Silvia, "Manifold Migrations," 272–273. For a Cuban perspective on the 1990s migration see, Aja Díaz, "La emigración de Cuba en los años noventa."

20. New Jersey Department of Human Services, *Public Assistance Manual.*

21. Pedraza, Silvia, "Manifold Migrations," 272–273.

22. Elián González left Cuba on a raft with his mother and others in November 1999. He was the only survivor when the raft capsized. The boy's Miami relatives wanted him to stay in the United States. His father, who lives in Cuba, wanted Elián to be returned to him. This case opened up a seven-month international custody dispute that ended with a U.S. immigration raid of the Miami relatives' home in order to hand over the boy to the father, who had come to the United States to pick him up.

23. Interview with Lourdes Méndez, September 22, 2003, Interview took place at the Hudson County Department of Human Services in Jersey City, N.J. Also see, Henken, "Balseros, Boteros, and El Bombo: Post 1994 Cuban Immigration to the United States and the Persistence of Special Treatment."

24. This has happened with other groups before. The Germans are one example. See Lowenstein, *Frankfurt on the Hudson: The German-Jewish Community of Washington Heights*, 255.

CHAPTER 2

1. New Jersey Department of Labor, *New Jersey Population Trends, 1790–2000.* Statistically, Hudson County is the equivalent to what the census calls the Jersey City Standard Metropolitan Area (SMSA), or Primary Metropolitan Statistical Area (PMSA) in 2000.

2. See Seward, *Union City: 50th Anniversary, 1925–1975.*

3. U.S. Bureau of the Census, Census of the Population, 2000, Hudson County, New Jersey, *General Demographic and Social Characteristics;* Center for Children and Technology, *The Transformation of Union City: 1989 to Present.*

4. Forero, "How 'Fomentenses' Came to the U.S. and Reshaped Hudson County."

5. See Censuses of Population and Housing, *New Jersey Population Trends, 1790 to 2000;* Brait, "The Cubans of Union City"; Prohías and Casal, *The Cuban Minority in the United States.*

6. Rogg and Santana Cooney, *Adaptation and Adjustment of Cubans: West New York, New Jersey,* 13; *New Jersey Population Trends,* 37. In the smaller town of West New York, the concentration of Cubans has even been higher than in Union City. Although the total number of Cubans was higher in Union City in 1999 (15,054) than in West New York (12,502), the proportion of Cubans relative to the general population was higher in West New York (32.8%) than in Union City (25.9%).

7. Bischoff, "Caribbean Peoples of New Jersey: An Overview"; Dolce "Faces of Immigration: The Cubans of New Jersey"; Prieto, *Reinterpreting an Immigration Success Story.* Figures vary slightly from one source to the other, but they are very close.

8. Prohías and Casal, *The Cuban Minority in the United States.*

9. Interview with Lourdes Gil, July 9, 2001.

10. State of New Jersey, Public Welfare Statistics for the Month of November, 1975; Interview with Ms. Angelica Harrison, Director of Hudson County Division of Social Services, July 31, 2001.

11. See Rogg and Santana Cooney, 15–19. In my study of Cuban women in Hudson County (Prieto 1984), I obtained very similar findings. The percentage on race composition is from my sample.

12. Findings in the West New York study by Rogg and Santana Cooney on this issue are identical to results for Union City in my 1980s research.

13. Rogg and Santana Cooney, 21—23.

14. Estévez, "Resettling the Cuban Refugees in New Jersey," 29.

15. Ibid., 33

16. Ibid., 30

17. State of New Jersey, Refugee Resettlement Program, Attachment to Circular Letter No. 80–11–9, 1.

18. Portes and Rumbaut, 241 and 23. There were also increasing numbers of migrants escaping repressive military, right-wing dictatorships in Latin America, which made it necessary to change the refugee law. However, during the Reagan administration, more people escaping communist countries, primarily from South Asia and eastern Europe, were granted political asylum than those fleeing noncommunist dictatorships such as Guatemala and El Salvador.

19. Estévez, 29–33. Also, interview with Iraida Iturralde, who worked with the Refugee Program of the IRC helping the refugees for almost four years (interviewed on August 8, 2001).

20. Interview with Iraida Iturralde, August 8, 2001. This comment was made to her by a friend.

21. Pedraza, Silvia, "Manifold Migrations," 273. Also see Ackerman, "The *Balsero* Phenomenon, 1991–1994"; Ackerman and Clark, *The Cuban Balseros: Voyage of Uncertainty.*

22. Interview with Lourdes Méndez, September 22, 2003, and interview with Scott Wasmuth, Director of Social Services, International Institute of New Jersey, September 22, 2003. The interviews took place at the Hudson County Department of Social Services.

23. Interview with Lourdes Méndez.

24. For a moving presentation of the *balsero* migration, see the film *Balseros* (Cuban Rafters), written by Carles Bosch and David Trueba, directed by Carles Bosch and Joseph Domenech. A Seventh Art Films Release in association with HBO/Cinemax Documentary Films, 2002.

25. U.S. Census of Population and Housing, Profile 1, *General Characteristics of the Population.* Prepared by New Jersey State Data Center, 1981, 1991.

26. Morrill, *"Cubans Head to Bergen Suburbs."*

27. Ibid.

28. U.S. Bureau of the Census, *American Community Survey 2006.*

CHAPTER 3

1. The term commonly used by white Americans to describe Cubans was "Spanish." To this day many non-Spanish-speaking residents use that term to categorize all Spanish-speaking nationalities.

2. Interview with Miguel Miqueli, August 21, 2001.

3. See Portes and Stepick, *City on the Edge: The Transformation of Miami;* Tully Tapia, "Two States Differ on Bilingual Ed's Value."

4. Bonacich, Light, and Choy Wong, "Koreans in Business"; Wilson and Portes, "Immigrant Enclaves: An Analysis of the Labor Market Experience of Cubans in Miami"; Portes and Rumbaut, *Immigrant America.*

5. Portes and Rumbaut, 21.

6. Interview with Dionisio Villanueva, Juan L. Martínez Miguel Miqueli, and Félix Noel Barrera, August 21, 2001; Rodríguez Zaldívar and Madán, *Páginas de Oro del Exilio Cubano 1959–1983*, 91.

7. Interview with Dionisio Villanueva, August 7, 2001.

8. Interview with Dionisio Villanueva, Juan L. Martínez, Miguel Miqueli, and Félix Noel Barrera, August 21, 2001.

9. Interviews with Rolando Alum, especially May 1, 2002.

10. Diaz-Briquets, Sergio, "Cuban-Owned Businesses in the United States," 60. The comparative proportion of Cuban-owned firms relative to the Cuban population is almost as high in other Cuban communities in the United States as in Miami. The Jersey City SMSA is a case in point. U.S. Bureau of the Census. 1977 Economic Census, Survey of Minority-Owned Business Enterprises; US. Bureau of the Census. 1987 Economic Census, Survey of Minority-Owned Business Enterprises.

11. U.S. Bureau of the Census, 1992 Economic Census, Survey of Minority-Owned Business Enterprises.

12. U.S. Bureau of the Census. 1997 Economic Census, *Survey of Minority-Owned Business Enterprises.* .

13. U.S. Bureau of the Census, *Basic Demographic Characteristic*s, Hudson County, New Jersey, 1980, 2000. Conversation with Ms. Katie Russell from the U.S. Bureau of the Census. The last Survey of Minority-Owned Business Enterprises is from 2002. I was not able to find statistics on Hispanics broken down by ethnicity in that report.

14. Both *La Esquina Habanera* and *Havana Bay Coffee* have closed recently, further reinforcing the decline of the Cuban economic enclave.

15. Oquendo, David, narration in documentary *Rumbo a la Rumba,* a film by Juan Carlos Rojas in cooperation with the New School for Social Research (New School University), a Havana on the Hudson Project, Union City, NJ, 2002.

16. As was said in Chapter 1, the complex topic of race will be further discussed in Chapter 7. For now, terms like black and white only denote phenotypical characteristics.

17. Basch, "The Vincentians and Grenadians: The Role of Voluntary Associations in Immigrant Adaptation to New York City."

18. Pessar and Graham, "Dominicans: Transnational Identities and Local Politics."

19. Interview with Julia Valdivia, September 22, 2003.

20. Prohías and Casal, *The Cuban Minority in the United States.*

21. Interview with Lidia Gil-Ramos, June 24, 2001, and Durán, "Tertulias de Antaño." Typescript, n.d. from the author's collection.

22. Interview with Lidia Gil-Ramos, June 24, 2001.

23. Shortly after I attended that party, *Tertulias* had to stop its activities. Ms. Lidia Gil-Ramos fell ill and could not direct the organization any more. There is talk that another group of members is going to resume activities. Manito (mentioned at the beginning of this chapter) will lend his locale on Sundays so that *Tertulias* meetings can take place.

24. Pérez, "Cuban Journalism in Exile," 91.

25. Interview with Manuel Pérez, August 29, 2001.

26. Pérez, "Cuban Journalism in Exile."

27. Interview with Dionisio Villanueva, Juan L. Martínez, Miguel Miqueli, and Félix N. Barrera, August 21, 2001.

28. Comas, Lourdes, ed. *West New York Leones Cubanos de Hudson, 20 Aniversario.*

29. *Revista Oficial de la Asociación Nacional de Mujeres Cubano-Americanas de New Jersey,* [Official Magazine of the National Association of Cuban American Women NACAW, New Jersey Chapter], 29.

30. The day care is licensed and sponsored by the local board of education as part of a special program for disadvantaged children.

31. Traditionally, children in Latin America received toys and gifts on Three Kings Day, not so much on Christmas, as it is the custom in the United States. By celebrating the Three Kings Day, the Association maintains Cuban and Latin American culture alive.

32. Interview with Siomara Sánchez, October 15, 2003.

33 On the condition of anonymity, I was told that, at present, there is ethnic conflict at Palisades Medical Center. Some white American members of the board express fears that "this cannot become a 'Spanish' hospital." My interviewees added that, for an institution that receives federal and state monies for poor people access (most of whom are Hispanic because in the area the hospital is located over 75 percent of the population is Hispanic), their attitudes are very prejudicial. They do not have telephone recording prompts in Spanish, like other institutions do in heavily Spanish-speaking neighborhoods, and, in general, they are not welcoming of the Hispanic population.

CHAPTER 4

1. See Fox, "Honor, Shame, and Women's Liberation in Cuba." See Peristiany, *Honour and Shame: The Values of Mediterranean Society* for a discussion of these cultural norms. For example, the basic elements in these codes are "honor" and "vergüenza," (translated as honor and shame). These qualities imply a sensitivity and consciousness of public opinion and the judgment of others. Honor and vergüenza, although important for everybody, were crucial for women. Also see Martínez-Alier, *Marriage, Class, and Colour in Nineteenth Century Cuba,* the most thorough analysis on sexual values and racial attitudes in Cuba so far. She also examines the relationship between female honor (virginity and virtue) and the protection and/or achievement of the family's social status.

2. Valdés, "The Historical Context of the Cuban Family." Typescript, n.d. From the author's collection. Nelson Valdés is a Cuban sociologist who has written about the family and gender relations in Cuba.

3. O'Connor, *The Origins of Socialism in Cuba.*

4. See Casal, *Images of Cuban Society Among Pre and Post Revolutionary Novelists;* Kaufman Purcell, "Modernizing Women for a Modern Society: The Cuban Case"; Pérez-Stable, *The Cuban Revolution: Origins, Course, and Legacy;* República de Cuba, *Censos de Población, Viviendas y Electoral.* 1943, 1953.

5. República de Cuba, *Censos de Población, Viviendas y Electoral,* 1953.

6. Women were always active in public life in Cuba. Many middle-class and working-class women were active politically, especially in the 1933 revolution against Machado, and later in the 1959 Revolution against Batista. The majority

of women who could, however, subscribed to the ideology that placed them at home.

7. See JUCEPLAN (Junta Central de Planificación) "Aspectos Demográficos de la Fuerza Laboral Femenina en Cuba."

8. Ibid.,19.

9. Farber, Interview, *International Socialist Review.*

10. ONE (Oficina Nacional de Estadísticas), *Cuba en Cifras, Cuba in Figures.*

11. For information about the changes in gender relations and the situation of Cuban women before and after the revolution, see González Pagés, *En busca de un espacio: Historia de mujeres en Cuba.*

12. As of November 8, 2004, the Cuban government prohibited the circulation of dollars in the country. Cuban citizens with dollars could exchange them for convertible pesos until mid-November, and tourists can exchange dollars for the Cuban currency once they arrive in Cuba. Exchanging dollars for convertible pesos carries a twenty percent tax. Since Raúl Castro was elected as President by the Cuban Parliament in February 2008, he has announced that changes will be coming in the currency and salary structures of the country to increase the standard of living of Cubans.

13. U.S. Bureau of the Census, Census of Population, 1980, *General Social and Economic Characteristics;* U.S. Bureau of the Census , Census of Population, 1980, *General Social and Economic Characteristics,* New Jersey.

14. Santana Cooney and Ortiz, "Hispanic Female Participation in the Labor Force: A Comparative Analysis of Puerto Ricans, Mexicans, and Cubans."

15. Safa, "The Differential Incorporation of Hispanic Women Migrants into the U.S. Labor Force."

16. López, "Disentangling Race-Gender Work Experiences: Second Generation Caribbean Young Adults in New York City."

17. Earlier in this chapter, I discussed the growth in employment for women in the 1950s. Also, my interviewees came to this country a few years after the revolutionary government started to encourage a higher participation of women in the labor force. Both circumstances may have affected a higher labor-force participation rate than expected in the sample.

18. Yans-McLauglin, "Patterns of Work and Family Organization: Buffalos's Italians."

19. Cohen, "Italian American Women in New York City, 1900–1950: Work and School."

20. Weinberg Stahl, *The World of Our Mothers,* 208–211.

21. Friedman-Kasaba, *Memories of Migration: Gender, Ethnicity, and Work in the Lives of Jewish and Italian Women in New York, 1870–1924.*

22. Virginia Domínguez addressed similar points when she said that the high labor-force participation of early Cuban migrant women was adaptive and did not represent a radical departure from tradition. Cuban women worked in such numbers because of the "catastrophic loss of status incurred by migrating to the United States." See Domínguez, Virginia, "The Nature of Change: Cuban Women in the United States." M. Patricia Fernández-Kelly and Anna M. García make a very similar point. See note 28.

23. Citations for interviews conducted in earlier studies will vary from the general format used in this book.

24. Berger, "Dominicans Gaining on Puerto Ricans in the City."

25. Pessar and Graham, "Dominicans: Transnational Identities and Local Politics."

26. For a compilation of works on Cuban American women see Stoner and Serrano Pérez, *Cuban and Cuban American Women: An Annotated Bibliography.*

27. Ferre, "Employment Without Liberation: Cuban Women in the United States."

28. Fernández-Kelly and García, "Power Surrendered, Power Restored: The Politics of Work and Family Among Hispanic Garment Workers in California and Florida."

29. The results of the follow-up study were published in Prieto, "Cuban Women in New Jersey: Gender Relations and Change" and "Continuity or Change?: Two Generations of Cuban American Women." The discussion of this section will draw on those publications.

30. Pérez, "Immigrant Economic Adjustment and Family Organization: The Cuban Success Story Reexamined."

31. Ibid., 13.

32. U.S. Bureau of the Census, *Average Household Size Census 2000*; U.S. Bureau of the Census, *Average Household Size Census 2000, Hudson County.*

33. U.S. Bureau of the Census, *Family Type by Presence and Age of Own Children, Racial or Ethnic Grouping: Cuban, Hudson County*U.S. Bureau of the Census, *General Population Characteristics,* New Jersey.

34. Fox, "Honor, Shame, and Women's Liberation in Cuba"; Peristiany, *Honour and Shame: The Values of Mediterranean Society;* and Valdés, "The Historical Context of the Cuban Family."

35. Interview with Lourdes Méndez, September 22, 2003.

CHAPTER 5

1. Crahan, Margaret, "Cuba" In Sigmund, Religious Freedom and Evangelization in Latin America, 89–91. The Jewish community numbered approximately 12,000 in 1959.

2. Although there is religious diversity in the migration, especially when considering the social class and geographic differences of the migrants, this chapter will only focus on the role of Catholicism.

3. Williams, *Religion of Immigrants from India and Pakistan: New Threads in the American Tapestry,* cited in Warner, *Introducing the New Ethnic and Immigrant Congregations Project,* 4. For discussions on this topic see PARAL (Program for the Analysis of Religion Among Latinos), *The National Survey of Leadership in Latino Parishes and Congregations: A Summary Report* ; Greeley, *The Denominational Society* and *The Catholic Myth: The Behavior and Beliefs of American Catholics;* Smith, "Religion and Ethnicity in America."

4. Interview with Father Joseph Fahey, C.P., November 21, 2003; Durán, "La Caridad del Cobre en North Hudson." The monastery closed as living quarters in

1979, but the Passionists remained in charge of St. Michael's Church until 1981 when it merged with St. Joseph. The last mass in St. Michael's Church was on November 2, 1981 (The Passionist Archives, 526 Monastery Place, Union City, NJ). The Virgin of El Cobre's full name in Spanish is *Nuestra Señora de la Caridad del Cobre.* Many authors use the English translation Our Lady of Charity. Throughout this work, I will refer to her as the Virgin of El Cobre.

5. Interview with Father Joseph Fahey, C.P., November 21, 2003.

6. Interview with Nora de Cárdenas, January 23, 2004.

7. The statue at the House of Charity is not the original one brought to St. Michael's Monastery. That one remains at St. Joseph and St. Michael's Church.

8. I want to acknowledge the Cushwa Center for the Study of American Catholicism at Notre Dame University for granting me a financial award to conduct an ethnography at St. Augustine Church. Part of the discussion of St. Augustine Church in this chapter is based on that enthnographic work.

9. Interview with Father Michael Feketie, December 18, 2001.

10. Interview with María de los Angeles García, former associate director of the Newark Archdiocese–Catechesis for Hispanics, March 1, 2000. As diocesan president of Acción Católica during that period in Cuba, Ms. García participated in the design and implementation of these programs.

11. According to some sources, a *batey* is the traditional Taíno meeting place of the yucayeke (village) and its people (http://www.taino-tribe.org/irc.htm). Other authors claim that the term means the hamlet on a plantation/cane field. See Alum, Rolando, "El parentesco ritual en un batey dominicano/Ritual Kinship in a Dominican Batey," 26: 11–36 and "The Dominican Republic," 1185–1193.

12. Interviewed on October 1, 2002. Since this interview took place, the non-Cuban Hispanic membership has increased even more, in particular from Mexico. There are also some recent Cuban immigrants.

13. Interview with Father Pedro Navarro, October 1, 2002.

14. Conferencia de Obispos Católicos de Cuba, Secretariado General, *La voz de la Iglesia: 100 Documentos Episcopales*; Fernández, *Religión y Revolución en Cuba*, 55.

15. Fernández, 38–41.

16. Ibid., 37.

17. Ibid., 40–41.

18. Crahan, "Cuba" " 93–94.

19. Fernández, 88–89.

20. Ibid., 104.

21. Crahan, 93.

22. Ibid., 94–96.

23. Alfonso, *Cuba, Castro y los Católicos*, 132–170.

24. Ibid., 172–173; Fernández, 124–125. Many authors are critical of the Vatican policy at the time. Some in exile emphasize the fact that Msgr. Zacchi "imposed the Roman line," which overrode the bishops' authority and was only partially sensitive to Cuban reality. A letter from a group, "Cuban Priests in the Diaspora," which met in Venezuela in 1969, urged the Vatican not to forget "those who suffer the rigor of Marxism-Leninism, that is, many in jail, or those who,

harassed by the government, were forced to flee the country." However, many admit that Msgr. Zacchi's tenure in Cuba created wider channels of communication and improved relations between Church and state.

25. Conde, *Operation Pedro Pan,* 98. Also see Torres, *The Lost Apple,* 81.

26. Conferencia de Obispos Católicos de Cuba, *La voz de la Iglesia,* 171–174.

27. Ibid., 175.

28. Ibid., 185–186. The letter was published on September 3, 1969.

29. In a period of institutional weakness, when there were not many priests, lay Catholics had taken over many functions in their parishes. Their help was invaluable, and when they left, the Cuban church felt even more deprived.

30. Alfonso, *Cuba, Castro y los Católicos,* 177. In Cuba there was discontent in some quarters about the bishops' position. Some priests did not even read the letters in their Sunday masses, and some who did expressed their opposition after reading them.

31. Wenski, "Ties Between the Cuban Catholic Church and the Archdiocese of Miami." 14. Also, interview with María de los Angeles García, March 1, 2000. Both Wenski and García said that Cubans in the United States had a higher level of church participation than they did in Cuba. As noted earlier in this chapter, religion serves as a vehicle for immigrant integration into the new society. Cubans in particular may have sought help in religion to offset the dislocations of exile.

32. As a result of the Dialogue, 3,000 political prisoners were released and thousands of Cuban Americans began to travel to the island every year. The 1980s opened a new era in relations between Cubans and Cuban Americans. Cuban American academics participated at conferences in Cuba and Cuban academics began to attend professional meetings in the United States. However, in June, 2004, George W. Bush implemented measures that severely restricted travel to Cuba with the purpose of strengthening the embargo against the island.

33. Wenski, "Ties Between the Cuban Catholic Church and the Archdiocese of Miami," 14–15.

34. Conferencia de Obispos Católicos de Cuba, *La voz de la Iglesia,* 212.

35. Castro, Transcripts, Speech to the Jamaican Council of Churches, November 20, 1977 in Crahan, 104.

36. Crahan, 107.

37. Conferencia de Obispos Católicos de Cuba, *La voz de la Iglesia,* 218.

38. Encuentro Nacional Eclesial Cubano (ENEC), *Documento Final,* 209.

39. Conferencia de Obispos Católicos de Cuba, *La voz de la Iglesia,* 424–425.

40. The discussion on the pope's visit to Cuba is largely based on my participation in the event. I conducted a number of interviews by telephone or in person with pilgrims from Miami, Washington, New Jersey, and New York. References from interviews, conversations, magazines, and my own observations reflect the general mood among Cuban American Catholics at that time concerning John Paul II's visit to the island. I want to thank the Program for the Analysis of Religion Among Latinos (PARAL) of the Office of Research for Religion in Society and Culture of Brooklyn College, CUNY, for sponsoring our delegation's trip to Cuba during the pope's visit.

41. Conferencia de Obispos Católicos de Cuba, *La voz de la Iglesia,* 430.

42. See Comunidades de Reflexión Eclesial Cubana en la Diáspora, CRECED, *Documento Final.*

43. See Ramírez, "Visita del Papa crea contradicciones entre fé y política." IPS Latin America, January 19, 1998, http//www.ipslatam.net/.

44. Wenski, "Ties Between the Cuban Church and the Archdiocese of Miami," 15–16.

45. Nuñez, "La visita del Papa ha dejado una marca irreversible."

46. *Revista Maryknoll,* " Nuevos Caminos y Viejos Andares" Testimony of José Andreas Rionda.

47. Telephone interview with Clara Baloyra, September 22, 1998.

48. Telephone interview with José Manuel Hernández, June 23, 1999.

49. See Cantero, Araceli, "Vió una iglesia vibrante y encarnada durante un recorrido de varias diócesis y encuentro con laicos y obispos."

50. Ibid. Father Espino stayed in Cuba from 1999 to 2004.

51. Boza Masvidal, *Revista Ideal,* n.p.

52. Román, *Revista Ideal,* n.p.

53. See *Zenit, el mundo visto desde Roma,* "En Cuba estamos reducidos al silencio"; *La presencia social de la iglesia: Instrucción teológico pastoral.*

54. The change after 1998 has been remarkable given the climate of intolerance that existed before. Examples of this intolerance toward the Cuban clergy were the critics who lashed out at Cardinal Jaime Ortega when he visited Miami and New Jersey in 1994. In both places there were demonstrations against him outside the churches where he was officiating. Nonetheless, even at the time, the number of people who welcomed him inside the temples was much higher than those protesting outside.

CHAPTER 6

1. Portes and Rumbaut, *Immigrant America* 24.

2. The Bay of Pigs is an area that encompasses several beaches, among them Playa Larga and Playa Girón. Cuba refers to the invasion as Playa Girón because the exiles were defeated there. U.S. documents use the term Bay of Pigs.

3. Draper, *Castro's Revolution: Myths and Realities,* 100–101.

4. García, *Havana USA: Cuban Exiles and Cuban Americans in South Florida 1959–1994,* 126.

5. Ibid., 127.

6. Ibid., 130.

7. Pérez, *Cuba: Between Reform and Revolution,* 230.

8. Ibid., 236.

9. Ibid., 244.

10. Task Force on Memory, Truth, and Justice, *Cuban National Reconciliation,* 17.

11. Ibid., 19.

12. Blight and Kornbluh, *Politics of Illusion: The Bay of Pigs Invasion Reexamined,* 22.

13. These two New Jersey-born groups were very different. Abdala was a political group composed of young intellectuals. Their base was in Elizabeth, New Jersey. Years after its inception, Abdala developed an institutional affiliation with the Social Democrats in the United States (SDUSA). Omega 7 was always a radical, militant, and violent organization.

14. Anonymous interview, August 21, 2001. Many of my sources will remain anonymous because of the sensitive nature of this subject.

15. Anonymous interview, August 18, 2001.

16. Anonymous interview, September 22, 2003.

17. U.S. Department of Justice, FBI Report, 3.

18. Ibid., 6

19. Ibid. Also see Arboleya, *The Cuban Counterrevolution,* 171–172.

20. U.S. Department of Justice, FBI Report, 8.

21. Ibid., 6.

22. Council on Hemispheric Affairs, "Unfinished Business: Why Luis Posada Carriles, an Admitted Cuban Exile Terrorist, Should Face Justice in Venezuela," 1.

23. A discussion about the CANF will follow in this chapter.

24. Bardach and Rother, "Key Cuba Foe Claims Exile Backing," 11.

25. Ibid.

26. Corral and Chardy, "Posada habla en Miami desde su refugio."

27. The details of this controversial case are still unfolding. An El Paso federal judge dismissed the charges against Posada Carriles after finding fault with a government interview with him. After posting a $350,000 bond and being under 24-hour house arrest, Posada Carriles is at this time free in Miami. The U.S. government could appeal this decision. Since May 2007, the United States and Cuba began to cooperate in the search for evidence on Posada Carriles' alleged bombing of hotels in Havana and the death of an Italian national in those bombings.

28. Alpha 66, *Our History.* http://www.alpha66.org/

29. See Chapter 2.

30. García, 146.

31. Advertisement for the Cuban American National Foundation in *Girón* newspaper, Miami, June, 1982, 4. Cited in García, María Cristina, 147.

32. Canedy, "Heir to a Cuban Exile Leader is Finding His Own Voice."

33. Ibid.

34. Ibid.

35. On May 20th, there are usually parades in areas of Cuban concentration celebrating what exiles consider the day of Cuban independence in 1902. This date is not recognized in Cuba since it is thought to be an independence mediated by U.S. intervention.

36. Grenier and Pérez, *The Legacy of Exile: Cubans in the United States,* 98.

37. Ibid.

38. Interview with Remberto Pérez, August 9, 2005.

39. Varoqua, " N.J. Political History Full of Scandals."

40. Kocieniewski, "Corzine Forgave $470,000 Loan to Friend Who Runs State Union," 1.

41. Hernandez, "New Jersey Power Broker Extends His Reach: As Influence Grows in Congress, Menendez is Keeping His Options Open," B5.

42. See Connors, *A Cycle of Power: The Career of Jersey City Mayor Frank Hague.*

43. Seward, *Union City, 50th Anniversary, 1925–1975,* 55.

44. Rosero, "Former Mayor, State Senator, and Assemblyman William Musto Dies at 88," 2.

45. Ibid.

46. Ibid.

47. Edge, "The Inside Edge."http://www.politicsnj.com,/

48. Biography of the Honorable Robert Menendez, Jersey City's District Office.

49. Hernandez, B1.

50. Herszenhorn and Strunsky, "Deals, Debts, and the Choice for Speaker in New Jersey," F1.

51. Ibid., F5.

52. Ibid.

53. Wong, "Mayor of Union City Resigns Under Fire; Rival Replaces Him."

54. Hernandez, B5.

55. This is increasingly the case in Miami, as the cosmopolitan area is receiving diverse groups, especially from Latin America. However, because of the high concentration of Cubans, Cuban political figures and the Cuban electorate still carry a lot of weight.

56. As mentioned in previous chapters, in June 2004, after this interview was conducted, President Bush introduced the harshest measures so far to toughen the embargo against Cuba since this law was put in place. As part of those measures, Cubans in the United States cannot visit their relatives regularly. They are only allowed to go once every three years and they need to be first-degree relatives: parents, siblings, children. Aunts, uncles, and cousins do not count as family.

57. Grenier and Pérez, 95. Also see Jacobs, "The Cuban-American Heartland, Northern Chapter."

58. Cuba Study Group, "2008 Cuban/US Transition Poll," Institute for Public Opinion Research/Florida International University, Brookings Institution, 2008. http://www.fiu.edu/~ipor/cuba-t/

CHAPTER 7

1. Rogg, *The Assimilation of Cuban Exiles,* 2.

2. See Gordon, *Assimilation in American Life.*

3. See Portes and Zhou, "The New Second Generation: Segmented Assimilation and its Variants," 491–522. Jensen and Chitose, "Today's Second Generation: Evidence from the 1990 Census," 83.

4. Gorelick, *City College and the Jewish Poor,* 95–96.

5. See Blauner, *Racial Oppression in America,* 19–81.

6. For an application of this concept to the Haitian community in the United States see Laguerre, *Diasporic Citizenship: Haitian Americans in Transnational*

America, 190. For an excellent analysis of trends in immigration research and a discussion of these concepts, see Pedraza, "Immigration in America at the Turn of This Century: Assimilation or Diasporic Citizenship?," 377–381. Also, for a study of transnationalism using the example of Mexicans in New York, see Smith, "Mexicans: Social, Educational, Economic, and Political Problems and Prospects in New York," in Foner, 2001, 275–300, as well as his many other publications on the subject.

7. Ore, *The Social Construction of Difference and Inequality,* 1.

8. Ibid., 9. The changes to the 2000 U.S. census were justified by "the increasing diversity of our nation's population stemming from growth in interracial marriages and immigration." U.S. Bureau of the Census 2000; Racial and Ethnic Classifications Used in Cesus 2000 and Beyond." (http://www.census.gov/dmd/www/2000quest.html).

9. Bonilla-Silva and Glover, "'We Are All Americans:' The Latin Americanization of Race Relations in the United States," 150.

10. Ibid.

11. Bobo, "Inequalities that Endure? Racial Ideology, American Politics, and the Peculiar Role of the Social Sciences," 15–16.

12. See Torres-Saillant, "The Tribulations of Blackness: Stages in Dominican Racial Identity," 126–127. Also see Bailey, *Language, Race, and Negotiation of Identity: A Study of Dominican Americans.*

13. Bonilla-Silva and Glover, 164.

14. For example, part of this new racial pride includes self-identifying as Afro-Cuban. Yesenia certainly does. Most older black Cubans would not use that classification.

15. See Pérez, "Immigrant Economic Adjustment and Family Organization: The Cuban Success Story Reexamined."

16. See Prieto, "Cuban Women in the U.S. Labor Force: Perspectives on the Nature of Change."

17. The figure for my study sample was even higher in the 1980s (68.2%). Cubans migrated to the United States in their peak productive years (37.5 median age in 1980 as opposed to 23.2 for the whole population, 21.8 for Mexican Americans, and 22.3 for Puerto Ricans).

18. López, *La autobiografía hispana contemporánea en los Estados Unidos: A través del caleidoscopio,* 5—6.

19. Ibid., 7.

20. Portes and Rumbaut, *Immigrant America,* 114.

21. Ibid., 115–116.

22. Ibid., 6. Also see Portes, ed. *The New Second Generation.*

23. *Catholic New York,* "Looking Forward on Immigration," 10.

24. Ibid.

25. Preston and Connelly, "Immigration Bill Provisions Gain Wide Support in Poll," 1.

26. Ibid.

27. Ibid.

28. Huntington, "The Hispanic Challenge"; Huntington, *Who Are We? The Challenges to America's National Identity.*

29. Huntington, "The Hispanic Challenge," 1.

30. Ibid., 3–5.

31. Drezner, "Hash of Civilizations," 2.

32. Ibid.

33. Ibid.

34. Fukuyama, "Identity Crisis: Why We Shouldn't Worry About Mexican Immigration."

35. Ibid., 4. It should be noted that part of Fukuyama's argument is based on religion, too.

36. Drezner, 2.

37. Huntington, "The Hispanic Challenge," 12.

38. Ibid.

Bibliography

Ackerman, Holly. "The *Balsero* Phenomenon." *Cuban Studies* 26 (1996): 169–200.

Ackerman, Holly, and Juan M. Clark. *The Cuban Balseros: Voyage of Uncertainty.* Miami: Cuban American National Council, 1995.

Acosta-Belén, Edna., and Carlos E. Santiago. *Puerto Ricans in the United States: A Contemporary Portrait.* Boulder, CO: Lynne Rienner, 2006.

Aja Díaz, Antonio. "La emigración de Cuba en los años noventa." *Cuban Studies* 30 (1999): 1–25.

Alfonso, Pablo. *Cuba, Castro y los Católicos.* Miami: Hispamerican Books, 1985.

Alonso, Aurelio. *Iglesia Católica y política revolucionaria en Cuba.* La Habana: Editorial Ciencias Sociales, 1997.

Alpha 66. *Our History: Cuban Freedom Fighters in Quest of the Liberation of Our Homeland.* Public document, http://alpha66.org/english/our/%20history.htm. Retrieved on July 14, 2005.

Alum, Rolando. "The Dominican Republic." In Delury, G., ed. *World Encyclopedia of Political Systems and Parties,* New York: Facts on File, 1983: 1185–1193.

———. "El parentesco ritual en un batey dominicano/Ritual Kinship in a Dominican Batey." *Revista EME-EME Estudios Dominicanos* 26 (1997): 11–36.

———, and Luis Alum, Review of "The Assimilation of Cuban Exiles: The Role of Community and Class," by Eleanor Rogg . *International Migration Review* 12 (Spring 1978): 143–144.

Amaro, Nelson, and Alejandro Portes. "Una Sociología del Exilio: Situación de los Grupos Cubanos en los Estados Unidos." *Aportes* 23 (1972): 6–24.

Anderson, Nels. *The Hobo.* Chicago: University of Chicago Press, 1923.

Arboleya, Jesús. *The Cuban Counterrevolution.* Translated by Rafael Betancourt. Athens: Ohio University Center for International Studies, Ohio University, 2000.

Bach, Robert L. "The New Cuban Immigrants: Their Background and Prospects." *Monthly Labor Review* 103 (1980): 39–46.

Bailey, Benjamin. *Language, Race, and Negotiation of Identity: A Study of Dominican Americans.* New York: LFB Scholarly Publishing, 2002.

Bardach, Ann L., and Larry Rother. "Key Cuba Foe Claims Exile Backing." *The New York Times,* July 12, 1998: 11.

Bash, Linda. "The Vincentians and Grenadians: The Role of Voluntary Associations in Immigrant Adaptation to New York City." In Foner, Nancy, ed. *New Immigrants in New York,* New York: Columbia University Press, 1987: 160–162.

Berger, Joseph. "Dominicans Gaining on Puerto Ricans in the City," *The New York Times,* October 9, 2003: B–1 Metro Section.

Bischoff, Henry. "Caribbean Peoples of New Jersey: An Overview." *New Jersey History* 113: 1,2 (Spring/Summer, 1995): 1–30.

———. *Immigration Issues.* Westport, CT: Greenwood Press, 2002.

Blauner, Robert. *Racial Oppression in America.* New York: Harper and Row, 1972.

Blight, James, and Peter Kornbluh. *Politics of Illusion: The Bay of Pigs Invasion Reexamined.* Boulder, CO: Lynne Reinner Publishers, 1988.

Bobo, Lawrence, D. "Inequalities that Endure? Racial Ideology, American Politics, and the Peculiar Role of the Social Sciences." In Krysan, Maria, and Amanda E. Lewis, eds. *The Changing Terrain of Race and Ethnicity.* New York: Russell Sage Foundation, 2004: 13–42.

Bonacich, Edna, Ivan Light, H. and Charles Choy Wong. "Koreans in Business." *Society* 14:6 (1977): 54–59.

Bonilla-Silva, Eduardo, and Karen S. Glover. "'We Are All Americans:' The Latin Americanization of Race Relations in the United States." In Krysan, Maria and Amanda E. Lewis, eds. *The Changing Terrain of Race and Ethnicity.* New York: Russell Sage Foundation, 2004: 149–183.

Boza Masvidal, Eduardo, Bishop Msgr. Interview by the Ideal Staff. *Revista Ideal,* No. 283, 1988, n.p.

Brait, Susan. "The Cubans of Union City." *New Jersey Monthly,* March 1981: 73–91.

Canedy, Dana. "Heir to a Cuban Exile Leader is Finding His Own Voice." *The New York Times,* September 2, 2001: 12, National Report.

Cantero, Araceli. "Vió una iglesia vibrante y encarnada durante un recorrido de varias diócesis y encuentro con laicos y obispos." *La voz católica,* March 11, 1999.

Casal, Lourdes. *Images of Cuban Society Among Pre and Post Revolutionary Novelists.* Ph.D. dissertation, The New School for Social Research, New York, NY, 1975.

Castro, Fidel. *Transcripts.* Speech to the Jamaican Council of Churches, November 20, 1977, in Crahan, "Cuba," 104.

Catholic New York. (2007) Looking forward on immigration. Editorial. May 24.

Center for Children and Technology. *The Transformation of Union City: 1989 to Present.* New York: Education Development Center, 2000.

Cobas, José A., and Jorge Duany. *Cubans in Puerto Rico: Ethnic Economy and Cultural Identity.* Gainesville: University Press of Florida, 1995.

Cohen, Miriam. "Italian American Women in New York City, 1900–1950: Work and School." In Cantor, Milton and Laurie Bruce, eds. *Class, Sex, and the Woman Worker.* Westport, CT: Greenwood Press, 1977: 120–143.

Comas, Lourdes, ed. *West New York Leones Cubanos de Hudson, 20 Aniversario.* Union City, NJ: Open Mind Designs, 1999.

Comunidades de Reflexión Eclesial Cubana en la Diáspora, CRECED, *Documento Final.* Hato Rey, Puerto Rico, Ramallo Bros. Printing, 1996.

Conde, Yvonne, M. *Operation Pedro Pan: The Untold Exodus of 14,048 Cuban Children.* New York: Routledge Press, 1999.

Conferencia de Obispos Católicos de Cuba. Secretariado General. *La voz de la iglesia: 100 documentos episcopales.* Mexico, D.F.: Obra Nacional de la Buena Prensa, 1995.

———. "La Presencia Social de la Iglesia: Instrucción Teológico-Pastoral," Pastoral Letter, Festivity of the Virgin of El Cobre, September 8, 2003.

Connors, Richard. *A Cycle of Power: The Career of Jersey City Mayor Frank Hague.* Metuchen, NJ: Scarecrow Press, Inc.1971.

Corral, Oscar, and Alfonso Chardy. "Posada habla en Miami desde su refugio," *The Miami Herald* (El Nuevo Herald. com), May 17, 2005.

Council on Hemispheric Affairs. "Unfinished Business: Why Luis Posada Carriles, an Admitted Cuban Exile Terrorist, Should Face Justice in Venezuela." Press Release. August 11, 2005.

Crahan, Margaret. "Cuba." In Sigmund, Paul, ed. *Religious Freedom and Evangelization in Latin America.* Maryknoll, N.Y.: Orbis Books, 1999: 87–112.

Cuba Study Group. "2008 Cuba/US Transition Poll," Institute for Public Opinion Research/Florida International University, Brookings Institution, 2008, http://www.fiu.edu/~ipor/cuba-t/. Retrieved on January 28, 2009.

Díaz-Briquets, Sergio. "Cuban-Owned Businesses in the United States." *Cuban Studies* 14:2 (1984): 57–64.

Dolce, Phillip C. "Faces of Immigration: The Cubans of New Jersey." In Yans-McLaughlin, Virginia, ed. *The Teaching of History: Ellis Island and American Immigration.* New Brunswick, NJ, 1985: 1–10.

Dominguez, Virginia. "The Nature of Change: Cuban Women in the United States." Paper presented at the Conference on Women and Change, Boston University, Boston, MA, May 6–7, 1977.

———. "Sex, Gender, and Revolution: The Problem of Construction and the Construction of a Problem." *Cuban Studies* 17 (1987): 7–23.

Draper, Theodore. *Castro's Revolution: Myths and Realities.* New York: Frederick A. Praeger Publishers, 1962.

Drezner, Daniel W. "Hash of Civilizations." *The New Republic* March 3, 2004. Online, http://www.danieldrezner.com/policy/hash.htm. Retrieved December 4, 2008.

Duany, Jorge. "Neither Golden Exile nor Dirty Worm: Ethnic Identity in Recent Cuban-American Novels." *Cuban Studies* 23 (1993): 167–183.

Durán, Aleida. "La Caridad del Cobre en North Hudson," *Noche de gala de la Caridad, 2003. Libro Programa.* North Bergen, NJ: Navea Printing, 2003.

Edge, Wally."The Inside Edge," April 22, 2002: 3. Online, http://www.politicsNJ.com. Retrieved on August 24, 2005.

Eickmann, Walter T. *History of West New York.* Published under the auspices of the Golden Jubilee Committee, West New York, NJ, 1948.

Encuentro Nacional Eclesial Cubano (ENEC). *Documento Final.* Rome, Italy: Tipografía Don Bosco, 1987.

Estévez, Guillermo A. "Resettling the Cuban Refugees in New Jersey." *Migration Today* 11:4,5 (1983): 28–33.

Farber, Samuel. *The Origins of the Cuban Revolution Reconsidered.* Chapel Hill: University of North Carolina Press, 2006.

———. Interview: Anthony Arnove and Ahmed Shawki interview Sam Farber on "Castro's Cuba in Perspective." *International Socialist Review* No. 36 (July-August, 2004).

Fernández, Damián. *The Politics of Passion.* Gainesville: University Press of Florida, 2000.

Fernández, Manuel. *Religión y Revolución en Cuba.* Miami: Saeta Ediciones, 1984.

Fernández-Kelly, María Patricia, and Anna M. García. "Power Surrendered, Power Restored: The Politics of Work and Family Among Hispanic Garment Workers in California and Florida." In Tilly, Louise, and Patricia Gurin, eds. *Women, Politics, and Change.* New York: Russell Sage Foundation, 1990: 130–149.

Ferre, Myra Marx. "Employment Without Liberation: Cuban Women in the United States." *Social Science Quaterly* 60 (June 1979). 35–50.

Foner, Nancy, ed. *New Immigrants in New York.* New York: Columbia University Press, 1987.

———. *New Immigrants in New York.* Revised Edition. New York: Columbia University Press, 2001.

Forero, Juan. "How 'Fomentenses' Came to the U.S. and Reshaped Hudson County." *The Jersey Journal,* Section A–2, August 23, 1999.

Fox, Geoffrey E. "Honor, Shame, and Women's Liberation in Cuba." In Pescatello, Ann, ed. *Female and Male in Latin America.* 273–292.

Friedman-Kasaba, Kathie. *Memories of Migration: Gender, Ethnicity, and Work in the Lives of Jewish and Italian Women in New York, 1870–1924.* Albany: State University of New York Press, 1996.

Fukuyama, Francis. "Identity Crisis: Why We Shouldn't Worry About Mexican Immigration." *Slate* June 4, 2004. Online, http://www.slate.com/id2101756/. Retrieved December 4, 2008.

Gabaccia, Donna, ed. *Seeking Common Ground: Multidisciplinary Studies of Immigrant Women in the United States.* Westport, CT: Greenwood Press, 1992.

García, Cristina. *Dreaming in Cuban.* New York: Alfred A. Knopf, 1992.

García, María Cristina. *Havana USA: Cuban Exiles and Cuban Americans in South Florida 1959–1994.* Berkeley: University of California Press, 1996.

Glick Schiller, Nina, and Eugene Fouron Georges. *George Woke Up Laughing: Long Distance Nationalism and the Search for Home.* Durham, NC: Duke University Press, 2001.

Glick Schiller, Nina, Linda Basch, and Cristina Szanton-Blanc, eds. *Towards a Transnational Perspective on Migration: Race, Class, Ethnicity, and Nationalism Reconsidered.* New York: New York Academy of Sciences, 1992.

Goldin, Liliana R., ed. *Identities on the Move: Transnational Processes in North America and the Caribbean Basin.* Albany, NY: Institute for Mesoamerican Studies, State University of New York, 1999.

González Pagés, Julio César. *En busca de un espacio: Historia de mujeres en Cuba.* La Habana: Editorial Ciencias Sociales, 2003.

Gordon, Milton. *Assimilation in American Life.* New York: Oxford University Press, 1964.

Gorelick, Sherry. *City College and the Jewish Poor: Education in New York, 1880–1924.* New Brunswick, NJ: Rutgers University Press, 1981.

Greeley, Andrew. *The Denominational Society.* Glenview, IL: Scott Foresman, 1972.

———. *The Catholic Myth: The Behavior and Beliefs of American Catholics.* New York: Charles Scribner's Sons, 1990.

Grenier, Guillermo J., and Lisandro Pérez. *The Legacy of Exile: Cubans in the United States.* Boston: New Immigrant Series, Allyn and Bacon, 2003.

Handlin, Oscar. *The Uprooted: The Epic Story of the Great Migration that Made the American People.* Boston: Little, Brown, 1951.

Haslip-Viera, Gabriel, and Sherrie L. Baver, eds. *Latinos in New York: Communities in Transition.* Notre Dame, IN: University of Notre Dame Press, 1996.

Henken, Ted. "*Balseros, Boteros* and *El Bombo*: Post-1994 Cuban Immigration to the United States and the Persistence of Special Treatment," *Latino Studies* 3:3 (2005): 393–416.

Hernández, Rafael. "La política de los Estados Unidos hacia Cuba y la cuestión de la migración." *Cuadernos de Nuestra América* 2:3 (1985): 75–100.

Hernández, Rafael, and Redi Gomis. "Retrato del Mariel: el ángulo socioeconómico." *Cuadernos de Nuestra América* 3:5 (1986): 124–151.

Hernandez, Raymond. "New Jersey Power Broker Extends His Reach: As Influence Grows in Congress, Menendez is Keeping His Options Open." *The New York Times,* July 3, 2001: B5, Metro Section.

Herszenhorn, David, and Steven Strunsky. "Deals, Debts, and the Choice for Speaker in New Jersey." *The New York Times,* December 3, 2001: F1,5.

Hollingshead, August B., and F.C. Redlich. *Social Class and Mental Illness: A Community Study.* New York: John Wiley and Sons, 1958.

Hondagneu-Soleto, Pierrette, ed. *Gender and U.S. Immigration.* Berkeley: University of California Press, 2003.

Huntington, Samuel P. "The Hispanic Challenge." *Foreign Policy* (March/April 2004).

———. *Who Are We? The Challenges to America's National Identity.* New York: Simon and Schuster, 2004.

Jacobs, Andrew. "The Cuban-American Heartland, Northern Chapter." *The New York Times,* April 11, 2000: B1, Metro Section.

Jensen, Leif, and Yoshimi Chitose. "Today's Second Generation: Evidence from the 1990 Census." In Portes, Alejandro, ed. *The New Second Generation.* New York: Russell Sage Foundation, 1996 82–107.

JUCEPLAN, *Aspectos Demográficos de la Fuerza Laboral Femenina en Cuba.* La Habana: Dirección Nacional de Estadísticas, 1975.

Kaufman Purcell, Susan. "Modernizing Women for a Modern Society: The Cuban Case." In Pescatello, Ann, ed. *Female and Male in Latin America.* Pittsburgh: University of Pittsburgh Press, 1970.

Kefalas, Maria. *Working Class Heroes: Protecting Home, Community, and Nation in a Chicago Neighborhood.* Berkeley: University of California Press, 2003.

Kelly, Oliver, ed. *The Portable Kristeva.* New York: Columbia University Press, 2002.

Kocieniewski, David. "Corzine Forgave $470,000 Loan to Friend Who Runs State Union." *The New York Times,* August 4, 2005: 1.

Krysan, Maria, and Amanda E. Lewis, eds. *The Changing Terrain of Race and Ethnicity.* New York: Russell Sage Foundation, 2004.

Kwong, Peter. *The New Chinatown.* New York: Hill and Wang, 1988 (revised 1996).

Laguerre, Michel S. *Diasporic Citizenship: Haitian Americans in Transnational America.* New York: St. Martin's Press, 1998.

Light, Ivan H., and Parminder Bhachu, eds. *Immigration and Entrepreneurship: Culture, Capital, and Ethnic Networks.* New Brunswick, NJ: Transaction Publishers, 2004.

López, Iraida. *La autobiografía hispana contemporánea en los Estados Unidos: A través del caleidoscopio.* Lewiston, NY: Edwin Mellen Press, 2001: 5–6.

López, Nancy. "Disentangling Race-Gender Work Experiences: Second Generation Caribbean Young Adults in New York City." In Hondagneu-Soleto, Pierrette, ed. *Gender and U.S. Immigration.* Berkeley, CA: University of California Press, 2003.

Lowenstein, Steven M. *Frankfurt on the Hudson: The German-Jewish Community of Washington Heights, 1933–1983, Its Structure and Culture.* Detroit, MI: Wayne State University Press, 1989: 255–269.

Lyon, Larry. *The Community in Urban Society.* Prospect Heights, IL: Waveland Press, 1989 (reissued in 1999).

Martínez-Alier, Verena. *Marriage, Class, and Colour in Nineteenth Century Cuba.* Cambridge, UK: Cambridge University Press, 1974.

Masud-Piloto, Félix. "The Mariel Boatlift of 1980: Consequences of a Politicized Migration Policy." *Dialogo* 7 (Spring 2003). Chicago: Center for Latino Research, DePaul University: 25–30.

Menendez, Robert, Honorable. *Biography.* Jersey City's District Office, Jersey City, N.J.

Morril, Jennifer. "Cubans Head to Bergen Suburbs," *The Jersey Journal,* May 24, 2001: 1, Section 1.

Mortimer, Delores M., and Roy Bryce-Laporte, eds. *Female Immigrants to the United States: Caribbean, Latin American and African Experiences.* Washington, DC: Research Institute on Immigration and Ethnic Studies, Smithsonian Institution, 1981.

New Jersey Department of Human Services. *Public Assistance Manual. Refugee Resettlement Program.* December, 1982.

New Jersey Department of Labor. *New Jersey Population Trends, 1790–2000.* Trenton, NJ: NJSDC 2000 Census Publication, Division of Labor Market and Demographic Research, New Jersey State Data Center, August, 2001.

New York Times. "Newest Immigrants Head Straight to New Jersey's Suburbs." March 10, 2001: B1, Metro Section.

North Jersey Media Group. "N.J. Political History full of Scandals," August 13, 2004, http://www.northjersey.com/page.php?qstr=eXJpcnk3ZjczN2Y3dn . . . (URL no longer available.)

Nuñez, Pedro, Rev. "La visita del Papa ha dejado una marca irreversible." *Mensaje* (February/March, 1998): 6–7.

O'Connor, James. *The Origins of Socialism in Cuba.* Ithaca, NY: Cornell University Press, 1970.

Oficina Nacional de Estadísticas (ONE). *Cuba en Cifras, Cuba in Figures.* La Habana, July, 2003.

Ojito, Mirta. "You Are Going to El Norte." *The New York Times Magazine,* April 23, 2000. Online, http://query.nytimes.com/gst/fullpage.html?res=9A05EFDC1231F930A15757C0A9669C8B63&n=Top/Reference/Times%20Topics/People/O/Ojito,%20Mirta&scp=20&sq=ojito%20mirta&st=cse. Retrieved December 4, 2008.

——— *Finding Mañana: A Memoir of a Cuban Exodus,* New York: Penguin Books, 2006.

Ore, Tracy E. *The Social Construction of Difference and Inequality.* Second Edition. New York: McGraw Hill, 2003.

PARAL (Program for the Analysis of Religion Among Latinos). *The National Survey of Leadership in Latino Parishes and Congregations: A Summary Report.* Brooklyn, NY: Office of Publications, Brooklyn College, 2002.

Patillo-McCoy, Mary. *Black Picket Fences: Privilege and Peril Among the Black Middle Class.* Chicago: University of Chicago Press, 1999.

Pedraza, Silvia. *Political Disaffection in Cuba's Revolution and Exodus.* New York: Cambridge University Press, 2007.

———. "Cuba's Refugees: Manifold Migrations." In Pedraza, Silvia, and Rubén G. Rumbaut, eds. *Origins and Destinies: Immigration, Race, and Ethnicity in America.* Belmont, CA: Wadsworth Publishing Co., 1996: 263–279.

———. "Immigration in America at the Turn of this Century: Assimilation or Diasporic Citizenship?," *Contemporary Sociology* 28:4 (1999): 377–381.

Pedraza-Bailey, Silvia. *Political and Economic Migrants in America: Cubans and Mexicans.* Austin, TX: University of Texas Press, 1985.

Pérez, Humberto. "Cuban Journalism in Exile." In Rodríguez Zaldívar, Rodolfo, and Bienvenido Madán, eds. *Páginas de Oro del Exilio Cubano 1959–1983.* Publisher unknown.

Pérez, Lisandro. "Immigrant Economic Adjustment and Family Organization: The Cuban Success Story Reexamined." *International Migration Review* 20 (Spring 1986): 4–20.

Pérez, Louis A. Jr. *Cuba: Between Reform and Revolution.* New York: Oxford University Press, 1998.

Pérez-Firmat, Gustavo. *Life on the Hyphen: The Cuban-American Way.* Austin: University of Texas Press, 1994.

Pérez-Stable, Marifeli. *The Cuban Revolution: Origins, Course, and Legacy.* Second Edition. New York: Oxford University Press, 1999.

Peristiany, J.G. *Honour and Shame: The Values of Mediterranean Society.* Chicago: Chicago University Press, 1966.

Pescatello, Ann, ed. *Female and Male in Latin America.* Pittsburgh, PA: University of Pittsburgh Press, 1970.

Pessar, Patricia R., and Pamela M. Graham. "Dominicans: Transnational Identities and Local Politics." In Foner, Nancy, ed. *New Immigrants in New York,* 2001: 251–273.

Portes, Alejandro, ed. *The New Second Generation.* New York: Russell Sage Foundation, 1996.

Portes, Alejandro, and Rubén G. Rumbaut. *Immigrant America: A Portrait.* Berkeley: University of California Press, 1996.

Portes, Alejandro, and Alex Stepick. *City on the Edge: The Transformation of Miami.* Berkeley: University of California Press, 1993.

Portes, Alejandro, and M. Zhou. "The New Second Generation: Segmented Assimilation and Its Variants." *Annals of the American Academy of Political and Social Sciences* 530 (November 1993): 74–96.

Powell, Michael. "Gone is the Swaggering Prince of Prosecution." *The New York Times*, April 1, 2007. Online, http://www.nytimes.com. Retrieved December 4, 2008.

Poyo, Gerald E. *"With All and for the Good of All": The Emergence of Popular Nationalism in the Cuban Communities of the United States, 1848–1898.* Durham, NC: Duke University Press, 1989.

Preston, Julia, and Marjorie Connelly. "Immigration Bill Provisions Gain Wide Support in Poll." *The New York Times*, May 25, 2007: 1.

Prieto, Yolanda. *Reinterpreting an Immigration Success Story: Cuban Women, Work, and Change in a New Jersey Community.* Ph.D. dissertation, Rutgers, The State University of New Jersey, New Brunswick, NJ, 1984.

———. "Cuban Women in the U.S. Labor Force: Perspectives on the Nature of Change." In "Sex, Gender, and Revolution." Domínguez, Virginia R. and Yolanda Prieto, Guest Editors, *Cuban Studies* 17 (1987): 73–91.

———. "Cuban Women in New Jersey: Gender Relations and Change." In Gabaccia, Donna, ed. *Seeking Common Ground: Multidisciplinary Studies of Immigrant Women in the United States.* 185–201.

———. "Continuity or Change?: Two Generations of Cuban American Women." *New Jersey History* 113:1–2 (1995): 47–59.

———. *The Catholic Church and the Cuban Diaspora,* Washington, DC: Georgetown University Cuba Occasional Paper Series, Caribbean Project, Center for Latin American Studies, 2001.

———. "Cuban-American Catholics and National Reconciliation: The Impact of the Pope's Visit to Cuba." In Stevens-Arroyo, Anthony M. ed. *Papal Overtures in a Cuban Key.* 83–99.

Prohías, Rafael, and Lourdes Casal. *The Cuban Minority in the United States: Preliminary Report on Need Identification and Program Evaluation.* Boca Raton: Florida Atlantic University, Cuban National Planning Council, 1973.

Ramírez Calzadilla, Jorge. *Religión y relaciones sociales: un estudio sobre la significación sociopolítica de la religión en la sociedad cubana.* La Habana: Editorial Academia, 2000.

Ramírez, Lyng-Hou, "Visita del Papa crea contradicciones entre fé y política," *Inter-Press Service Latin America(IPS).* Montevideo, Uruguay, January 19, 1998.

Online, http//www.ipslatam.net/. (URL no longer available.)

República de Cuba. *Censos de Población, Viviendas y Electoral.* Informes Generales. La Habana, 1943.

———. *Censos de Población, Viviendas y Electoral.* Informes Generales. La Habana, 1953.

Revista Maryknoll. "Nuevos caminos y viejos andares," Testimony of José Andreas Rionda, May, 1998.

Revista Oficial de la Asociación Nacional de Mujeres Cubanoamericanas de New Jersey (Official Magazine of the National Association of Cuban American Women NACAW [New Jersey Chapter], 308 38th Street, Union City, NJ), November 7, 1999.

Rieder, Jonathan. *Canarsie: The Jews and Italians of Brooklyn Against Liberalism.* Cambridge, MA: Harvard University Press, 1985.

Rodríguez Zaldívar, Rodolfo, and Bienvenido Madán. *Páginas de Oro del Exilio Cubano, 1959–1983.* 1983.

Rogg, Eleanor Meyer. *The Assimilation of Cuban Exiles: The Role of Community and Class.* New York: Aberdeen Press, 1974.

Rogg, Eleanor Meyer, and Rosemary Santana Cooney. *Adaptation and Adjustment of Cubans: West New York, New Jersey.* Bronx, NY: Hispanic Research Center, Fordham University, 1980.

Román, Agustín Msgr. Interview by the Ideal Staff. *Revista Ideal* No. 283 (1998).

Rosero, Jessica. "Former Mayor, State Senator, and Assemblyman William Musto Dies at 88," *Hudson Reporter,* March 5, 2006.

Safa, Helen I. "The Differential Incorporation of Hispanic Women Migrants Into the U.S. Labor Force." In Mortimer, Delores M. and Roy Bryce-Laporte, eds. *Female Immigrants to the United States: Caribbean, Latin American, and African Experiences.* Washington, DC, Research Institute on Immigration and Ethnic Studies, Smithsonian Institution, 1981.

———. *The Myth of the Male Breadwinner.* Boulder, CO: Westview Press, 1995.

Sanchez-Korrol, Virginia. *From Colonia to Community: The History of Puerto Ricans in New York.* Berkeley: University of California Press, 1994.

Santana-Cooney, Rosemary, and Vilma Ortiz. "Hispanic Female Participation in the Labor Force: A Comparative Analysis of Puerto Ricans, Mexicans, and Cubans." Paper presented at the Population Association of America Meeting, New York, NY, 1981.

Scott, Joan W. "The Evidence of Experience." *Critical Inquiry* (Summer, 1991): 773–797.

Seward, Steve. *Union City: 50th Anniversary, 1925–1975.* Union City Public Library, n.d.

Smith, Robert. *Mexican New York: Transnational Lives of New Immigrants.* Berkeley: CA: University of California Press, 2005.

———. "Mexicans: Social, Educational, Economic, and Political Problems and Prospects in New York." In Foner, Nancy, ed. *New Immigrants in New York.* Revised Edition. New York: Columbia University Press, 2001.

Smith, Timothy. "Religion and Ethnicity in America." *American Historical Review* 83. Cited in Warner, Stephen R. *Introducing the New Ethnic and Immigrant Congregations Project,* Chicago: Office of Social Science Research, University of Illinois at Chicago, 1993.

State of New Jersey, Department of Human Services, Division of Public Welfare. *Guidelines.* November 24, 1980.

State of New Jersey, Department of Institutions and Agencies, Division of Public Welfare, Fiscal and Management Operations. *Public Welfare Statistics for the Month of November, 1975.* April 14, 1976.

Stevens-Arroyo, Anthony M. *Papal Overtures in a Cuban Key: The Pope's Visit and Civic Space for Cuban Religion.* Scranton, PA: University of Scranton Press, 2002.

Stoner, K. Lynn. *From the House to the Streets: The Cuban Woman's Movement for Legal Reform, 1898–1940.* Durham, NC: Duke University Press, 1991.

Stoner, K. Lynn, and Hipólito Serrano Pérez. *Cuban and Cuban American Women: An Annotated Bibliography.* Wilmington, DE: Scholarly Resources, 2000.

Task Force on Memory, Truth, and Justice. *Cuban National Reconciliation.* Miami: Latin American and Caribbean Center, Florida International University, 2003.

Tilly, Louise, and Patricia Gurin, eds. *Women, Politics, and Change.* New York: Russell Sage Foundation, 1990.

Torreira Crespo, Ramón, and José Buajasan Marrawi. *Operación Peter Pan: Un caso de guerra psicológica contra Cuba.* La Habana: Editora Política, 2000.

Torres, María de los Angeles. *In the Land of Mirrors: Cuban Exile Politics in the United States.* Ann Arbor: University of Michigan Press, 1999.

———. *The Lost Apple: Operation Pedro Pan, Cuban Children in the U.S., and the Promise of a Better Future.* Boston: Beacon Press, 2003.

Torres-Saillant, Silvio. "The Tribulations of Blackness: Stages in Dominican Racial Identity." *Latin American Perspectives,* Issue 100, 25:3 (1998): 126–146.

Tully Tapia, Sarah. "Two States Differ on Bilingual Ed's Value," www.azstarnet.com The Online Service of the Arizona Daily Star, . April 11, 2000. Online, http://www.azstarnet.com/bilingual/day3–1.html. Retrieved December 4, 2008.

U.S. Bureau of the Census. 1977 Economic Census, Survey of Minority-Owned Business Enterprises. Washington, DC, March, 1981.

———. Census of Population, 1980, *General Social and Economic Characteristics,* Vol. 1 Series, PC-80–1-CI. Washington, DC: U. S. Department of Commerce, 1983.

———. Census of Population, 1980, *General Social and Economic Characteristics, New Jersey.* Washington, DC: U.S. Department of Commerce, December, 1983.

———. 1987 Economic Census, Survey of the Minority-Owned Business Enterprises. Washington, DC, March, 1991.

———. Current Population Survey, data transcribed from *Employment and Earnings.* Washington, DC: U.S. Department of Commerce, 1991.

———. U.S. Census of Population and Housing, Profile 1 *General Characteristics of the Population.* Summary Tape File 1. Prepared by the New Jersey State Data Center. Trenton, NJ: New Jersey Department of Labor, May 1981, May 1991.

———. 1992 Economic Census, Survey of Minority-Owned Business Enterprises. Washington, DC, March, 1996.

———. *Average Household Size, Census 2000, Hudson County.* Washington, DC: PCT8, Summary File 4 (SF4) Sample Data, U.S. Department of Commerce, 2000.

———. *Average Household Size, Census 2000, United States.* Washington, DC: Summary File 4 (SF4), Sample Data, U.S. Department of Commerce, 2000.

———. *Basic Demographic Characteristics,* Washington, DC: 2000.

———. *Family Type by Presence and Age of Own Children, Racial or Ethnic Grouping: Cuban, Hudson County.* Washington, DC: Summary File 2 (SF2), U.S. Department of Commerce, 2000.

———. *Sex and Age by Employment Status, Racial or Ethnic Groupings, Hudson County, N.J.* Washington, DC: PCT79, Summary File 4 (SF 4) Sample Data, U.S. Department of Commerce, 2000.

———. *Sex by Age by Employment Status, Racial or Ethnic Groupings, United States.* Census Summary File 4 (SF4) Sample Data. Washington, DC: U.S. Department of Commerce, 2000.

———. 1997 Economic Census, *Survey of Minority-Owned Business Enterprises*. Washington, DC: March, 2001.

———. *General Demographic and Social Characteristics, Hudson County, New Jersey, 2000*, released May 23, 2002. http://www.census.gov. Retrieved on April 15, 2005.

———. *American Community Survey*, Washington, DC: 2006.

———. U.S. Census of the Population 2000. Table DT-1, *Profile of General Demographic and Social Characteristics, 2000*, updated May 5, 2006. http://www.census.gov. Retrieved on April 15, 2005.

———. "Racial and Ethnic Classifications Used in Census 2000 and Beyond," April 10, 2008. (http://www.census.gov/dmd/www/2000quest.html)

U.S. Department of Justice, Federal Bureau of Investigation. *Omega 7* Cuban Information Archives, Washington, DC: October 29, 1993. Online, http://cuban-exile.com_001–025/doc0011.html. Retrieved December 4, 2008.

U.S. Department of State, *A Report of the Cuban-Haitian Task Force*, Washington, DC: Government Printing Office, 1980.

Valdés, Nelson P. "The Historical Context of the Cuban Family." Typescript, n.d., author's collection.

Warner, Stephen R. *Introducing the New Ethnic and Immigrant Congregations Project.* Chicago: Office of Social Science Research, University of Illinois at Chicago, July 1993.

Warren, Roland L., and Larry Lyon. *New Perspectives on the American Community.* Chicago: Dorsey Press, 1988.

Weinberg, Sydney Stahl. *The World of Our Mothers.* Chapel Hill: University of North Carolina Press, 1988.

Wenski, Thomas G., Msgr. "Ties Between the Cuban Catholic Church and the Archdiocese of Miami." Unpublished paper delivered at the XII International Congress of the Latin American Studies Association (LASA), Miami, March 16–18, 2000, 14–15.

Whyte, William Foote. *Street Corner Society.* Chicago: University of Chicago Press, 1955.

Williams, Raymond Brady. *Religion of Immigrants from India and Pakistan: New Threads in the American Tapestry.* Boston: Cambridge University Press, 1988.

Wilson, Kenneth L., and Alejandro Portes. "Immigrant Enclaves: An Analysis of the Labor Market Experience of Cubans in Miami." *American Journal of Sociology* 86:2 (1980): 295–319.

Wilson, William Julius, and Richard P. Taub. *There Goes the Neighborhood: Racial, Ethnic, and Class Tensions in Four Chicago Neighborhoods and Their Meaning for America.* New York: Alfred A. Knopf, 2006.

Wirth, Louis. *The Ghetto,* Chicago: University of Chicago Press, 1928.

———. "Urbanism as a Way of Life." Reprinted in Warren, Roland and Larry Lyon, eds. *New Perspectives on the American Community.* Chicago: Dorsey Press, 1983.

Wong, Edward. "Mayor of Union City Resigns Under Fire; Rival Replaces Him." *The New York Times,* October 25, 2000. Online, http://query.nytimes.com/gst/fullpage.html?res=9406EFDE1231F936A15753C1A9669C8B63&scp=1&sq=Mayor+of+Union+City+Resigns+Under+Fire&st=nyt. Retrieved October 31, 2008.

Yans-McLaughlin, Virginia. "Patterns of Work and Family Organization: Buffalo's Italians." *Journal of Social History* 2 (Autumn, 1971).
Zenit, el mundo visto desde Roma (Agencia de Noticias). "En Cuba estamos reducidos al silencio." Interview with Cardinal Jaime Lucas Ortega y Alamino, Havana, January 14, 2004.
Zorbaugh, Harvey. *Gold Coast and Slum.* Chicago: University of Chicago Press, 1929.

Index

Page numbers in *italics* indicate photographs or figures.

A. Holthausen (store), 40
Abdala, 119, 179n13
Academia Amador, 56–57
academies, 56–57
Acción Católica (Catholic Action), 89
Afro-Cubans, 52–53, 85, 146–48 *see also* immigrant stories; Mariel boatlift refugees
Agrarian Reform, 96–97
Alfonso, Octavio, 133
Alpha 66, 119, 121, 123–25
Alum, Rolando, 48
Amador, Antonio, 57
Amarilis (dance academy), 57
Anthony's Pharmacy, 41
anti-Castro politics: Catholic Church and, 98–100; of Cuban immigrants, 46–62, 98–100, 113, 120–29; economic and social organizations and, 46–62; *periodiquitos,* 57–58; radical organizations and, 120–29
anti-communist sentiments, 3, 28, 95, 115, 160–61
Antonia, María, 147
Antonio Maceo Brigade, 120, 137
Arango, José Obdulio, 133
Archdiocese of Newark, 88, 91, 101
Areíto, 120
Arocena, Eduardo, 121–22
Arteaga, Manuel (cardinal of Havana), 87
Asociación Católica Padre Félix Varela (Felix Varela Catholic Association), 102
Asociación de la Caridad (Virgen de la Caridad Association), 88
Asociación de Mujeres Cubano-Americans de New Jersey (Association of Cuban American Women of NJ), 59–61, 119
Asociaciones de Presos Políticos (Association of Political Prisoners), 119
assassinations, 121
assimilation theories, 141–44, 159
Association of Cuban Journalists in Exile (Colegio de Periodistas Cubanos en el Exilio), 57
associations and organizations, 41–42, 44–48, 53–56, 119–29, 137–38 *see also* political organizations; social clubs; specific organizations
asylum, political, 10, 13, 123, 155, 169n12, 171n18
Avance (Advance) (newspaper), 58
Azúcar Restaurant, 51, 142

Bahamas, 117
Baloyra, Clara, 107
balseros (raft refugees), 3, 33–35, 81–84
Bandera (restaurant/supermarket), *45*
banks, 41–42, 46

Barrera, Félix, 45
Batista government, resistance to, 23, 96, 114
Bay of Pigs invasion, 98, 116, 118, 121, 134, 136, 178n2
Bello, Deisy, 36
Bello, Julio, 22, 36
Bergen County, NJ, 35–36
Bergenline Avenue: bodegas, 39–40; changes, 49–50; commercial center, 19, 44; extortion, 19; parades, 30; photos, *19, 21, 40*; restaurants, *47*
Betto, Frei, 103
BHE (New Jersey Bureau of Hispanic Enterprise), 48
Bidot, Carlos, 58
bilingual education, 42, 159
Blauner, Robert, 143
blue-collar immigrants, 9, 28
Bobo, Lawrence, 145
bodegas, 39–40, 44, *45*, 49
Bohemia (magazine), 58
bombings, 121, 179n27
Bonilla-Silva, Eduardo, 145
Borrero, Gerson, 130
Bosch Avila, Orlando, 122
Boza Masvidal, Eduardo (Auxiliary Bishop of Havana), 88, 102, 109
breweries, 19
Brigada 2506, 115, 118
Bush, George W. and Bush administration, 107, 136, 153, 177n32, 180n56
businesses: associations, 41–42, 44–48; catering to Cubans, 41; Cuban owned, 39–41, 43–46, 51–52, 172n10; and second generation Cubans, 52–53

Caibarién (municipo), 55
California and bilingual education, 42
Camagüey, Cuba, 3
Camajuaní (municipo), 55
Camarioca, Cuba, 9
Camiñas, Fr., 128
CANF (Cuban American National Foundation), 122, 126–28, 135
Caribbean Relief Program, 30
Caribe Express, 52, 150
Caritas, 105, 109
Carter, Jimmy and Carter administration, 12, 120
Casa de la Caridad (House of Charity), 88, 93
Case, Clifford, 131
Castro, Fidel: anti-Castro movements, 46–62, 98–100, 113, 120–29; Catholic Church and, 95–111; CIA plots to overthrow, 115, 122; Cuban Lions Club, 59; leader of anti-Batista rebels, 23; *periodiquitos*, 57–58; support from Cuban immigrants, 114 *see also* Cuban Revolution
catechesis, 89, 93–94
Catholic Action (Acción Católica), 89
Catholic Charities, 28, 90
Catholic Church, 28; anti-Castro politics, 98–100; Archdiocese of Newark, 88, 91, 101; assistance to immigrants, 41, 88, 90–92, 177n31; Batista government, resistance to, 96; and Castro, 95–111; communism and, 97–98, 103; in Cuba, 85–86, 96–111, 176–77n24; Latin American immigrants and, 93–95; on migration from Cuba, 98–99, 103–4; as social center, 91 *see also* specific churches
Catholic Working Youth (Juventud Obrera Católica), 97, 109
Celia Cruz Way (street), *162*
census data: Cuban population in Hudson County, 25–26; Cuban population in Union City, 35–36, 170n6; Cuban population in U.S., 6; household size, 76; multiracial category, 144–45, 182n8; racial and ethnic categorization, 144–45; women in the workforce, 70
Central Intelligence Agency (CIA) and anti-Castro activities, 115, 122
chain migration effect, 28
Chamber of Commerce (Cámera de Comercio), 46
children (Operación Pedro Pan), 7, 99–100, 128
churches, assistance to immigrants, 41, 88, 90–92, 177n31
Church World Service, 8
cigar manufacturing, 6
Clinton, Bill and Clinton administration, 125, 136
Cohen, Miriam, 69
Colarusso, Florence, 22–23
cold war, 8 *see also* Bay of Pigs invasion; Soviet Union and Cuba; U.S. foreign policy and Cuba
communism and the Catholic Church, 97–98, 103
community building, 43
Condis, Dalia, 57
Confraternity of the Virgen of El Cobre, 88
Congreso Nacional Católico (National Catholic Congress), 97

Congressmen and women, Cuban American, 128–30, 133
Constitution of 1940, 118
Continental furniture, 46
Cooney, Rosemary Santana, 28, 67
Coordinación de Organizaciones Revolucionarias Unidas (Coordination of United Revolutionary Organizations), 120
corruption and politics, 129–31, 134
Corzine, Jon, 129–30
CRP (Cuban Refugee Program, Hudson County), 8, 41, 55, 90
Cuba: Afro-Cubans in, 146–48; Catholic Church in, 85–86, 95–111, 176–77n24; devaluation of professions, 66–67, 81; nationalization of private property, 2, 28, 66; papal visit, 104–11, *108*, 151, 177n34; political culture, 117–19; reconciliation with Cuban immigrants, 102, 104, 109, 111–12, 125, 137–38; religion in, 85–86, 103, 111, 175n1; and sexuality, 78; Soviet Union and, 115, 152; travel to by immigrants, 52, 82, 104–9, *108*, 150–51, 180n56; U.S. dollars and, 11–12, 14, 66, 82, 174n12; and U.S. foreign policy, 115–20, 153–56; women in the workforce, 63–67
Cuban Adjustment Act, 8, 11, 13, 34
Cuban Bridges (Puentes Cubanos), 137
Cuban Change (Cambio Cubano), 125, 137
Cuban Committee for Democracy, 137
Cuban Consensus (Consenso Cubano), 137
Cuban Day Parade, 30
Cuban-Haitian Entrant Program, 12, 31
Cuban immigrants to the U.S.: overview, 5–14; prior to Revolution, 21–25; first wave after Revolution, 6–9, 25–35; second wave, 9, 28; third wave, 9–10 (*see also* Mariel boatlift refugees); fourth wave, 10–12 (*see also balseros* refugees); anti-Castro politics of, 46–62, 98–100, 113, 120–29; anti-communist sentiments, 3, 28, 95, 115, 160–61; assimilation, 141–44; Castro, support for, 114; Catholic Church and, 41, 88, 90–92, 177n31; and discrimination, 10, 31–33, 93, 132, 155; diversity of Cuban communities, 14–15; feeling of betrayal by U.S., 116, 123, 136; identity formation, 151–53; and papal visit to Cuba, 105–11; political participation, 113–17, 125–37, 161–62; preferential treatment for Cuban immigrants, 12–13, 155; and race, 144–48; reconciliation with Cuba, 102, 104, 109, 111–12, 125, 137–38; relationship with Latin American immigrants, 83, 161; resentment of "new Cubans" by "first exiles," 13, 36, 61, 82–83, 150, 161; and U.S. foreign policy, 12, 115–20, 126, 153–56; in U.S. Congress, 128–30, 133 *see also* women, in the workforce
Cuban Lions Club (Leones Cubanos en el Exilio), 58–59
"Cuban loan," 27
Cuban missile crisis, 116, 152
Cuban National Ecclesiastic Encounter (Encuentro Nacional Eclesial Cubano), 104
Cuban Nationalist Movement (Movimiento Nacionalista Cubano), 119–21
Cuban Power (Poder Cubano), 120
Cuban Refugee Center, 26
Cuban Refugee Emergency Center, 8
Cuban Refugee Program (CRP), Hudson County, 8, 41, 55, 90
Cuban Research Institute, 138
Cuban Revolution, 6, 66, 96–101, 118 *see also* Castro, Fidel
Cuban Revolutionary Council, 115–16
Cuban Welfare Program, 27
Cuba-Peru Crusade, 30
Cuba Study Group, 137–38
cultural assimilation, 141, 151–53
cultural preservation, 59–61, 68–69, 71–72, 86, 142–43, 173n31

Dade County, FL, 25
Dávila Colón, Nidia, 133
DeFino, Anthony, 55
del Valle, Msgr. Raúl, 102
Democratic Party, 116, 126, 129–31, 133–34, 136
30 de Noviembre (November 30th), 119
devaluation of professions in Cuba, 66–67, 81
diasporic citizenship, 143–44
Díaz, Manny, 133
Díaz, Sammy, 108–9
Díaz Balart, Lincoln and Mario, 128
Directorio Revolucionario Estudiantil (Revolutionary Student Directorate), 115
discrimination: of Afro-Cubans, 146–48; assimilation and, 159; against Cuban immigrants, 132; by Cuban immigrants, 93; against Haitian refugees, 12; against Hispanic population, 173n33; against Mariel boatlift refugees, 10, 13, 31–33, 155 *see also* race
dispersion of immigrants, 35–36, 138, 149–50, 158–59

diversity and politics, 135
diversity in the Catholic Church, 93–95
divorce, 75–77
Docampo, Justica, 57
dollars in Cuba, 11–12, 14, 66, 82, 174n12
domestic service jobs, 64–66
Dominican immigrants, 49, 51, 54, 71, 146
Drezner, Daniel, 156–57
Durán, Aleida, 29, 58, 127

economic opportunity as motive for immigration, 2, 5, 12, 22, 81, 131
education, 27, 42, 56–57, 61, 159
educational loans, 27
Eisenhower, Dwight D. and Eisenhower administration, 8, 115
El Almacén el Español, 52
El Amor Todo lo Espera (Love Hopes for All Things), 104
El Clarín (The Trumpet), 58
El Club Amigos e Hijos de Fomento (municipo), 55, 119
El Condor, 120
elderly, 55–56, 75
El Diálogo (the Dialogue), 101–2, 120, 127, 137, 177n32
Elena Mederos Award, 60
El Escambray, Cuba, 124
El Especial (The Special) (newspaper), 58
El Heraldo de la Semana (The Weekly Herald), 58
El Independiente (The Independent) (newspaper), 58
El Nuevo Hudson (newspaper), 58
embroidery industry, 2, 19
Encuentro Nacional Eclesial Cubano (Cuban National Ecclesiastic Encounter), 104
English as a second language programs, 42
Epiphany, 60
ESL (English as a second language) programs, 42
Espino, Fr. José Joaquín, 109
Estelita Santaló (singer), 91
Estévez, Guillermo, 32
ethnic enclaves, 2, 43–62, 168n1
ethnicity and race, 144–48
Europa, Eunice, 42, 158–59
exiles, definition, 169n12
exit permits, 7

Fahey, Fr. Joseph, 28
family: assistance to new arrivals, 41; family economics, 77; importance of, 44, 75–77, 80; location of, 29, 35 *see also* women, in the workforce
Father Luis, 28
Favalora, John Clement (Archbishop of Miami), 105
Federación Mercantil Hispana (Hispanic Mercantile Federation), 41–42, 44–48
Feketie, Fr. Michael, 89–91, 159–60
Felix Varela Catholic Association (Asociación Católica Padre Félix Varela), 102
Fernández, Ariel, 147–48
Fernández-Kelly, M. Patricia, 71
Fernández-Selier, Yesenia, 147–48, 161–62
Ferree, Myra Marx, 71
fertility of Cuban women, 76
"first exiles" and resentment of "new Cubans," 13, 36, 61, 82–83, 150, 161
Florida, 2, 6, 42 *see also* Miami, FL
Florio, James and Florio administration, 129
Fomento, Cuba, 2, 22, 55
Forero, Juan, 23
Franklin, Benjamin, 156
Freedom Flights, 9
Friedman-Kasaba, Kathie, 69
Friendship Foundation (Fundación Amistad), 137
Fukuyama, Francis, 157
Fundación Amistad (Friendship Foundation), 137
funeral homes, 44
furniture stores, 41, 46

Galaor, Don, 58
García, Anna M., 71
García, Dionisio (Bishop of Bayamo-Manzanillo), 111
García, Raúl "Rudy," 134–35
García Rodríguez, Félix, 121
Gatherings of Yesterday (Tertulias de Antaño), 55–56
gender and immigration, 148–49
gender dynamics, 71–75
Gil, Lourdes, 26, 36
Gil-Ramos, Lidia, 55–56, 172n23
globalization and immigration, 5
Glover, Karen S., 145
González, Aracelio, 46
González, Elián, 13, 126–27, 136–37, 169n22
Gordon, Milton, 141
Gorelick, Sherry, 143
Graham, Pamela, 71
Grammy Awards, Latin, 126–27
Gras, Ernesto, 46

Grey, Fr. Martin, 28
grocery stores *see* bodegas
Guantanamo Bay, U.S. Naval base, 11
Guarini, Frank, 134
Guerra (War) (newspaper), 58
guest worker program, 154
Güines (municipo), 55
Gutiérrez Menoyo, Eloy, 124–25, 137

Hague, Frank, 130
Haitian immigration, 12–13, 31
Harrison, Angelica, 27
Havana, Cuba, 28, 81
Havana Bay Coffee, 52
Helms-Burton Act, 125–26, 136
Hernández, José Manuel, 108
Hernandez, Raymond, 132
Hernández Restaurant, 40
The Hispanic Challenge (Huntington), 156
Hispanic Mercantile Federation (Federación Mercantil Hispana), 41–42, 44–48
históricos (first arrivals) *see* Cuban immigrants to the U.S., first wave after Revolution
Hoffman, Harold, 129
Holy Family Church, 88, 102
homosexuality, 80
honor and vergüenza (honor and shame), 173n1
House of Charity (Casa de la Caridad), 88, 93
Hudson Avenue, 39
Hudson County, NJ, 17, 25; Cuban population, 25–26, 76; Division of Social Services, 27, 41; politics, 130, 133–34; women in the workforce, 149 *see also* Union City, NJ; West New York, NJ
Hudson County Cuban Refugee Program (CRP), 8, 41, 55, 90
The Hudson Dispatch (newspaper), 58, 127
Hungarians, 8
hunger strikes, 32
Hunter, Bill, 42
Huntington, Samuel P., 156–59
hypo-descent, rule of, 144–45

Ibarria, Antonio, 46
identity formation of immigrants, 151–53
illegal or undocumented immigration, 153–54
immersion programs, 42
immigrants and immigration: assimilation theories, 141–44; attitudes towards, 20, 156–59; entrepreneurship, 43–46; gender and, 148–49; geographic area concentrations, 4, 168n7; identity formation, 151–53; illegal or undocumented immigration, 153–54; integration *versus* assimilation, 142, 158–59; legal status, 169n12; and religion, 149–50; shift to non-white, 4, 153; transnational migrations, 4, 52, 82, 143–44, 150–51; and women in the workforce, 68–69 *see also* Cuban immigrants to the U.S.; economic opportunity as motive for immigration; political conflict as motivation for immigration; professional status of immigrants; religious immigrants
immigrant stories: Alberto (Cuban American), 50; author's, 1–2, 39, 86, 110, 160; Benito (jewelry store owner), 49–50; Berta (St. Augustine member), 92; Clara Baloyra (pilgrim to Cuba), 107; Dalia (St. Augustine member), 94–95; Delia (Cuban immigrant), 160–61; Dionisio Villanueva (anti-communist immigrant), 25; Doris (Afro-Cuban woman), 146; Elsa (Mariel refugee), 80–81; Ernesto (Parish Council member), 91, 93; Eva (working woman), 72–73; Evelio (St. Augustine member), 94; Guillermo Estévez (on Mariel boatlift refugees), 32; Humberto (student), 35; José Andreas Rionda (pilgrim to Cuba), 107; José (on working women), 74; Laura (doctor), 81; Lilia (St. Augustine member), 93; Luisa (Cuban Refugee Program worker), 27; Luisa (on Miami), 36; Luis *(balsero)*, 34; Manuel (Afro-Cuban man), 147; Manuel and Lyda Rodríguez (early Union City immigrants), 22–23, 25; Manuel (recent Cuban immigrant), 35; Manuel (restaurant owner), 50–51; Margaret (Italian American), 20; María Antonia (Afro-Cuban woman), 147; Maria de los Angeles (mother), 79; María (Ecuadorian St. Augustine member), 94; María (lottery system immigrant), 35; Mariana (single mother), 83, 149; Marina (working woman), 73; Maritza (St. Augustine member), 94; Marta (working woman), 73; Omar and Elsa *(balseros)*, 34–35; Oscar (drapery business owner), 51, 142; Pedro (on working women), 74–75; Roberto (on working women), 74–75; Silverio Rodríguez (Alpha 66 member), 23, 25, 124–25, 152; Susan (German American), 20; Yesenia Fernández-Selier (Afro-Cuban woman), 147–48, 161–62 *see also* businesses, Cuban owned

indefinite voluntary departure status, 7
Información (Information) (newspaper), 58
Inguaggiato, Anthony, 41
Institute for Public Opinion Research, 138
integration *versus* assimilation, 142, 158–59
intermarriage, 142
internal colonialism model, 143
International Institute of New Jersey, 33
International Rescue Committee (IRC), 8, 30, 33
Italian immigrants, 68–69, 157
Iturralde, Iraida, 31

Jaclyn's handbag factory, *82*
jewelry stores, 46, 49–50
Jewish immigrants, 69
Jews in Cuba, 85, 175n1
Jiménez, Yiyo, 58
John Paul II (pope), 104–11, 151, 177n34
journalists, 58
July 26th Revolutionary Movement, 114–15, 125 *see also* Cuban Revolution
Juventud Obrera Católica (Catholic Working Youth), 97, 109

Katz, Carla, 129
Kean, Thomas, 48
Kennedy, John F. and Kennedy administration, 8, 115–16, 134, 136, 152
Kenny, John V., 130
Kugelman, Fr. Richard, 28

Labrada, Guillermo, 39
La Casa Tony (furniture store), 46
La Defensa (shoe store), 46
La Esquina Habanera (club), 52
"la generación de Mariel" *see* Mariel boatlift refugees
laissez-faire racism, 145
La Razón (Reason) (newspaper), 58
La Rosa, Catherine, 42
Las Villas province, 2–3.
Latin American immigrants: and the Catholic Church, 93–95; racial classifications, 146; relationships with Cuban immigrants, 83, 161; and sexuality, 78; in Union City, 3, 48, 159; and women in the workforce, 67–68, 70–71, 83
Latin Grammy Awards, 126–27
La Tribuna (The Forum), 58
La Voz (The Voice) (newspaper), 58
lawyers, 60
Legion of Mary, 89
Leones Cubanos en el Exilio (Cuban Lions Club), 58–59
Letelier, Orlando, 121
Liceo Cubano, 40, 53–54, 132
Lions Club, 58–59
López, Iraida, 151
lottery system, 11–12, 33, 81
Madán, Bienvenido, 58
Maná (journalist), 58
Manito (second-hand furniture store), 41, 172n23
Manolo La Cachita Restaurant, *47*
maps: of Hudson County, NJ, *18*; Union City, *24*
Marazul Tours, 52, 150
Mariel boatlift refugees: and the Asociación de Mujeres Cubano-Americans, 61; demographic information, 30; discrimination against, 10, 13, 31–33, 155; events leading to, 9–10; including some blacks, mentally ill, and criminals, 10, 61, 80; in Union City, 3, 29–33; women and, 80–81
marielitos see Mariel boatlift refugees
Martí, José, 113, *114*
Martinéz, Juan L. (Kiko), 45
Martínez, Nivio, 133
Más Canosa, Jorge, 126–29
Más Santos, Jorge, 126–28
McGreevey, James, 129
Mederos, Elena, 60
Meehan, William, 130
Méndez, Lourdes, 34
Menendez, Robert, 128–35
men on women in the workforce, 74–75, 78–79
methodology, xi–xiv, 67, 72, 167–68n11
Meurice, Msgr. Pedro, 103–4
Mexican American immigrants, 70, 156–57
Miami, FL: Catholic Church in, 101–2, 105, 109; as Cuban ethnic enclave, 25, 44, 158; politics, 135, 137–38
migratory accord between U.S. and Cuba (1994), 3
minority owned businesses, 39–41, 43–52, 172n10
Miqueli, Miguel, 45, 51
Morgado, Luis, 44
Morgado Funeral Home, 44
Movement of Revolutionary Recovery (Movimiento de Recuperación Revolucionaria), 115

Movimiento de Recuperación Revolucionaria (Movement of Revolutionary Recovery), 115
Movimiento Nacionalista Cubano (Cuban Nationalist Movement), 119–21
Movimiento Revolucionario del Pueblo (People's Revolutionary Movement), 115
Mr. Rojas (clothing store), 46, 88
multiracial category on census, 144–45, 181n8
municipos (hometown clubs), 55
Musto, William, 130–33

narcotics traffickers, 122
National Catholic Congress (Congreso Nacional Católica), 97
nationalization of private property in Cuba, 2, 28, 66
Navarro, Fr. Pedro, 92
Necker-Sharpe (funeral home), 44
Negrín, Eulalio, 121
"new Cubans" and resentment by "first exiles," 13, 36, 61, 82–83, 150, 161
New Jersey: minority businesses, 39–41, 43–52, 172n10; politics, 129–30 *see also* specific cities and counties
New Jersey Bureau of Hispanic Enterprise (BHE), 48
newspapers, 57–58, 123
New York City and Cuban immigration, 6, 136, 159
Nixon, Richard, 131
N.J. Division of Public Welfare, 27
Northeast Hispanic Catholic Center, 102
Novo, Guillermo, 121
Nuestra Cuba (Our Cuba) (newspaper), 58
Núñez, Fr. Pedro, 107

Ofensiva Revolucionaria (Revolutionary Offensive), 2, 28
Omega 7, 119, 121–22, 138, 179n13
Operación Pedro Pan (Operation Peter Pan), 7, 99–100, 128
Operation Mongoose, 116
Oquendo, David, 52
Oriente, Alexander V., 134
Orrico, James, 27
Ortega, Jaime (cardinal of Havana), 178n54
Ortiz, Vilma, 67
Oves, Francisco, 99

Palisade Avenue, 41
Palisades Medical Center, 173n33
papal visit to Cuba, 104–11, *108*, 151, 177n34
paramilitary groups, 119
Pardo, Rodolfo, 127
parole status, 7, 155
Passionist Order of priests, 86–87, 175–76n4
patriarchal cultural norms, 68–69, 71–72, 78
Pedraza, Silvia, 180–81n6
Pedro sin Pán (Peter Without Bread), 128
Pellicer, Miriam, 57
People's Revolutionary Movement (Movimiento Revolucionario del Pueblo), 115
Pérez, Dosinda, 42
Pérez, Elio, 46
Pérez, Jesús, 41
Pérez, Lisandro, 148
Pérez, Louis, 117
Pérez, Manuel, 29, 40, 46, 58
Pérez, Nick, 51
Pérez, Remberto, 127–29, 135
Pérez, Teresa, 51, 142
Pérez family, *26*
Pérez Serantes, Enrique (Archbishop of Santiago de Cuba), 96–97
Pérez Travel (travel agency), 40, 46
período especial (special period), 11, 35
periodiquitos (small newspapers), 57–58, 123
permanent residency status, 8
Peruvian Embassy, 10
Pessar, Patricia, 71
Peter Without Bread (Pedro sin Pán), 128
pharmacies, 41
Placetas, Cuba, 2
plantation economies, 64–65
Platt Amendment, 117
Playa Girón *see* Bay of Pigs invasion
Poder Cubano (Cuban Power), 120
polarization between rich and poor nations, 5
political conflict as motivation for immigration, 5, 152
political organizations, anti-Castro, 46–62, 98–100, 113, 120–29
political participation of Cuban immigrants, 113–17, 125–37, 161–62 *see also* Democratic Party; Republican Party
Portes, Alejandro, 152
Posada Carriles, Luis, 122–23, 179n27
poverty rates, 71
Premio Elena Mederos (Elena Mederos Award), 60
press, 57–58, 123, 137

professional status of immigrants, 2, 33–34, 56–57, 66–67, 81, 83, 147
professions, devaluation of, in Cuba, 66–67, 81
propaganda, anticommunist, 7–8
Protestant Church in Cuba, 85
Puentes Cubanos (Cuban Bridges), 137
Puerto Rican immigrants, 70, 71
Pulido, Juan, 121

queuing theory, 3–4
Quevedo, Oneida, 57
Quintero, Rafael, 118

race: anti black sentiments, 94–95; and division of labor, 64–65; and ethnicity, 144–48; Latin Americanization of race relations, 145; and racism, 145–48 *see also* Afro-Cubans; discrimination
Radio Mambí, 105
Radio Martí, 126
Raíces Habaneras (musical group), 52–53
Reagan, Ronald and Reagan administration, 125, 133, 171n18
real-estate businesses, 51
reconciliation among Cubans, 102, 104, 109, 111–12, 125, 137–38
Refugee Act of 1980, 12
Refugee Resettlement Program (RRP), 12, 31, 33, 81
refugee status, 155, 169n12, 171n18
relatives *see* family
religion and immigration, 149–50
religion in Cuba, 85–86, 103, 111, 175n1 *see also* Catholic Church
religious immigrants, 98–100
Reportaje Gráfico (Graphic Report) (newspaper), 58
Representatives, Cuban American, 128, 133
Republican Party, 116, 129, 131, 133–34, 136
restaurants, 40, 44, *45*, *47*, 50–51
Revolutionary Offensive (Ofensiva Revolucionaria), 2, 28
Revolutionary Student Directorate (Directorio Revolucionario Estudiantil), 115
Revolution of 1959 *see* Cuban Revolution
Rionda, José Andreas, 107
Roa-Kouri, Raúl, 122
Rodríguez, Manuel and Lyda, 22–23, 25
Rodríguez, Silverio, 23, 25, 124–25, 152
Rodríguez Fariña, Julio, 55
Rodríguez Zaldívar, Rodolfo, 58
Rogg, Eleanor M., 28, 54
Rojas, Nené, 46, 88
Román, Agustín (Auxiliary Bishop of Miami), 105, 110
Roosevelt Stadium, 87–88
Ros-Lehtinen, Ileana, 128
Ross, Alvin, 121
RRP (Refugee Resettlement Program), 12, 31, 33, 81
rumba, 52–53
Rumbaut, Rubén G., 152

Safa, Helen, 67–68
Saint Augustine parish, 28, 88–96, *90*, 111–12, 149–50
Saint Joseph and Saint Michael's R. C. Church, 87
Saint Joseph of the Palisades Church, 28, 55, 88
Saint Michael's Church, 86–88, 175–76n4
Saint Rocco Church, 88
Saladrigas, Carlos, 137
Sánchez, Siomara, 60–61, 83–84
Sánchez Parodi, Ramón, 122
Sancti Spíritus (municipo), 55
Santana, Armando, 121
Santería, 85
Schlezinger's (clothing store), 40
Second Escambray Front (Segundo Frente del Escambray), 115, 124
second generation Cubans: Adriana (on mothers), 77; Ana (working woman), 77; anti-Castro sentiment diminishing, 135, 138–39; Ariel Fernández (Afro-Cuban woman), 147–48; business owners, 52–53; daughters on mothers, 73, 77, 79; definition of, 168n10; Deisy Bello (on family), 36; Evelyn (on mothers), 77; and family economics, 77; Graciela (working woman), 73–74, 77; intermarriage, 142; Julio Bello (on family), 22, 36; Mariela (daughter), 79; political identification of, 152; Roberto (son), 79; Susy (high school student), 73–74, 79; and women in the workforce, 73–74
second-hand stores, 41
segmented assimilation, 142
Segundo Frente del Escambray (Second Escambray Front), 115, 124
self-actualization through work, 72–75
Senators, Cuban American, 128–30, 133
Serrano, José, 130

sexuality, 78–80
shoe stores, 46
shopping malls, 49–50
silk mills, 19
Sires, Albio, 128–30, 134–35
Sisters of Charity, 108
slavery, 64
social class *see* blue-collar immigrants; professional status of immigrants; white-collar workers
social clubs, 40, 53–56, 58–59, 132
Social Security, Supplemental Security Income (SSI), 27
Soviet Union and Cuba, 115, 152
SSI (Social Security, Supplemental Security Income), 27
structural assimilation, 141–42
suburbs, direct migration to, 4
sugar production, 6
Survey of Minority-Owned Business Enterprises, 49
Swiss embassy, 7

Tarallo, Jeffrey, 160, 162
Ten Years' War of Independence, 6
terrorist activities, 121–25, 138, 179n27
Tertulias de Antaño (Gatherings of Yesterday), 55–56
26th of July Movement, 23
The Jersey Journal (newspaper), 58
three-generation families, 75
Three Kings Day, 60, 173n31
Title VII, 42
transnational migrations, 4, 52, 82, 143–44, 150–51
travel agencies, 40, 52

Ugalde, Carlos, 46
Última Hora (The Last Hour) (newspaper), 58
Union City, NJ: historical background, 17–21; Cuban immigrants prior to Revolution, 21–25; first wave of Cuban immigrants after Revolution, 25–35; third wave of Cuban immigrants after Revolution (Mariel boatlift refugees), 3, 29–33; fourth wave of Cuban immigrants after Revolution, 35–36; anti-Castro organizations, 121–25, 127; assimilation or integration by immigrants, 143; associations and organizations, 53–56, 121–25, 127, 137–38; academies, 56–57; *balseros* refugees, 3, 33–35, 81–82; businesses, Cuban owned, 39–41, 43–46, 49–52; Castro's visits, 114; Catholic Church in, 86–96; Cuban Day Parade, 30; as Cuban ethnic enclave, 2, 44–62, 168n1; Cuban population, 170n6; dispersion of immigrants, 35-36, 138, 149–50, 158–59; embroidery industry, 2, 19; Latin American immigrants, 3, 48, 159; maps, *24*; and Mariel boatlift refugees, 3, 29–33; papal visit reaction, 110; politics and political organizations, 119–20, 129–30, 133–39, 162; press, 57–58; women in the workforce, 67–84 *see also* Hudson County
Union City Building Supply, 46
Unión de Cubanos en el Exilio (Union of Cubans in Exile), 88, 102
United Hebrew Immigrant Aid, 8
United States Catholic Conference, 8
Universidad de Villanueva, 97
U.S. dollars and Cuba, 11–12, 14, 66, 82, 174n12
U.S. foreign policy and Cuba, 12, 115–20, 153–56 *see also* Bay of Pigs invasion; cold war
U.S. immigration policy, 7, 12–13, 153–55, 162

Valdés Muñoz Conchita, 27
Valdivia, Julia *"La Alcaldesa"*, 131–32
Varela, Fr. Félix, 6, 102
Velázquez. Nidia, 130
vergüenza (shame), 173n1
Villa Clara province, Cuba, 2–3, 22, 28
Villanueva, Dionisio, 25, 45
violence and politics in Cuba, 118
Virgen de la Caridad Association (Asociación de la Caridad), 88
virginity, 64, 78–79, 173n1
Virgin of El Cobre, 85, 87–88, 110, 176n7
visa waiver program, 7

Weinberg, Sydney Stahl, 69
West New York, NJ, 25, 55, 67, 134, 170n6
West New York Leones Cubanos de Hudson (Cuban Lions Club), 59
"wet foot-dry foot" policy, 11, 155
white-collar workers, 28, 65–66 *see also* professional status of immigrants
Who Are We? The Challenges to America's National Identity (Huntington), 156
Williams, Harrison A. Jr., 129
women: associations, 59–61; *balseros* refugees, 81–84; on the Mariel boatlift, 80–81;

Yolanda Prieto is Professor Emerita of Sociology in the Scho
Science and Human Services of Ramapo College of New Jersey